enVision® Integrated

MATHEMATICS III

Student Companion

Boston, Massachusetts Chandler, Arizona
Glenview, Illinois New York, New York

ISBN-13: 978-1-4183-1761-4
ISBN-10: 1-4183-1761-6

1 19

Contents

enVision Integrated MATHEMATICS III

About the Authors

Authors

Dan Kennedy, Ph.D

- Classroom teacher and the Lupton Distinguished Professor of Mathematics at the Baylor School in Chattanooga, TN
- Co-author of textbooks *Precalculus: Graphical, Numerical, Algebraic* and *Calculus: Graphical, Numerical, Algebraic, AP Edition*
- Past chair of the College Board's AP Calculus Development Committee.
- Previous Tandy Technology Scholar and Presidential Award winner

Eric Milou, Ed.D

- Professor of Mathematics, Rowan University, Glassboro, NJ
- Member of the author team for Pearson's **enVision**math**2.0** 6-8
- Member of National Council of Teachers of Mathematics (NCTM) feedback/advisory team for the Common Core State Standards
- Author of *Teaching Mathematics to Middle School Students*

Christine D. Thomas, Ph.D

- Professor of Mathematics Education at Georgia State University, Atlanta, GA
- Past-President of the Association of Mathematics Teacher Educators (AMTE)
- Past NCTM Board of Directors Member
- Past member of the editorial panel of the NCTM journal *Mathematics Teacher*
- Past co-chair of the steering committee of the North American chapter of the International Group of the Psychology of Mathematics Education

Rose Mary Zbiek, Ph.D

- Professor of Mathematics Education, Pennsylvania State University, College Park, PA
- Series editor for the NCTM *Essential Understanding* project

Contributing Author

Al Cuoco, Ph.D

- Lead author of CME Project, a National Science Foundation (NSF)-funded high school curriculum
- Team member to revise the Conference Board of the Mathematical Sciences (CBMS) recommendations for teacher preparation and professional development
- Co-author of several books published by the Mathematical Association of America and the American Mathematical Society
- Consultant to the writers of the Common Core State Standards for Mathematics and the PARCC Content Frameworks for high school mathematics

EXPLORE & REASON

A diver is doing ocean search-and-rescue training. The graph shows the relationship between her depth and the time in seconds since starting her dive.

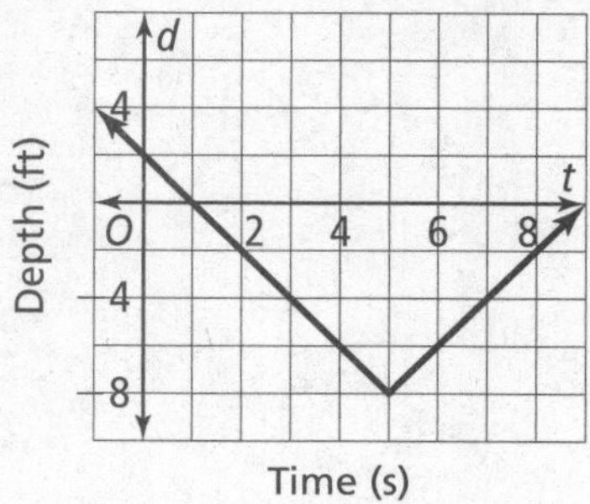

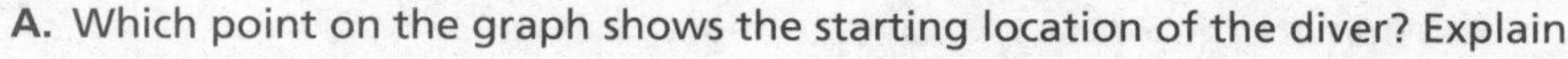

A. Which point on the graph shows the starting location of the diver? Explain.

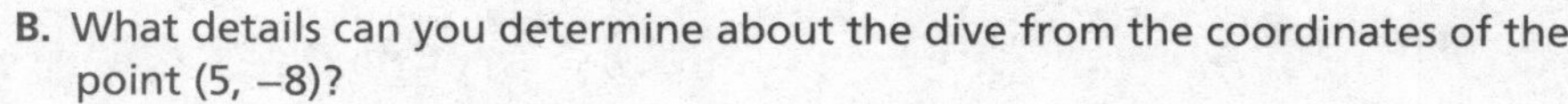

B. What details can you determine about the dive from the coordinates of the point (5, −8)?

C. What is the average speed of the diver's descent? How can you tell from the graph?

D. Communicate Precisely What does the V-shape of the graph tell you about the dive? What information does it not tell you about the dive?

HABITS OF MIND

Reason What do the points where the graph intersects the *x*-axis tell you about the dive?

1-1 Key Features of Functions

PearsonRealize.com

Assess

EXAMPLE 1  **Try It! Understand Domain and Range**

1. What are the domain and range of each function? Write the domain and range in set-builder notation and interval notation.

a. $y = |x - 4|$ **b.** $y = 6x - 2x^2$

EXAMPLE 2  **Try It! Find x- and y-intercepts**

2. What are the x- and y-intercepts of $g(x) = 4 - x^2$?

HABITS OF MIND

Make Sense and Persevere A function does not have any x-intercepts. What might be true about its domain and range?

EXAMPLE 3  **Try It! Identify Positive or Negative Intervals**

3. a. For what interval(s) is the function $h(x) = 2x + 10$ positive?

b. For what interval(s) is the function negative?

Notes

Assess

EXAMPLE 4  **Try It!** Identify Where a Function Increases or Decreases

4. For what values of x is each function increasing? For what values of x is each function decreasing?

a. $f(x) = x^2 - 4x$

b. $f(x) = -2x - 3$

HABITS OF MIND

Use Structure Can a function be increasing and negative on the same interval? Explain.

EXAMPLE 5  **Try It!** Understand Average Rate of Change Over an Interval

5. What do the average rates of change of the function $y = |x| + 2$ over the intervals $[-2, 0]$, $[0, 3]$, and $[-2, 3]$ indicate about the function?

HABITS OF MIND

Construct Arguments If a function has a positive average rate of change over an interval, does that mean that the function must be increasing over that interval? Explain.

Do You UNDERSTAND?

1. ESSENTIAL QUESTION How do graphs and equations reveal information about a relationship between two quantities?

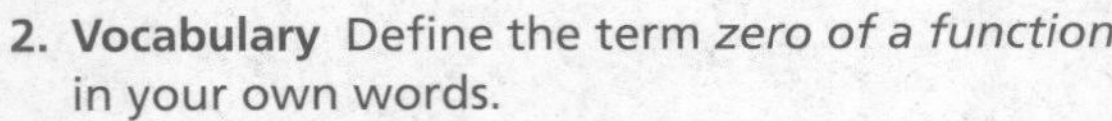

2. **Vocabulary** Define the term *zero of a function* in your own words.

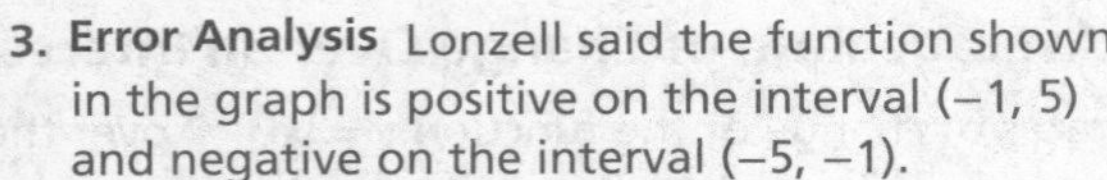

3. **Error Analysis** Lonzell said the function shown in the graph is positive on the interval (–1, 5) and negative on the interval (–5, –1).

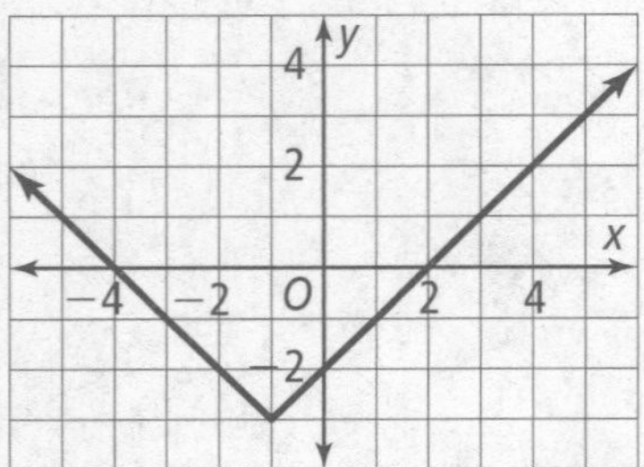

Identify and correct Lonzell's error.

Do You KNOW HOW?

Find each key feature.

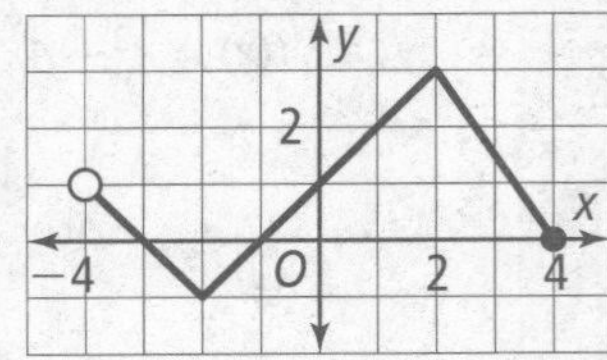

4. domain

5. range

6. *x*-intercept(s)

7. *y*-intercept(s)

8. interval(s) where the graph is positive

9. interval(s) where the graph is decreasing

10. interval(s) where the graph is increasing

11. rate of change on [–1, 4]

Activity

1-2 Transformations of Functions

EXPLORE & REASON

The graph of the function $f(x) = |x|$ is shown.

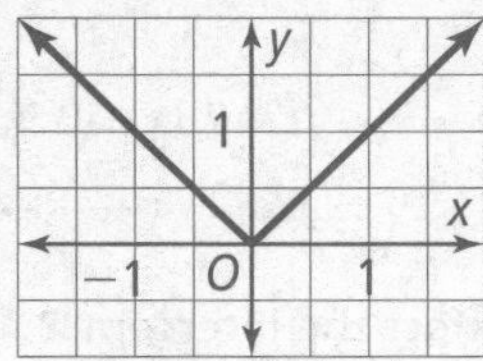

A. Graph the function $g(x) = |x + c|$ for each of several different values of c between −5 and 5.

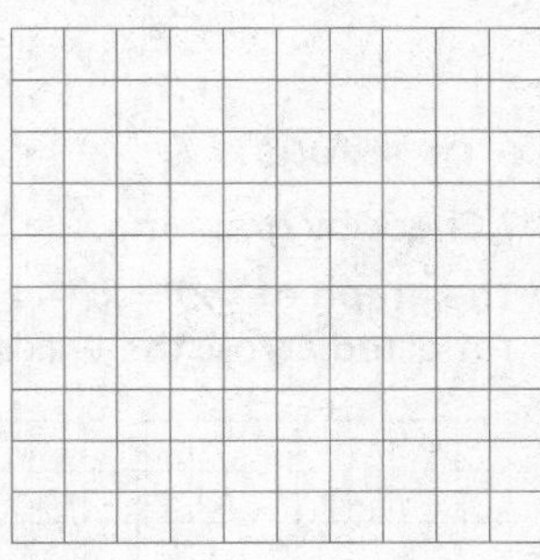

B. Look for Relationships Predict what will happen to the graph if c is a number greater than 100. What if c is a number between 0 and $\frac{1}{2}$?

HABITS OF MIND

Reason What happens to the graph if c is a negative number?

Assess

EXAMPLE 1

Try It! Translate a Function

1. a. How did the transformation of f to g in part (a) affect the intercepts?

   b. How did the transformation of f to g in part (b) affect the intercepts?

EXAMPLE 2

Try It! Reflect a Function Across the x- or y-Axis

2. What is an equation for the reflected graph? Check by graphing.

   a. the graph of $f(x) = x^2 - 2$ reflected across the x-axis.

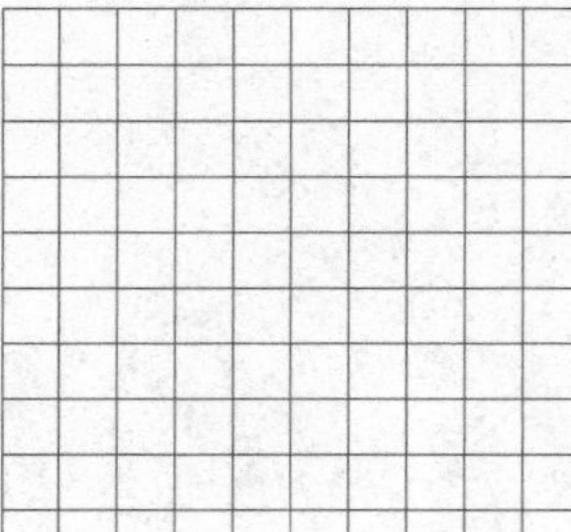

   b. the graph of $f(x) = x^2 - 2$ reflected across the y-axis.

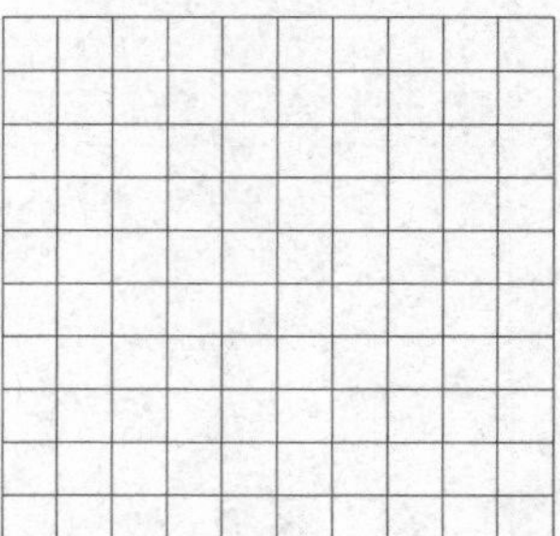

HABITS OF MIND

Look for Relationships How are the intercepts of a graph affected by reflection across the x-axis? Explain.

EXAMPLE 3

Try It! Understand Stretches and Compressions

3. Show that $j(x) = f\left(\frac{1}{2}x\right)$ is a horizontal stretch of the graph of f.

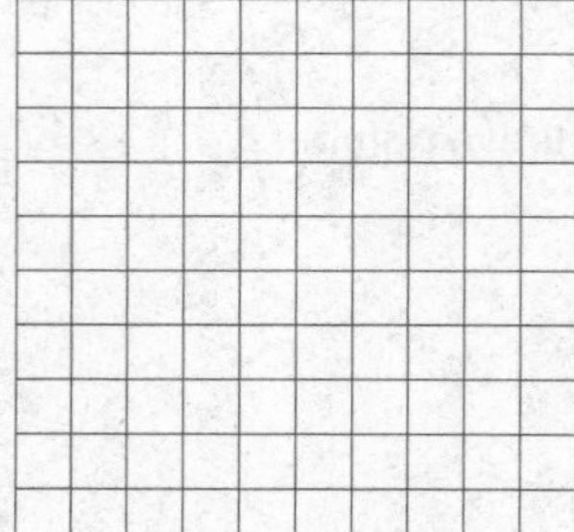

Notes

Assess

EXAMPLE 4

Try It! Graph a Combination of Transformations

4. Using the graph of f in Example 4, graph each equation.

a. $y = f(2x) - 4$

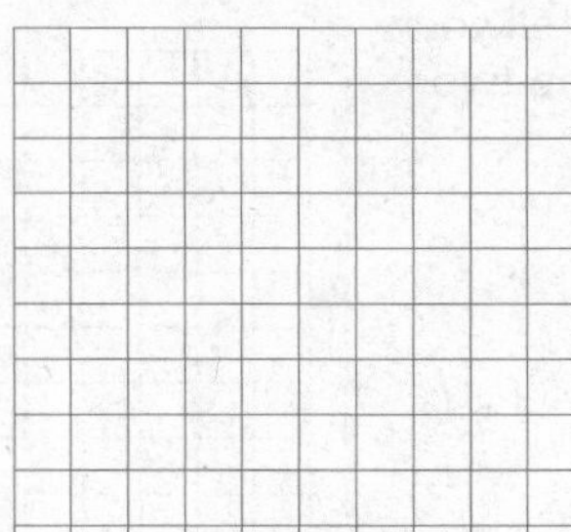

b. $y = f(2x - 3) - 2$

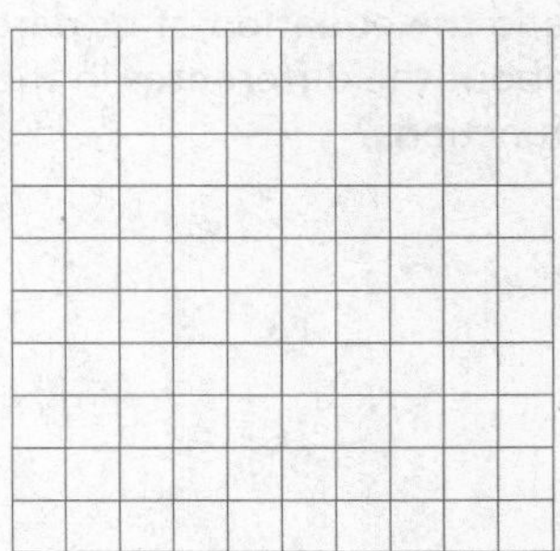

HABITS OF MIND

Model With Mathematics If the graph of a parent function is vertically stretched by a factor of 2 and then translated 3 units down, would you get the same graph if you translated the parent graph 3 units down first and then vertically stretched it by a factor of 2? Explain.

EXAMPLE 5

Try It! Identify Transformations From an Equation

5. What transformations of the graph of $f(x) = |x|$ are applied to graph the function g?

a. $g(x) = \frac{1}{2}|x + 3|$

b. $g(x) = -|x| + 2$

EXAMPLE 6

Try It! Write an Equation From a Graph

6. How would the graph and equation be affected if the train traveled twice as far in the same amount of time?

HABITS OF MIND

Make Sense and Persevere The function $f(x) = |x|$ is translated 3 units right and 2 units down, and then vertically stretched by a factor of 4. What is an equation for the transformed function g?

Assess

Do You UNDERSTAND?

1. ESSENTIAL QUESTION What do the differences between the equation of a function and the equation of its parent function tell you about the differences in the graphs of the two functions?

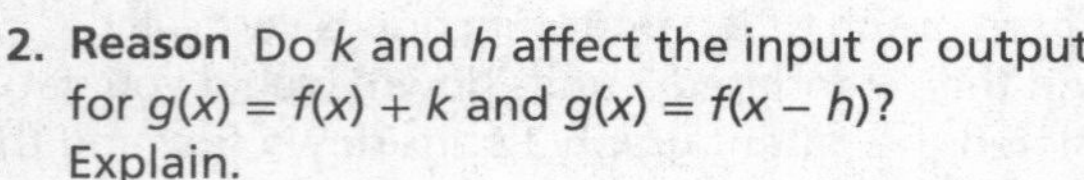

2. **Reason** Do k and h affect the input or output for $g(x) = f(x) + k$ and $g(x) = f(x - h)$? Explain.

3. **Error Analysis** Margo is comparing the functions $f(x) = |x|$ and $g(x) = |x + 1| - 5$. She said the graph of g is a vertical translation of the graph of f 5 units down and a horizontal translation of the graph of f 1 unit right. What is Margo's error?

Do You KNOW HOW?

Graph each function and its parent function.

4. $g(x) = |x| - 1$

5. $g(x) = (x - 3)^2$

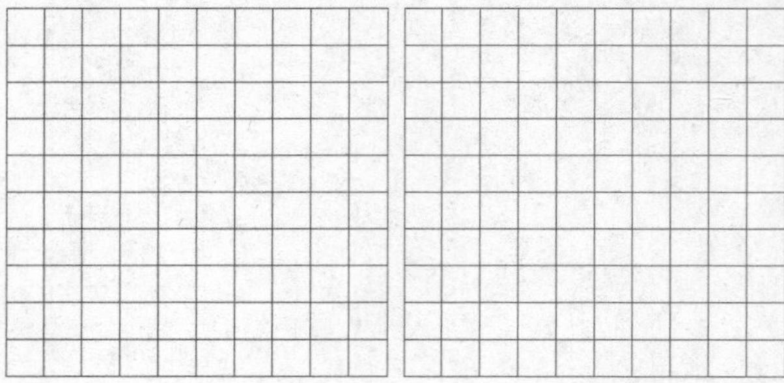

6. $g(x) = -|x|$

7. $g(x) = -x$

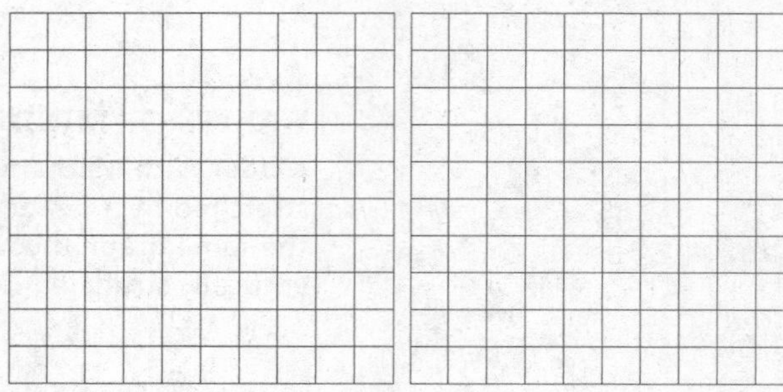

8. $g(x) = x^2 - 2$

9. $g(x) = \frac{1}{2}|x|$

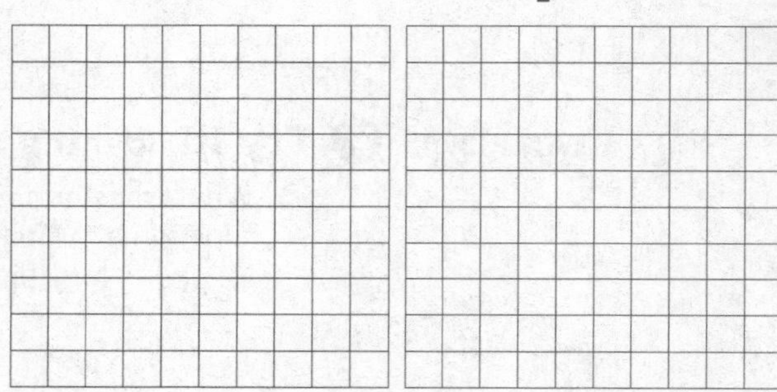

10. $g(x) = 4x$

11. $g(x) = |5x|$

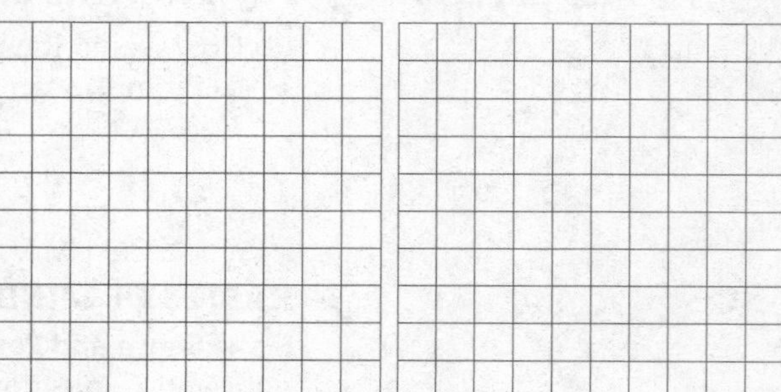

12. Which types of transformations in Exercises 4–11 do not change the shape of a graph? Which types of transformations change the shape of a graph? Explain.

1-3 Piecewise-Defined Functions

PearsonRealize.com

MODEL & DISCUSS

A music teacher needs to buy guitar strings for her class. At store A, the guitar strings cost $6 each. At store B, the guitar strings are $20 for a pack of 4.

A. Make graphs that show the income each store receives if the teacher needs 1–20 guitar strings.

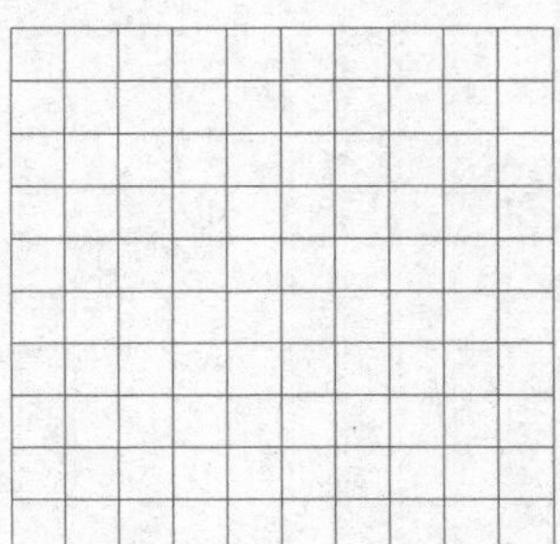

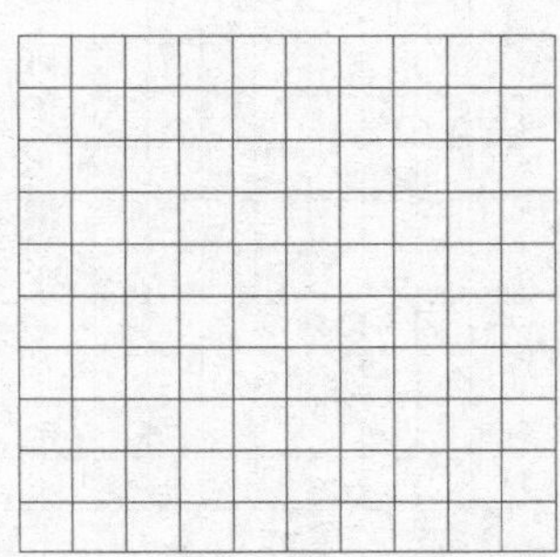

B. Describe the shape of the graph for store A. Describe the shape of the graph for store B. Why are the graphs different?

C. **Communicate Precisely** Compare the graphs for stores A and B. For what numbers of guitar strings is it cheaper to buy from store B? Explain how you know.

HABITS OF MIND

Communicate Precisely Why do you use dots rather than line segments to graph these two functions?

Notes

EXAMPLE 1 Try It! Model With a Piecewise-Defined Function

1. How much will Alani earn if she works:

   a. 37 hours? b. 43 hours?

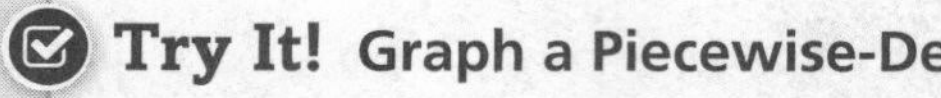

EXAMPLE 2 Try It! Graph a Piecewise-Defined Function

2. Graph the piecewise-defined function. What are the domain and range? Over what intervals is the function increasing or decreasing?

   a. $f(x) = \begin{cases} 2x + 5, & -6 \leq x \leq -2 \\ 2x^2 - 7, & -2 < x < 1 \\ -4 - x, & 1 \leq x \leq 3 \end{cases}$

   b. $f(x) = \begin{cases} 3, & -4 < x \leq 0 \\ -x, & 0 \leq x \leq 2 \\ 3 - x, & 2 < x < 4 \end{cases}$

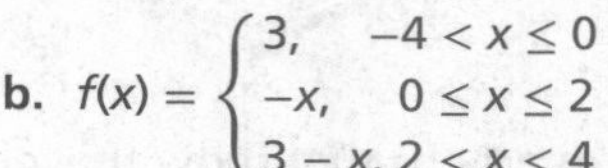

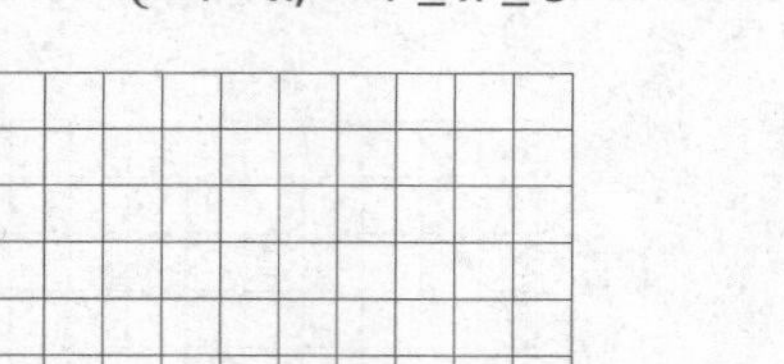

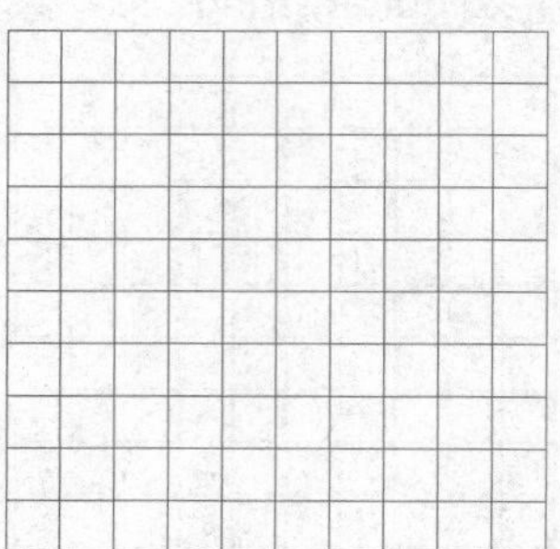

HABITS OF MIND

Reason Why is the interval for the domain of the second piece of the function in Try It! 2(a) defined using the $<$ symbol rather than the $\leq$ symbol?

EXAMPLE 3 Try It! Write a Piecewise-Defined Rule From a Graph

3. What rule defines the function in each of the following graphs?

a.

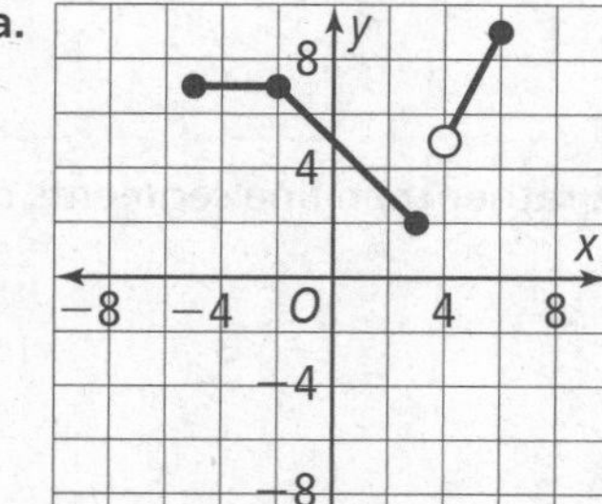

b.

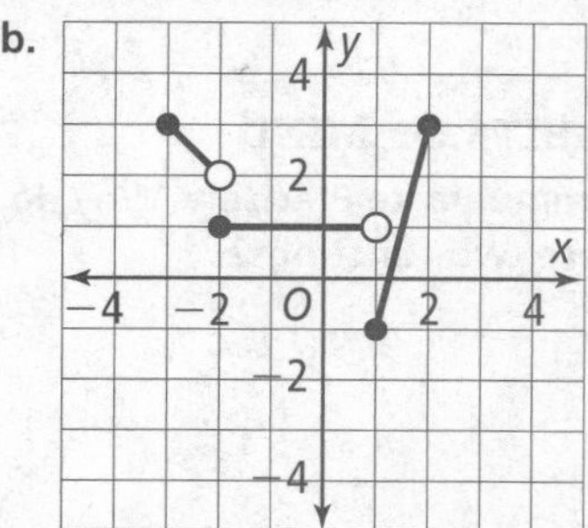

Notes

Assess

EXAMPLE 4 Try It! Write a Rule for an Absolute Value Function

4. How can you rewrite each function as a piecewise-defined function?

a. $f(x) = |-5x - 10|$ b. $f(x) = -|x| + 3$

HABITS OF MIND

Use Structure Why can the graph of an absolute value function also be defined as a piecewise-defined function?

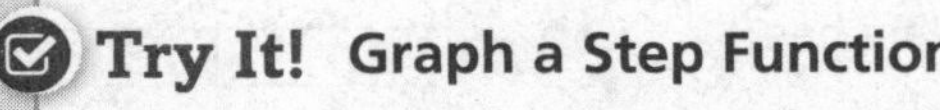

EXAMPLE 5 Try It! Graph a Step Function

5. The table below represents fees for a parking lot. Graph the function. What are the domain and range of the function? What are the maximum and minimum values?

Time	$0 < t \leq 3$h	$3 < t \leq 6$h	$6 < t \leq 9$h	$9 < t \leq 12$h
Cost	\$10	\$15	\$20	\$25

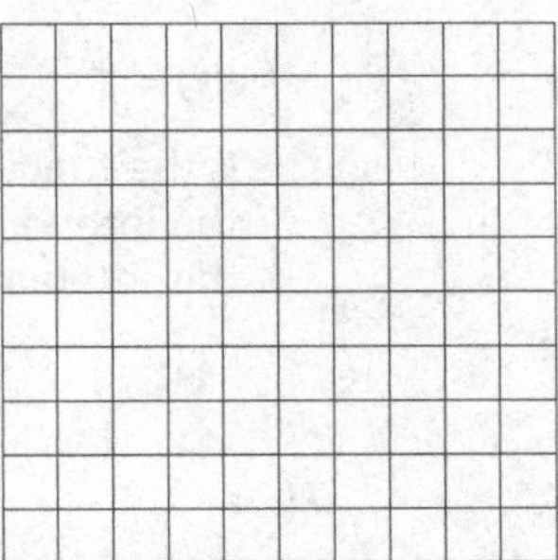

HABITS OF MIND

Make Sense and Persevere How would a piecewise-defined rule for the function in the Try It! show that the graph is a step function?

Assess

Do You UNDERSTAND?

1. ESSENTIAL QUESTION How do you model a situation in which a function behaves differently over different parts of its domain?

2. **Vocabulary** How do piecewise-defined functions differ from step functions?

3. **Error Analysis** Given the function

$$f(x) = \begin{cases} 2x + 5, & -2 < x \le 4 \\ -4x - 7, & 4 < x \le 9 \end{cases},$$

Rebecca says there is an open circle at $x = 4$ for both pieces of the function. Explain her error.

4. **Communicate Precisely** What steps do you follow when graphing a piecewise-defined function?

5. **Make Sense and Persevere** Is the relation defined by the following piecewise rule a function? Explain.

$$y = \begin{cases} 7x - 4, & x < 2 \\ -x + 5, & x \ge -2 \end{cases}$$

Do You KNOW HOW?

Graph the function.

6. $f(x) = \begin{cases} -x + 1, & -10 \le x < -3 \\ x^2 - 9, & -3 \le x \le 3 \\ 2x + 1, & 3 < x < 5 \end{cases}$

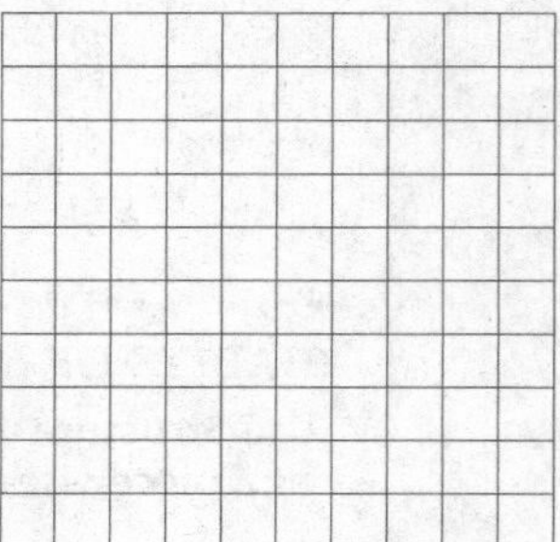

7. $g(x) = \begin{cases} 1, & 0 \le x < 2 \\ 3, & 2 \le x < 4 \\ 5, & 4 \le x < 6 \\ 7, & 6 \le x < 8 \end{cases}$

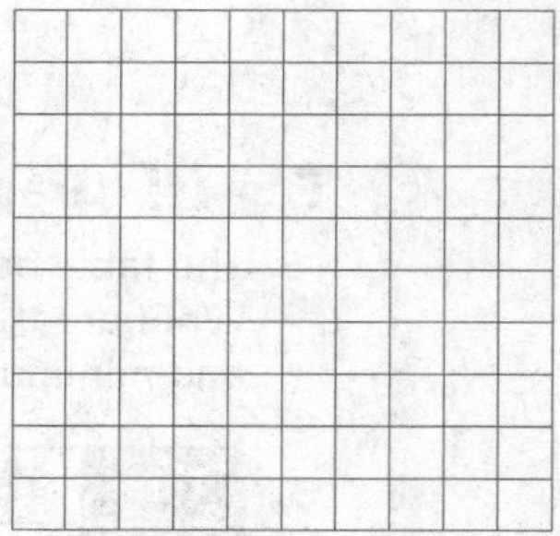

8. Given the function

$$f(x) = \begin{cases} -2x + 4, & 0 \le x < 8 \\ -5x + 11, & x \ge 8 \end{cases}$$

is the function increasing or decreasing over the interval [2, 7]? Find the rate of change over this interval.

9. What is the rule that defines the function shown in the graph?

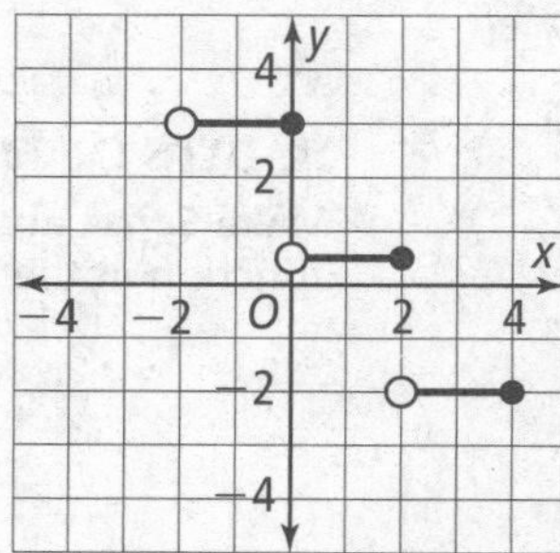

1-4 Arithmetic Sequences and Series

PearsonRealize.com

CRITIQUE & EXPLAIN

Yumiko and Hugo are looking at the table of data.

Input	Output
0	1
1	5
2	9
3	13
4	17

Yumiko writes

$f(1) = 1 + 4 = 5,$
$f(2) = f(1) + 4 = 5 + 4 = 9,$
$f(3) = f(2) + 4 = 9 + 4 = 13,$
$f(4) = f(3) + 4 = 13 + 4 = 17.$

Hugo writes $g(x) = 1 + 4x$.

A. Describe the pattern Yumiko found for finding an output value.

B. Describe the pattern Hugo found for finding an output value.

C. **Use Structure** Compare the two methods. Which method would be more useful in finding the 100th number in the list? Why?

HABITS OF MIND

Use Structure Find the average rate of change between a few pairs of points. What can you conclude about the function represented in the table?

EXAMPLE 1 Try It! Understand Arithmetic Sequences

1. Are the following sequences arithmetic? If so, what is the recursive definition, and what is the next term in the sequence?

   a. 25, 20, 15, 10, . . .

   b. 2, 4, 7, 12, 13, . . .

EXAMPLE 2 Try It! Translate Between Recursive and Explicit Forms

2. a. For the recursive definition $a_n = \begin{cases} 45, & n = 1 \\ a_{n-1} - 2, & n > 1 \end{cases}$, what is the explicit definition?

   b. For the explicit definition $a_n = 1 + 7(n - 1)$, what is the recursive definition?

EXAMPLE 3 Try It! Solve Problems With Arithmetic Sequences

3. Samantha is training for a race. The distances of her training runs form an arithmetic sequence. She runs 1 mi the first day and 2 mi the seventh day.

   a. What is the explicit definition for this sequence?

   b. How far does she run on day 19?

HABITS OF MIND

Use Appropriate Tools How can you use the recursive definition for an arithmetic sequence to find the 120th term?

Notes

Assess

EXAMPLE 4

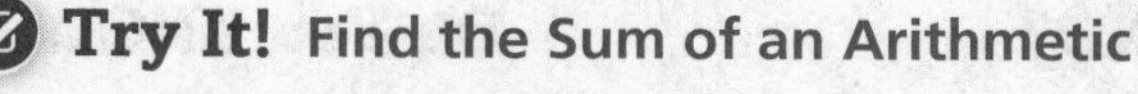

Try It! Find the Sum of an Arithmetic Series

4. Find the sum of each arithmetic series.

a. series with 12 terms, $a_1 = 3$ and $a_{12} = 25$

b. $5 + 11 + 17 + 23 + 29 + 35 + 41$

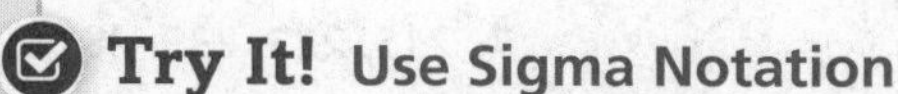

EXAMPLE 5

Try It! Use Sigma Notation

5. a. What is the sum of the series $\sum_{i=1}^{13} 3i + 2$?

b. How can you write the series $8 + 13 + 18 + \ldots + 43$ using sigma notation? What is the sum?

EXAMPLE 6

Try It! Use a Finite Arithmetic Series

6. A flight of stairs gets wider as it descends. The top stair is 15 bricks across, the second stair is 17 bricks across, and the third stair is 19 bricks across. What is the total number of bricks used in all 16 stairs?

HABITS OF MIND

Make Sense and Persevere What is the sum of the first 50 odd whole numbers? Explain how you found your answer.

Do You UNDERSTAND?

1. ESSENTIAL QUESTION What is an arithmetic sequence, and how do you represent and find its terms and their sums?

2. **Vocabulary** How do arithmetic sequences differ from arithmetic series?

3. **Error Analysis** A student claims the sequence 0, 1, 3, 6, . . . is an arithmetic sequence, and the next number is 10. What error did the student make?

4. **Communicate Precisely** How would you tell someone how to calculate $\sum_{n=1}^{5}(2n + 1)$?

Do You KNOW HOW?

Find the common difference and the next three terms of each arithmetic sequence.

5. $\frac{1}{4}, \frac{1}{2}, \frac{3}{4}, 1, \frac{5}{4}, \ldots$

6. 6, 1, −4, −9, −14, . . .

7. 215, 227, 239, 251, . . .

8. −4, −5, −6, −7, . . .

9. 4.1, 6.3, 8.5, 10.7, . . .

10. −17, −9, −1, 7, 15, . . .

11. In June, you start a holiday savings account with a deposit of $30. You increase each monthly deposit by $4 until the end of the year. How much money will you have saved by the end of December?

1-5
Solving Equations and Inequalities by Graphing

PearsonRealize.com

MODEL & DISCUSS

A homeowner has 32 feet of fencing to build three sides of a rectangular chicken run.

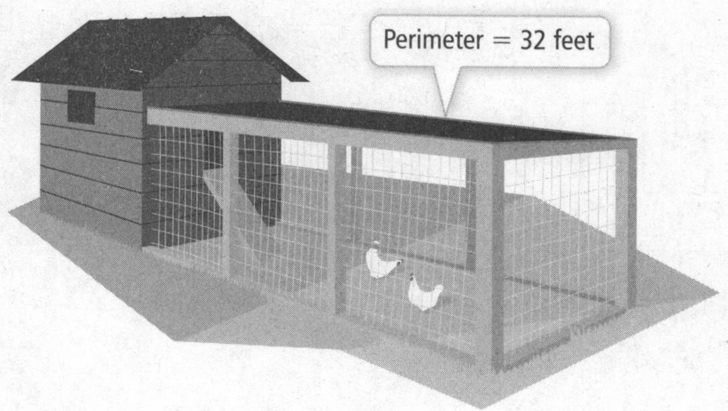

A. Make a table of values for the length, width, and area of different rectangles that will utilize 32 feet of fencing. Then write a function for the area, in terms of width, of a rectangular run using this much fencing.

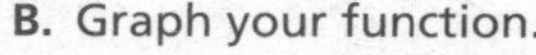

B. Graph your function.

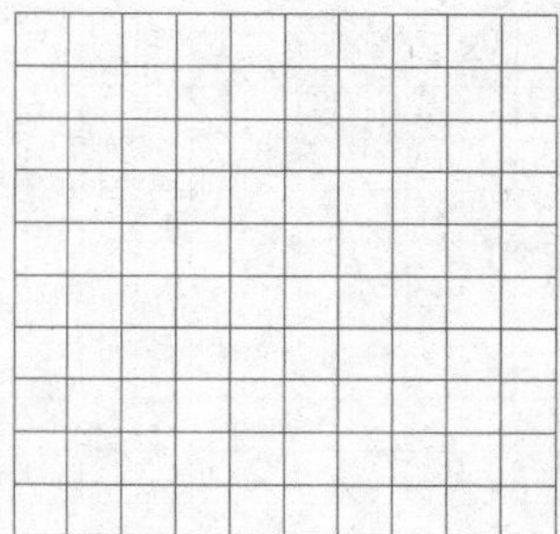

C. Reason Explain what happens where the graph intersects the *x*-axis.

HABITS OF MIND

Make Sense and Persevere For what widths will the area of the chicken run be at least 55 ft^2?

Notes

Assess

EXAMPLE 1

Try It! Use a Graph to Solve an Equation

1. Use a graph to solve the equation.

a. $5x - 12 = 3$

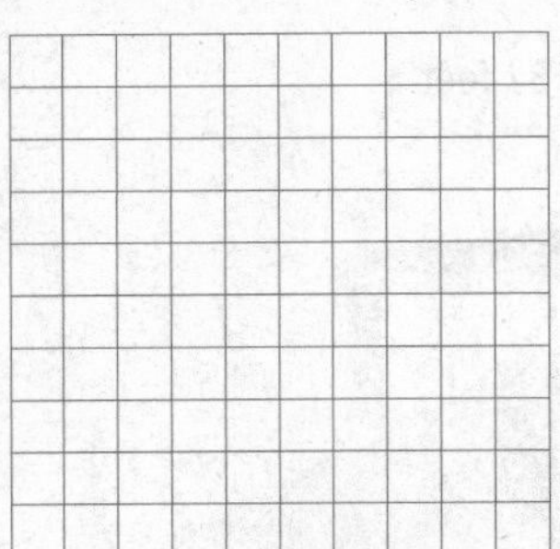

b. $-|x - 2| = -\frac{1}{2}x - 2$

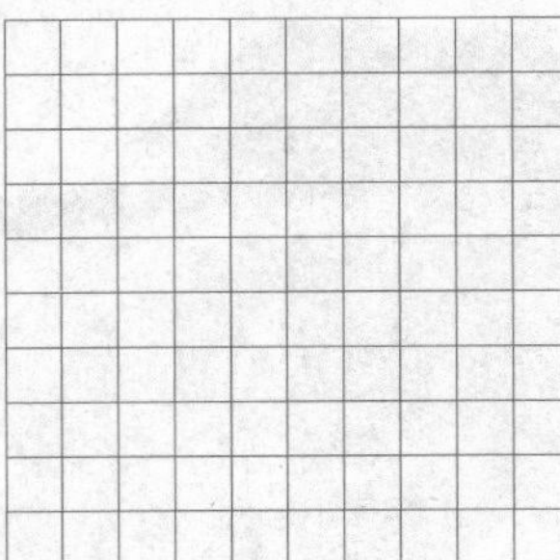

EXAMPLE 2

Try It! Solve a One-Variable Inequality by Graphing

2. Use a graph to solve each inequality.

a. $x^2 + 6x + 5 \geq 0$

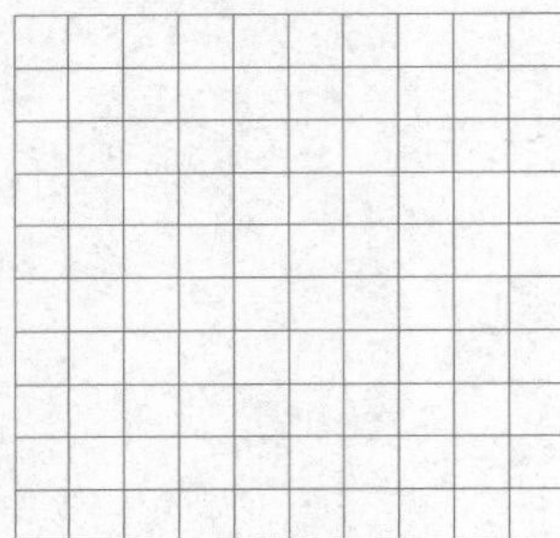

b. $x + 3 > 7 - 3x$

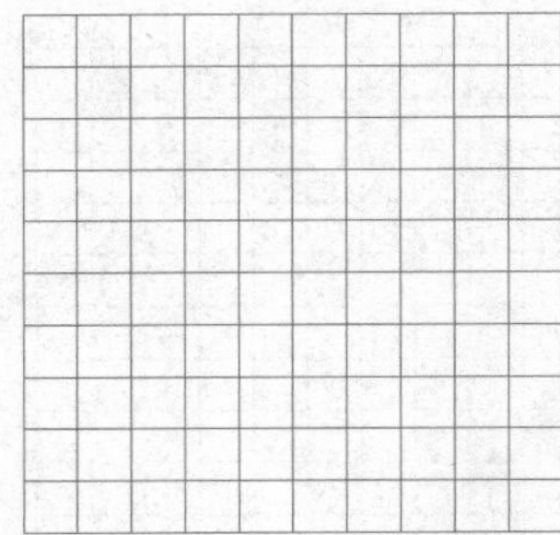

HABITS OF MIND

Use Structure How does a graph show the solution to an equation?

Notes

EXAMPLE 3

Try It! Use a Table to Solve an Equation

3. The equation $x^2 - 4x + 1 = x - 2$ has a second solution in the interval $4 < x < 5$. Use a spreadsheet to approximate this solution to the nearest thousandth.

EXAMPLE 4

Try It! Use Graphing Technology to Solve Equations

4. Use graphing technology to approximate the solutions of the equation $x^2 + 2x - 1 = |x + 2| + 2$ to the nearest tenth.

HABITS OF MIND

Use Appropriate Tools What are the advantages and disadvantages of using spreadsheets and graphing technology?

Do You UNDERSTAND?

1. ESSENTIAL QUESTION How can you solve an equation or inequality by graphing?

2. **Communicate Precisely** What is an advantage of solving an equation graphically by finding the points of intersection?

3. **Error Analysis** Ben said the graph of the inequality $-x^2 + 9 > 0$ shows the solution is $x < -3$ or $x > 3$. Is Ben correct? Explain.

Do You KNOW HOW?

4. Using the graph below, what is the solution to $-2x + 4 = -2$? How can you tell?

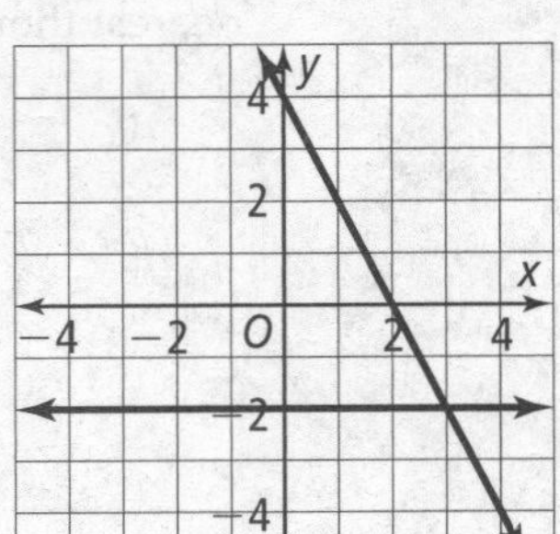

1-6

Linear Systems

PearsonRealize.com

EXPLORE & REASON

The graph shows two lines that intersect at one point.

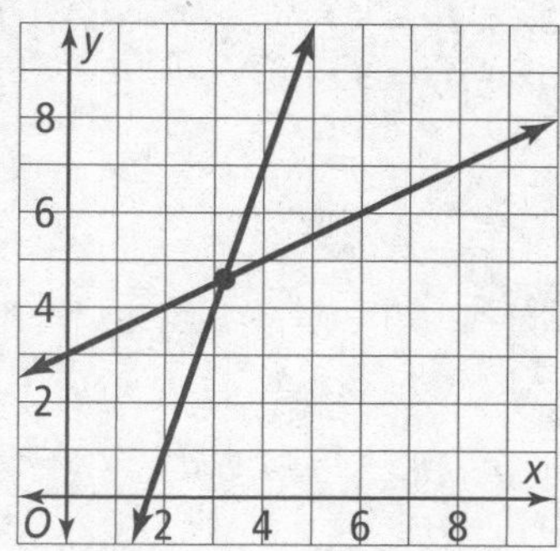

A. What are the approximate coordinates of the point of intersection?

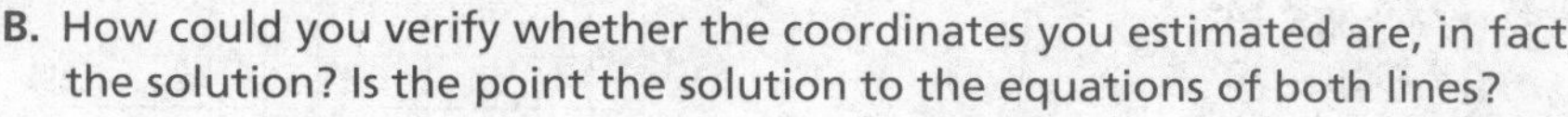

B. How could you verify whether the coordinates you estimated are, in fact, the solution? Is the point the solution to the equations of both lines?

C. Make Sense and Persevere Use your result to refine your approximation, and try again. Can you find the point of intersection this way? Is there a more efficient way?

HABITS OF MIND

Communicate Precisely The graphs of two equations appear to intersect at the point (2, 3). Does that guarantee that $x = 2$ and $y = 3$ is a solution to both equations? Explain.

Notes

EXAMPLE 1

Try It! Solve a System of Linear Equations

1. Solve each system of equations.

a. $\begin{cases} 2x + y = -1 \\ 5y - 6x = 7 \end{cases}$

b. $\begin{cases} 3x + 2y = 5 \\ 6x + 4y = 3 \end{cases}$

EXAMPLE 2

Try It! Solve a System of Linear Inequalities

2. Sketch the graph of the set of all points that solve this system of linear inequalities.

$\begin{cases} 2x + y \leq 14 \\ x + 2y \leq 10 \\ x \geq 0 \\ y \geq 0 \end{cases}$

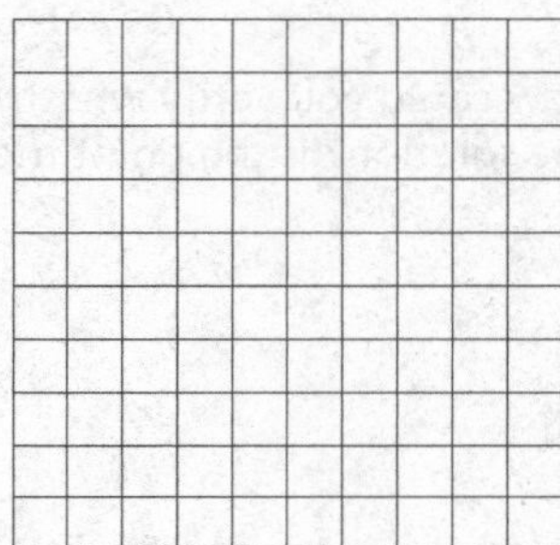

HABITS OF MIND

Make Sense and Persevere Is it possible to solve a system of linear inequalities using the same methods you used to solve a system of linear equations?

Notes

EXAMPLE 3 **Try It!** **Solve a System of Equations in Three Variables**

3. Solve the following systems of equations.

a. $\begin{cases} x + y + z = 3 \\ x - y + z = 1 \\ x + y - z = 2 \end{cases}$

b. $\begin{cases} 2x + y - 2z = 3 \\ x - 2y + 7z = 12 \\ 3x - y + 5z = 10 \end{cases}$

HABITS OF MIND

Generalize What is the goal of the substitution and elimination methods?

Do You UNDERSTAND?

1. ESSENTIAL QUESTION How can you find and represent solutions of systems of linear equations and inequalities?

2. **Error Analysis** Shandra said the solution of the system of equations $\begin{cases} 2x + y = 3 \\ -x + 4y = -6 \end{cases}$ is $(-1, 2)$. Is she correct? Explain.

3. **Communicate Precisely** Why is a system of linear inequalities often solved graphically?

4. **Make Sense and Persevere** How does knowing how to solve a system of two equations in two variables help you to solve a system of three equations in three variables?

5. **Vocabulary** What is the difference between a system of linear equations and a system of linear inequalities?

Do You KNOW HOW?

6. Solve the following system of equations.
$$\begin{cases} 2x + 2y = 10 \\ x + 5y = 13 \end{cases}$$

7. Graph the following system of inequalities.
$$\begin{cases} -x + 2y < 1 \\ x \geq 0 \\ y \geq 0 \end{cases}$$

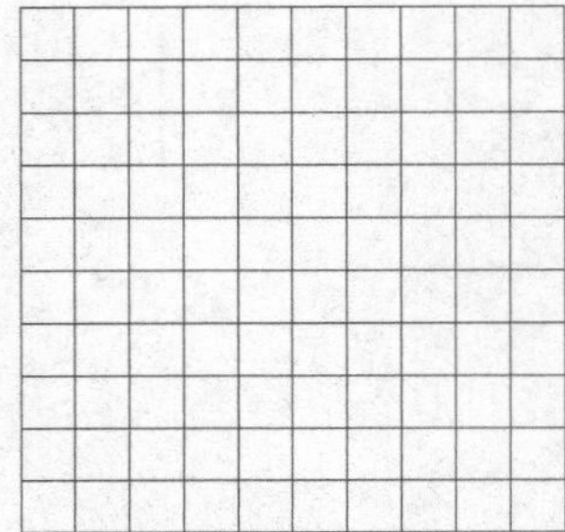

8. Solve the following systems of equations.
$$2x - y + z = 3$$
$$3x + y + 3z = 10$$
$$x - 2y - 2z = 3$$

9. Equations with two variables that are raised only to the first power represent lines. There are three possible outcomes for the intersections of two lines. Describe the outcomes.

Video

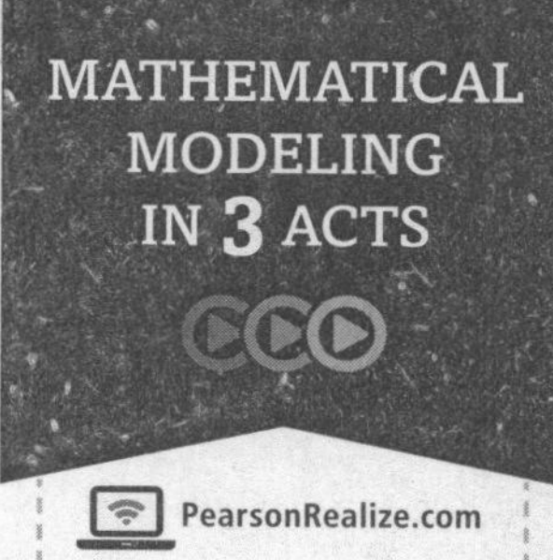

PearsonRealize.com

Current Events

You might say that someone who loses their temper has "blown a fuse." However, it's rare to hear about electrical fuses blowing these days. That's because most fuses have been replaced by circuit breakers. A fuse must be replaced once it's blown, but a circuit breaker can be reset.

Ask for permission to look at the electrical panel in your home. If there is a series of switches inside, each of those is a circuit breaker, designed to interrupt the circuit when the electrical current inside is too dangerous. How much electricity does it take to trip a circuit breaker? Think about this question during the Mathematical Modeling in 3-Acts lesson.

ACT 1 Identify the Problem

1. What is the first question that comes to mind after watching the video?

2. Write down the Main Question you will answer.

3. Make an initial conjecture that answers this Main Question.

4. Explain how you arrived at your conjecture.

5. What information will be useful to know to answer the main question? How can you get it? How will you use that information?

ACT 2 Develop a Model

6. Use the math that you have learned in the topic to refine your conjecture.

ACT 3 Interpret the Results

7. Did your refined conjecture match the actual answer exactly? If not, what might explain the difference?

EXPLORE & REASON

Consider functions of the form $f(x) = x^n$, where n is a positive integer.

A. Graph $f(x) = x^n$ for $n = 1$, 3, and 5. Look at the graphs in Quadrant I. As the exponent increases, what is happening to the graphs? Which quadrants do the graphs pass through?

B. Look for Relationships Now graph $f(x) = x^n$ for $n = 2$, 4, and 6. What happens to these graphs in Quadrant I as the exponent increases? Which quadrants do the graphs pass through?

C. Write two equations in the form $f(x) = x^n$ with graphs that you predict are in Quadrants I and II. Write two equations with graphs that you predict are in Quadrants I and III. Use graphing technology to test your predictions.

HABITS OF MIND

Construct Arguments Compare and contrast the end behavior of the graphs of $f(x) = x^n$ when $n = 1$, 3, & 5 with the graphs of $f(x) = x^n$ when $n = 2$, 4, & 10. Write a general statement that compares the end behavior of the graphs when the exponents are odd to the end behavior when the exponents are even.

Notes

EXAMPLE 1 **Try It!** **Classify Polynomials**

1. What is each polynomial in standard form. What are the leading coefficient, the degree, and the number of terms of each?

   a. $2x - 3x^4 + 6 - 5x^3$

   b. $x^5 + 2x^6 - 3x^4 - 8x + 4x^3$

EXAMPLE 2 **Try It!** **Interpret Leading Coefficients and Degrees**

2. Use the leading coefficient and degree of the polynomial function to determine the end behavior of each graph.

   a. $f(x) = 2x^6 - 5x^5 + 6x^4 - x^3 + 4x^2 - x + 1$

   b. $g(x) = -5x^3 + 8x + 4$

HABITS OF MIND

Communicate Precisely How does the leading coefficient help determine the end behavior of an even function?

EXAMPLE 3 **Try It!** **Graph a Polynomial Function**

3. Consider the polynomial function $f(x) = x^5 + 18x^2 + 10x + 1$.

   a. Make a table of values to identify key features and sketch a graph of the function.

   b. Find the average rate of change over the interval [0, 2].

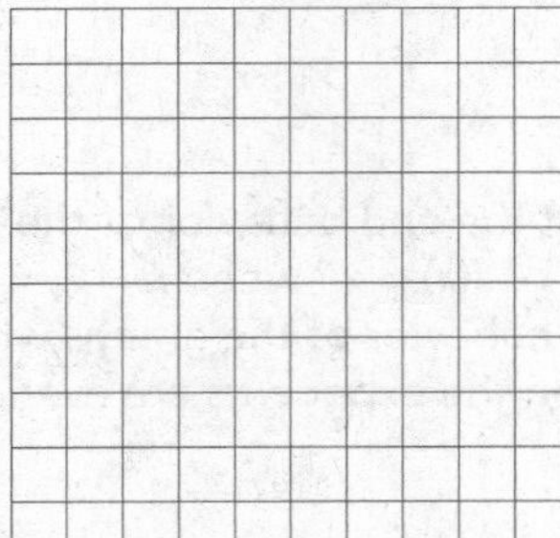

Notes

EXAMPLE 4

Try It! Sketch a Graph from a Verbal Description

4. Use the information below to sketch a graph of the polynomial function $y = f(x)$.

- $f(x)$ is positive on the intervals $(-2, -1)$ and $(1, 2)$.
- $f(x)$ is negative on the intervals $(-\infty, -2)$, $(-1, 1)$, and $(2, \infty)$.
- $f(x)$ is increasing on the intervals $(-\infty, -1.5)$ and $(0, 1.5)$.
- $f(x)$ is decreasing on the intervals $(-1.5, 0)$ and $(1.5, \infty)$.

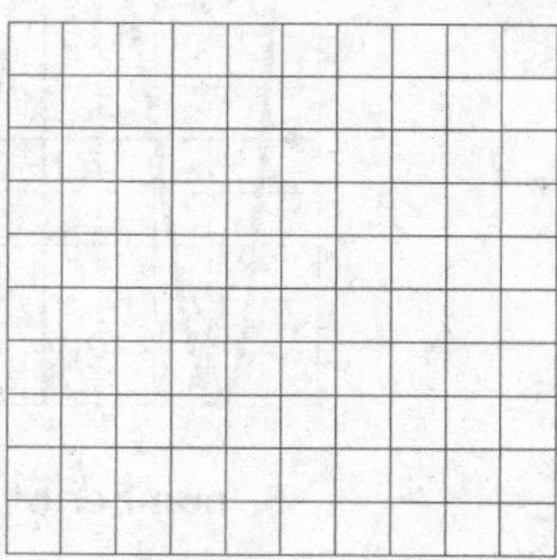

HABITS OF MIND

Generalize What can you tell about the graph of a function if its equation has an odd degree and a negative leading coefficient?

EXAMPLE 5

Try It! Interpret a Polynomial Model

5. Danielle is engineering a new brand of shoes. For x shoes sold, in thousands, a profit of $p(x) = -3x^4 + 4x^3 - 2x^2 + 5x + 10$ dollars, in ten thousands, will be earned.

a. How much will be earned in profit for selling 1,000 shoes?

b. What do the x- and y-intercepts of the graph mean in this context? Do those values make sense?

HABITS OF MIND

Use Appropriate Tools Estimate the turning point of the graph of $p(x) = -3x^4 + 4x^3 - 2x^2 + 5x + 10$. What does this point represent in the context of Try It! 5?

Do You UNDERSTAND?

1. ESSENTIAL QUESTION How do the key features of a polynomial function help you sketch its graph?

2. **Error Analysis** Allie said the degree of the polynomial function $f(x) = x^5 + 2x^4 + 3x^3 - 2x^6 - 9x^2 - 6x + 4$ is 5. Explain and correct Allie's error.

3. **Vocabulary** Explain how to determine the **leading coefficient** of a polynomial function.

4. **Look for Relationships** What is the relationship between the degree and leading coefficient of a polynomial function and the end behavior of the polynomial?

Do You KNOW HOW?

The graph shows the function $f(x) = x^4 + 2x^3 - 13x^2 - 14x + 24$. Find the following.

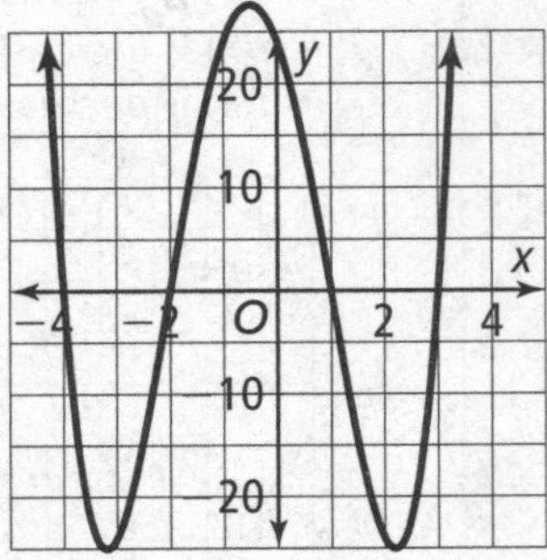

5. number of terms

6. degree

7. leading coefficient

8. end behavior

9. turning point(s)

10. x-intercept(s)

11. relative minimum(s)

12. relative maximum(s)

2-2 Adding, Subtracting, and Multiplying Polynomials

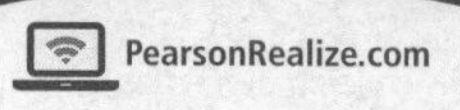

EXPLORE & REASON

Let S be the set of expressions that can be written as $ax + b$, where a and b are real numbers.

A. Describe the Associative Property, the Commutative Property, and the Distributive Property. Then, explain the role of each in simplifying the sum $(3x + 2) + (7x - 4)$ and identify the leading coefficient and the constant term in the result.

B. Is the sum you found in part A a member of S? Explain.

C. **Construct Arguments** Is the product of two expressions in S also a member of S? Explain why or produce a counterexample.

HABITS OF MIND

Construct Arguments Is the quotient of two expressions in S also a member of S? Explain why or produce a counterexample.

Notes

EXAMPLE 1  **Try It! Add and Subtract Polynomials**

1. Add or subtract the polynomials.

   a. $(4a^4 - 6a^3 - 3a^2 + a + 1) + (5a^3 + 7a^2 + 2a - 2)$

   b. $(2a^2b^2 + 3ab^2 - 5a^2b) - (3a^2b^2 - 9a^2b + 7ab^2)$

HABITS OF MIND

Generalize When can you combine two terms using addition or subtraction?

EXAMPLE 2  **Try It! Multiply Polynomials**

2. Multiply the polynomials.

   a. $(6n^2 - 7)(n^2 + n + 3)$

   b. $(mn + 1)(m^2n - 1)(mn^2 + 2)$

EXAMPLE 3  **Try It! Understand Closure**

3. Is the set of monomials closed under multiplication? Explain.

HABITS OF MIND

Construct Arguments Is the set of polynomials closed under multiplication? Explain.

Notes

EXAMPLE 4

Try It! Write a Polynomial Function

4. The cost of Carolina's materials changes so that her new cost function is $c(x) = 4x + 42$. Find the new profit function. Then find the quantity that maximizes profit and calculate the profit.

EXAMPLE 5

Try It! Compare Two Polynomial Functions

5. Compare the profit functions of two additional market sellers modeled by the graph of f and the equation $g(x) = (x + 1)(5 - x)$. Compare and interpret the y-intercepts of these functions and their end behavior.

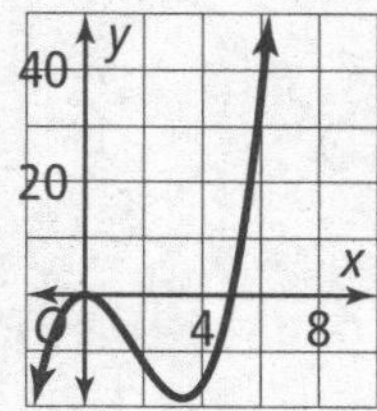

HABITS OF MIND

Make Sense and Persevere Find the quantity that maximizes profit for $g(x) = (x + 1)(5 - x)$. Calculate the profit.

Do You UNDERSTAND?

1. ESSENTIAL QUESTION How do you add, subtract, and multiply polynomials?

2. **Error Analysis** Chen subtracted two polynomials as shown. Explain Chen's error.

$p^2 + 7mp + 4 - (-2p^2 - mp + 1)$

$p^2 + 2p^2 + 7mp - mp + 4 + 1$

$3p^2 + 6mp + 5$ ✗

3. **Communicate Precisely** Why do we often write the results of polynomial calculations in standard form?

4. **Construct Arguments** Is the set of whole numbers closed under subtraction? Explain why you think so, or provide a counterexample.

Do You KNOW HOW?

Add or subtract the polynomials.

5. $(-3a^3 + 2a^2 - 4) + (a^3 - 3a^2 - 5a + 7)$

6. $(7x^2y^2 - 6x^3 + xy) - (5x^2y^2 - x^3 + xy + x)$

Multiply the polynomials.

7. $(7a + 2)(2a^2 - 5a + 3)$

8. $(xy - 1)(xy + 6)(xy - 8)$

9. The length of a rectangular speaker is three times its width, and the height is four more than the width. Write an expression for the volume V of the rectangular prism in terms of its width, w.

Activity

PearsonRealize.com

EXPLORE & REASON

Look at the following triangle. Each number is the sum of the two numbers diagonally above. If there is not a second number, think of it as 0.

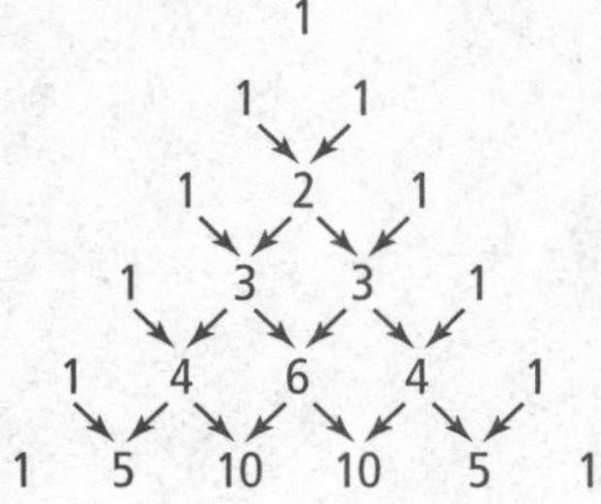

A. Write the numbers in the next 3 rows.

B. Look for Relationships What other patterns do you see?

C. Write a formula for the sum of the numbers in the nth row of the triangle.

HABITS OF MIND

Look for Relationships Create a triangle that starts with 2 instead of 1. How does this new triangle relate to the original triangle?

EXAMPLE 1

Try It! Prove a Polynomial Identity

1. Prove the Difference of Cubes Identity.

HABITS OF MIND

Reason Is the trinomial factor in the Difference of Cubes Identity a perfect square trinomial? Explain.

EXAMPLE 2

Try It! Use Polynomial Identities to Multiply Polynomials

2. Use polynomial identities to multiply each expression.

   a. $(3x^2 + 5y^3)(3x^2 - 5y^3)$

   b. $(12 + 15)^2$

EXAMPLE 3

Try It! Use Polynomial Identities to Factor Polynomials

3. Use polynomial identities to factor each polynomial or simplify each expression.

   a. $m^8 - 9n^{10}$

   b. $27x^9 - 343y^6$

   c. $12^3 + 2^3$

HABITS OF MIND

Look for Relationships What binomial has factors $(a - 3b)$ and $(a^2 + 3ab + 9b^2)$?

Notes

Assess

EXAMPLE 4 **Try It! Expand a Power of a Binomial**

4. Use Pascal's Triangle to expand $(x + y)^6$.

EXAMPLE 5 **Try It! Apply the Binomial Theorem**

5. Use the Binomial Theorem to expand each expression.

a. $(x - 1)^7$

b. $(2c + d)^6$

HABITS OF MIND

Use Structure For what binomial expression is the expansion $243x^5 - 405x^4y^2 + 270x^3y^4 - 90x^2y^6 + 15xy^8 - y^{10}$?

Do You UNDERSTAND?

1. ESSENTIAL QUESTION How can you use polynomial identities to rewrite expressions efficiently?

2. **Reason** Explain why the middle term of $(x + 5)^2$ is $10x$.

3. **Communicate Precisely** How are Pascal's Triangle and a binomial expansion, such as $(a + b)^5$, related?

4. **Use Structure** Explain how to use a polynomial identity to factor $8x^6 - 27y^3$.

5. **Make Sense and Persevere** What does C_3 represent in the expansion $C_0a^5 + C_1a^4b + C_2a^3b^2 + C_3a^2b^3 + C_4ab^4 + C_5b^5$? Explain.

6. **Error Analysis** Dakota said the third term of the expansion of $(2g + 3h)^4$ is $36g^2h^2$. Explain Dakota's error. Then correct the error.

Do You KNOW HOW?

Use polynomial identities to multiply each expression.

7. $(2x + 8y)(2x - 8y)$

8. $(x + 3y^3)^2$

Use polynomial identities to factor each polynomial.

9. $36a^6 - 4b^2$

10. $8x^6 - y^3$

11. $m^9 + 27n^6$

Find the term of each binomial expansion.

12. fifth term of $(x + y)^5$

13. third term of $(a - 3)^6$

Use Pascal's Triangle to expand each expression.

14. $(x + 1)^5$

15. $(a - b)^6$

Use the Binomial Theorem to expand each expression.

16. $(d - 1)^4$

17. $(x + y)^7$

Activity

2-4 Dividing Polynomials

PearsonRealize.com

EXPLORE & REASON

Benson recalls how to divide whole numbers by solving a problem with 6 as the divisor and 83 as the dividend. He determines that the quotient is 13 with remainder 5.

A. Explain the process of long division using Benson's example.

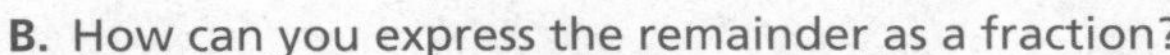

B. How can you express the remainder as a fraction?

C. Use Structure Use the results of the division problem to write two expressions for 83 that include the divisor, quotient, and remainder.

HABITS OF MIND

Look for Relationships If the remainder in a division problem is zero, what can you say about the dividend?

Assess

EXAMPLE 1  **Try It! Use Long Division to Divide Polynomials**

1. Use long division to divide the polynomials.

   a. $x^3 - 6x^2 + 11x - 6$ divided by $x^2 - 4x + 3$

   b. $16x^4 - 85$ divided by $4x^2 + 9$

EXAMPLE 2  **Try It! Use Synthetic Division to Divide by $x - a$**

2. Use synthetic division to divide $3x^3 - 5x + 10$ by $x - 1$.

HABITS OF MIND

Communicate Precisely Which method would you use to divide a polynomial by $x^2 + 5$? Why?

EXAMPLE 3  **Try It! Relate $P(a)$ to the Remainder of $P(x) \div (x - a)$**

3. Use synthetic division to show that the remainder of $f(x) = x^3 + 8x^2 + 12x + 5$ divided by $x + 2$ is equal to $f(-2)$.

Notes

EXAMPLE 4 **Try It! Use the Remainder Theorem to Evaluate Polynomials**

4. A technology company uses the function $R(x) = -x^3 + 12x^2 + 6x + 80$ to model expected annual revenue, in thousands of dollars, for a new product, where x is the number of years after the product is released. Use the Remainder Theorem to estimate the revenue in year 5.

EXAMPLE 5 **Try It! Use the Factor Theorem**

5. Use the Remainder and Factor Theorems to determine whether the given binomial is a factor of $P(x)$.

   a. $P(x) = x^3 - 10x^2 + 28x - 16$; binomial: $x - 4$

   b. $P(x) = 2x^4 + 9x^3 - 2x^2 + 6x - 40$; binomial: $x + 5$

HABITS OF MIND

Make Sense and Persevere Is $x - 2$ a factor of $x^5 + x^4 - 6x^3 + 2x^2 - 11x + 15$? If not, what is the remainder?

Do You UNDERSTAND?

1. ESSENTIAL QUESTION How can you divide polynomials?

2. **Error Analysis** Ella said the remainder of $x^3 + 2x^2 - 4x + 6$ divided by $x + 5$ is 149. Is Ella correct? Explain.

3. **Look for Relationships** You divide a polynomial $P(x)$ by a linear expression $D(x)$. You find a quotient $Q(x)$ and a remainder $R(x)$. How can you check your work?

Do You KNOW HOW?

4. Use long division to divide $x^4 - 4x^3 + 12x^2 - 3x + 6$ by $x^2 + 8$.

5. Use synthetic division to divide $x^3 - 8x^2 + 9x - 5$ by $x - 3$.

6. Use the Remainder Theorem to find the remainder of $2x^4 + x^2 - 10x - 1$ divided by $x + 2$.

7. Is $x + 9$ a factor of the polynomial $P(x) = x^3 + 11x^2 + 15x - 27$? If so, write the polynomial as a product of two factors. If not, explain how you know.

Activity

PearsonRealize.com

MODEL & DISCUSS

Charlie and Aisha built a small rocket and launched it from their backyard. The rocket fell to the ground 10 s after it launched. The height *h*, in feet, of the rocket relative to the ground at time *t* seconds can be modeled by the function shown.

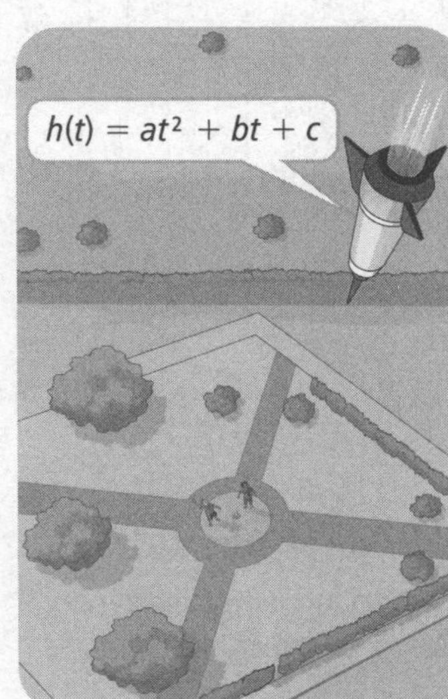

A. How are the launch and landing times related to the modeling function?

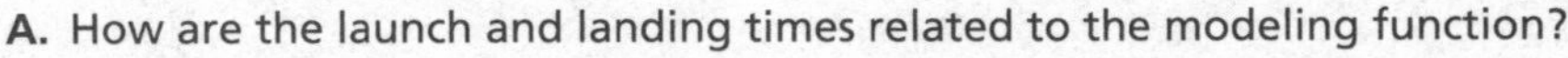

B. What additional information about the rocket launch could you use to construct an accurate model for the rocket's height relative to the ground?

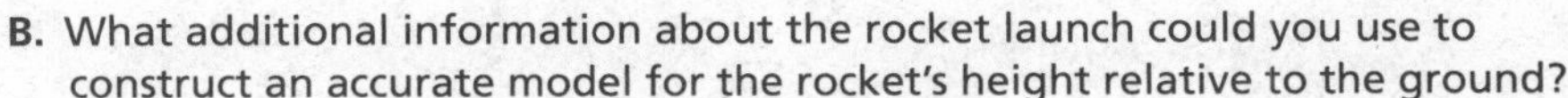

C. Construct Arguments Charlie believes that the function $h(t) = -16t^2 + 160t$ models the height of the rocket with respect to time. Do you agree? Explain your reasoning and indicate the domain of this function.

HABITS OF MIND

Reason In Charlie's function, what is the value of *c*? Why is this the correct value?

 Notes

Assess

EXAMPLE 1 **Try It! Use Zeros to Graph a Polynomial Function**

1. Factor each function. Then use the zeros to sketch its graph.

a. $f(x) = 4x^3 + 4x^2 - 24x$ b. $g(x) = x^4 - 81$

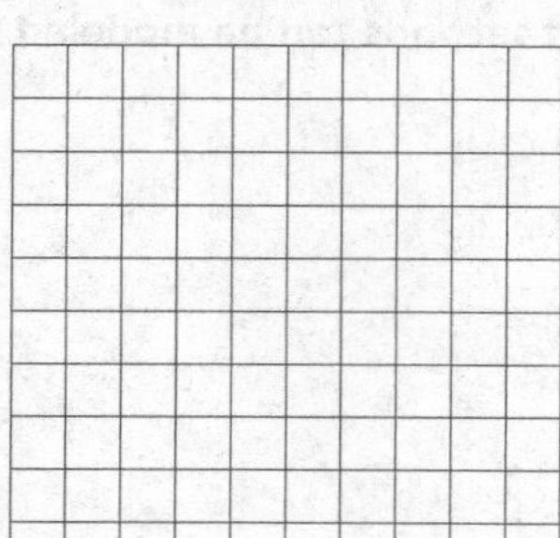

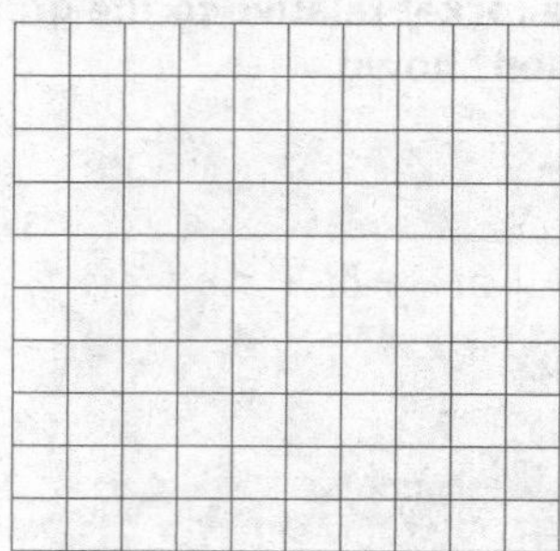

EXAMPLE 2 **Try It! Understand How a Multiple Zero Can Affect a Graph**

2. Describe the behavior of the graph of the function at each of its zeros.

a. $f(x) = x(x + 4)(x - 1)^4$ b. $f(x) = (x^2 + 9)(x - 1)^5(x + 2)^2$

HABITS OF MIND

Reason Do the values of a function always change from positive to negative or negative to positive on either side of a zero? Explain.

EXAMPLE 3 **Try It! Find Real and Complex Zeros**

3. What are all the real and complex zeros of the polynomial function shown in the graph?

a.

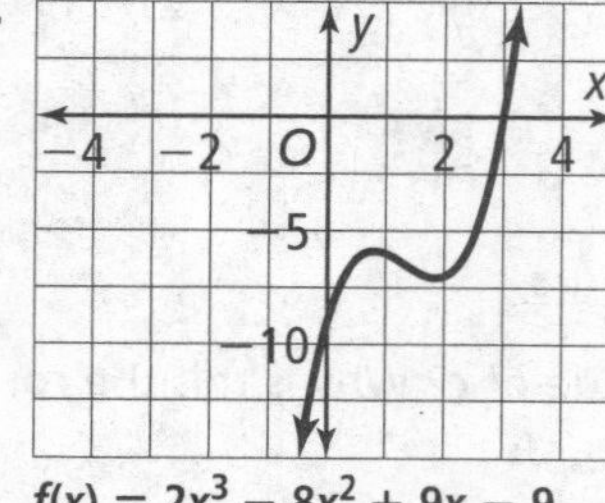

$f(x) = 2x^3 - 8x^2 + 9x - 9$

b.

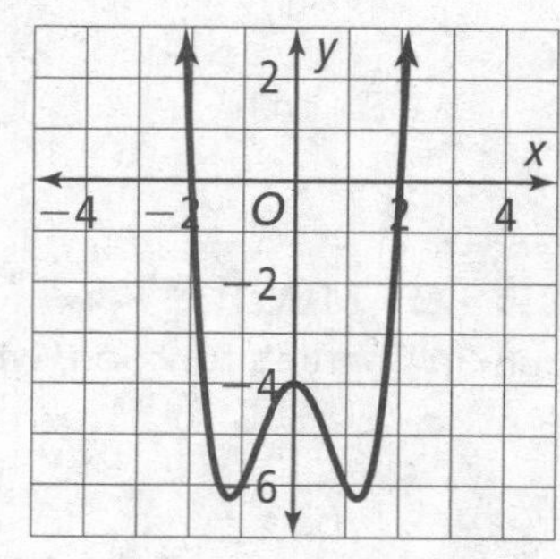

$f(x) = x^4 - 3x^2 - 4$

Notes

Assess

EXAMPLE 4

Try It! Interpret the Key Features of a Graph in Context

4. Due to a decrease in the cost of materials, the profit function for Acme Innovations has changed to $Q(x) = -x^3 + 10x^2 + 13x - 22$. How many lamps should they make in order to make a profit?

HABITS OF MIND

Make Sense and Persevere On a graph, how do complex roots differ from real roots?

EXAMPLE 5

Try It! Solve Polynomial Equations

5. What is the solution of the equation?

a. $x^3 - 7x + 6 = x^3 + 5x^2 - 2x - 24$

b. $x^4 + 2x^2 = -x^3 - 2x$

EXAMPLE 6

Try It! Solve a Polynomial Inequality by Graphing

6. What are the solutions of the inequality?

a. $2x^3 + 12x^2 + 12x < 0$

b. $(x^2 - 1)(x^2 - x - 6) > 0$

HABITS OF MIND

Use Structure How does solving $2x^3 + 12x^2 + 12x = 0$ help you to solve the inequality $2x^3 + 12x^2 + 12x < 0$?

Do You UNDERSTAND?

1. ESSENTIAL QUESTION How are the zeros of a polynomial function related to the equation and graph of a function?

2. **Error Analysis** In order to identify the zeros of the function, a student factored the cubic function $f(x) = x^3 - 3x^2 - 10x$ as follows:

$$f(x) = x^3 - 3x^2 - 10x$$
$$= x(x^2 - 3x - 10)$$
$$= x(x - 5)(x + 2)$$
$$x = 0, x = -5, x = 2$$

Describe and correct the error the student made.

3. **Make Sense and Persevere** Explain how you can determine that the function $f(x) = x^3 + 3x^2 + 4x + 2$ has both real and complex zeros.

Do You KNOW HOW?

4. If the graph of the function f has a multiple zero at $x = 2$, what is a possible exponent of the factor $x - 2$? Justify your reasoning.

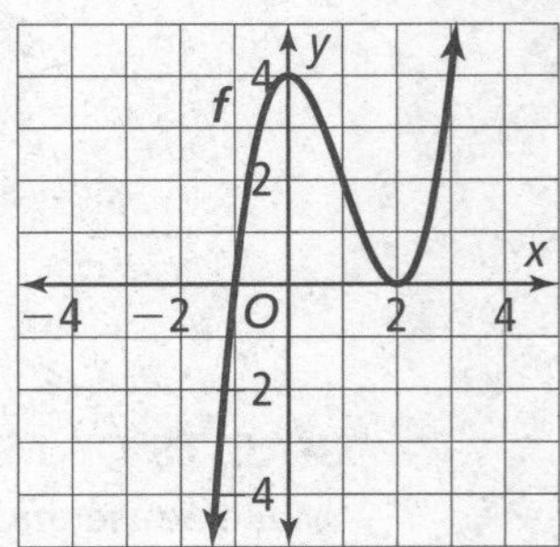

5. Energy Solutions manufactures LED light bulbs. The profit p, in thousands of dollars earned, is a function of the number of bulbs sold, x, in ten thousands. Profit is modeled by the function $-x^3 + 9x^2 - 11x - 21$. For what number of bulbs manufactured is the company profitable?

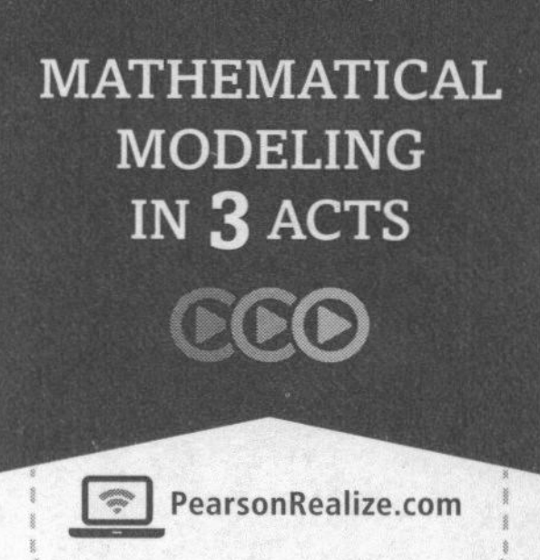

What Are the Rules?

All games have rules about how to play the game. The rules outline such things as when a ball is in or out, how a player scores points, and how many points a player gets for each winning shot.

If you didn't already know how to play tennis, or some other game, could you figure out what the rules were just by watching? What clues would help you understand the game? Think about this during the Mathematical Modeling in 3 Acts lesson.

ACT 1 Identify the Problem

1. What is the first question that comes to mind after watching the video?

2. Write down the Main Question you will answer.

3. Make an initial conjecture that answers this Main Question.

4. Explain how you arrived at your conjecture.

5. What information will be useful to know to answer the Main Question? How can you get it? How will you use that information?

Video

ACT 2 Develop a Model

6. Use the math that you have learned in the topic to refine your conjecture.

ACT 3 Interpret the Results

7. Did your refined conjecture match the actual answer exactly? If not, what might explain the difference?

CRITIQUE & EXPLAIN

Look at the polynomial functions shown.

$g(x) = x^2 - 7x - 18$
$h(x) = 5x^2 + 24x + 16$

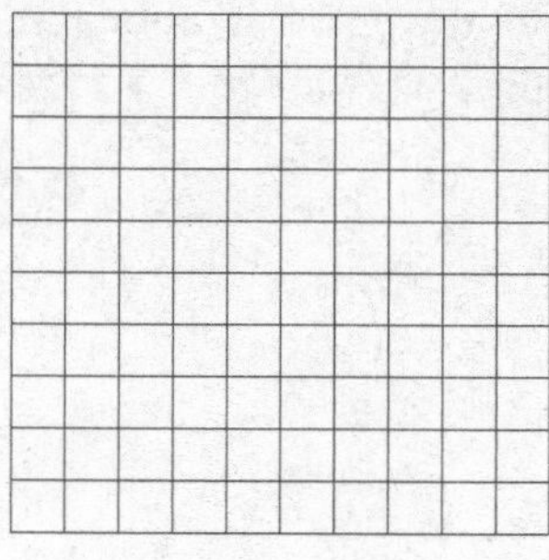

2-6 Theorems about Roots of Polynomial Equations

PearsonRealize.com

A. Avery has a conjecture that the zeros of a polynomial function have to be positive or negative factors of its constant term. Factor g completely. Are the zeros of g factors of -18?

B. Look for Relationships Now test Avery's conjecture by factoring $h(x)$. Does Avery's conjecture hold? If so, explain why. If not, make a new conjecture.

HABITS OF MIND

Use Structure For the factored function $k(x) = (ax + b)(cx + d)$, what are the coefficients in the expanded expression?

Notes

EXAMPLE 1

Try It! Identify Possible Rational Solutions

1. List all the possible rational solutions for each equation.

   a. $4x^4 + 13x^3 - 124x^2 + 212x - 8 = 0$

   b. $7x^4 + 13x^3 - 124x^2 + 212x - 45 = 0$

EXAMPLE 2

Try It! Use the Rational Root Theorem

2. A jewelry box measures $2x + 1$ in. long, $2x - 6$ in. wide, and x in. tall. The volume of the box is given by the function $v(x) = 4x^3 - 10x^2 - 6x$. What is the height of the box, in inches, if its volume is 28 in.^{3}?

HABITS OF MIND

Critique Arguments For the jewelry box, a student thought that the rational roots could be $\pm6, \pm3, \pm2, \pm1, \pm\frac{3}{2}, \pm\frac{1}{2}, \pm\frac{1}{4}$, using factors of -6 for the numerator and factors of 4 for the denominator of the possible rational roots. Is the student correct? Explain.

EXAMPLE 3

Try It! Find All Complex Roots

3. What are all the complex roots of the equation $x^3 - 2x^2 + 5x - 10 = 0$?

Notes

EXAMPLE 4

Try It! Irrational Roots and the Coefficients of a Polynomial

4. Suppose a quadratic polynomial function f has two complex zeros that are a conjugate pair, $a - bi$ and $a + bi$ (where a and b are real numbers). Are all the coefficients of f real? Explain.

HABITS OF MIND

Construct Arguments Could a polynomial equation with rational coefficients have two complex roots that are not conjugates as its only roots? Explain.

EXAMPLE 5

Try It! Write Polynomial Functions Using Conjugates

5. a. What is a quadratic equation in standard form with rational coefficients that has a root of $5 + 4i$?

   b. What is a polynomial function Q of degree 4 with rational coefficients such that $Q(x) = 0$ has roots $2 - \sqrt{3}$ and $5i$?

HABITS OF MIND

Reason Is it possible to write a polynomial function of degree 3 that has rational coefficients and zeros $2 - \sqrt{3}$ and $5i$? Explain.

Do You UNDERSTAND?

1. ESSENTIAL QUESTION How are the roots of a polynomial equation related to the coefficients and degree of the polynomial?

2. **Error Analysis** Renaldo said that a polynomial equation with real coefficients that has zeros $-1 + 2i$ and $3 + \sqrt{5}$ and has a degree of 4. Is Renaldo correct? Explain.

3. **Use Structure** A fifth degree polynomial $P(x)$ with rational coefficients has zeros $2i$ and $\sqrt{7}$. What other zeros does $P(x)$ have? Explain.

4. **Construct Arguments** If one root of a polynomial equation with real coefficients is $4 + 2i$, is it certain that $4 - 2i$ is also a root of the equation? Explain.

Do You KNOW HOW?

List all the possible rational solutions for each equation according to the Rational Roots Theorem. Then find all of the rational roots.

5. $0 = x^3 + 4x^2 - 9x - 36$

6. $0 = x^4 - 2x^3 - 7x^2 + 8x + 12$

7. $0 = 4x^3 + 8x^2 - x - 2$

8. $0 = 9x^4 - 40x^2 + 16$

A polynomial equation with rational coefficients has the given roots. List two more roots of each equation.

9. $1 + \sqrt{11}$ and $-3 + \sqrt{17}$

10. $5 + 12i$ and $-9 - 7i$

11. $12 + 5i$ and $6 - \sqrt{13}$

12. $5 - 15i$ and $17 + \sqrt{23}$

2-7 Transformations of Polynomial Functions

EXPLORE & REASON

Look at the polynomial graphs below.

$f(x) = x^2$

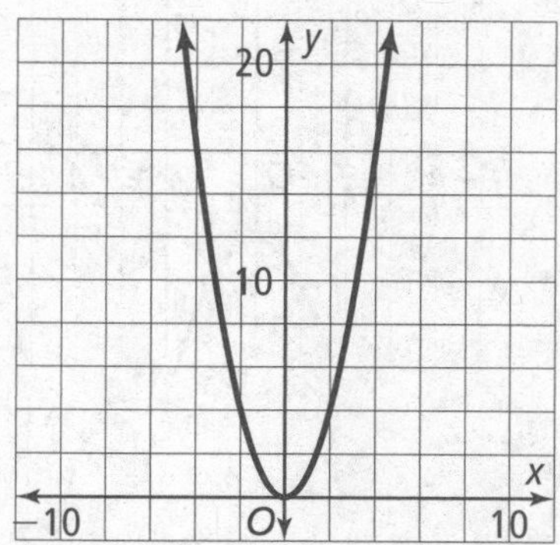

$g(x) = x^3$

A. Is the graph of *f* or *g* symmetric about the *y*-axis? Is the graph of *f* or *g* symmetric about the origin? Explain.

B. Look for Relationships Graph more functions of the form $y = x^n$ where *n* is a natural number. Which of these functions are symmetric about the origin? Which are symmetric about the *y*-axis? What conjectures can you make?

HABITS OF MIND

Look for Relationships Do you notice any other patterns among the functions with even degree or the functions with odd degree?

Notes

Assess

EXAMPLE 1  **Try It!** Identify Even and Odd Functions From Their Graphs

1. Classify the polynomial functions as even or odd based on the graphs.

a.
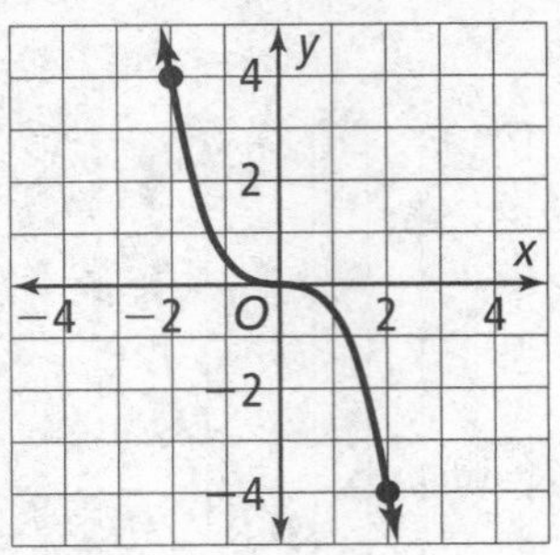

b.
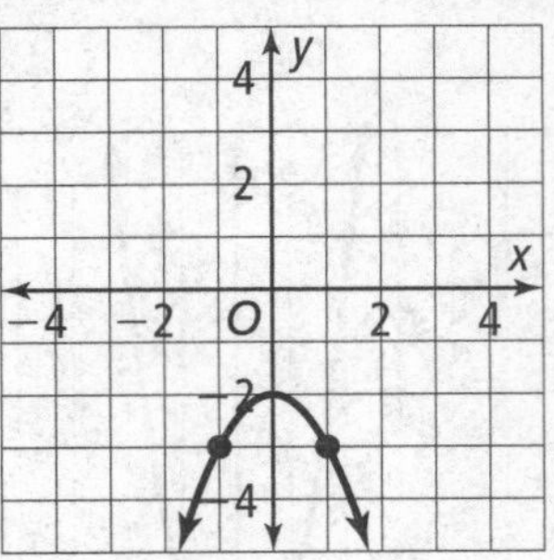

EXAMPLE 2  **Try It!** Identify Even and Odd Functions From Their Equations

2. Is the function odd, even, or neither?

a. $f(x) = 7x^5 - 2x^2 + 4$

b. $f(x) = x^6 - 2$

HABITS OF MIND

Make Sense and Persevere Why do you replace x with $-x$ when determining if a function is odd, even, or neither?

EXAMPLE 3  **Try It!** Graph Transformations of Cubic and Quartic Parent Functions

3. How does the graph of the function $g(x) = 2x^3 - 5$ differ from the graph of its parent function?

Notes

Assess

EXAMPLE 4 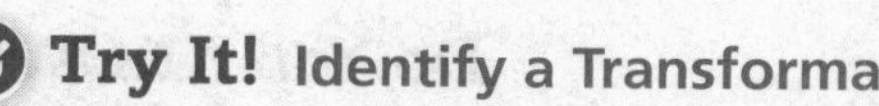

Try It! Identify a Transformation

4. Determine the equation of each graph as it relates to its parent cubic function or quartic function.

a.

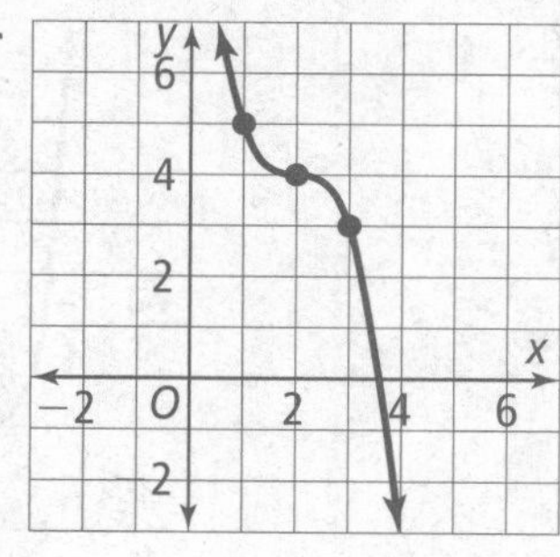

b.

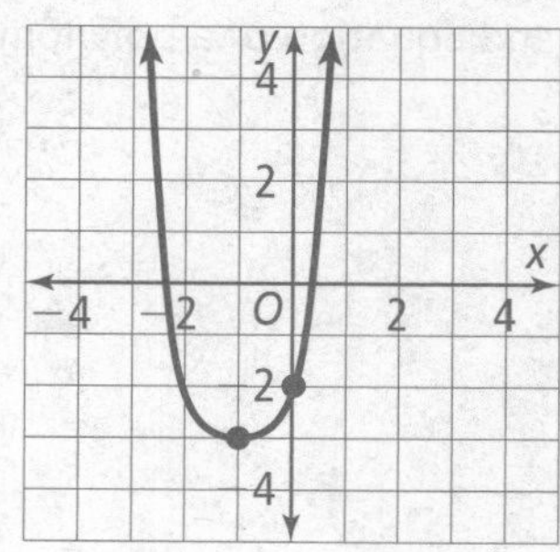

HABITS OF MIND

Look for Relationships What type of transformation would change a function's end behavior?

EXAMPLE 5 

Try It! Apply a Transformation of a Cubic Function

5. a. The volume of a cube, in cubic feet, is given by the function $V(x) = x^3$. Write a function for the volume of the cube in cubic inches if x is the edge length in feet.

b. A storage unit is in the shape of a rectangular prism. The volume of the storage unit is given by $V(x) = (x)(x)(x - 1) = x^3 - x^2$, where x is measured in feet. A potential customer wants to compare the volume of this storage unit with that of another storage unit that is 1 foot longer in every dimension. Write a function for the volume of this larger unit.

HABITS OF MIND

Critique Arguments A student thought that, for 5a, the new function should be $V(x) = 144x^3$. What are the two errors the student made?

Do You UNDERSTAND?

1. 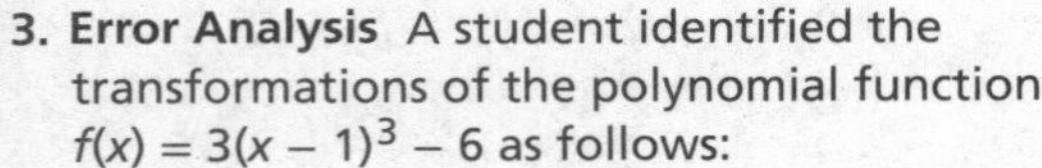

How are symmetry and transformations represented in the graph and equation of a polynomial function?

2. **Vocabulary** What is the difference between the graph of an even function and the graph of an odd function?

3. **Error Analysis** A student identified the transformations of the polynomial function $f(x) = 3(x - 1)^3 - 6$ as follows:

The function is shifted to the left 1 unit, stretched vertically, and is shifted downward 6 units.

Describe and correct the error the student made.

Do You KNOW HOW?

4. Classify the function on the graph as odd, even, or neither.

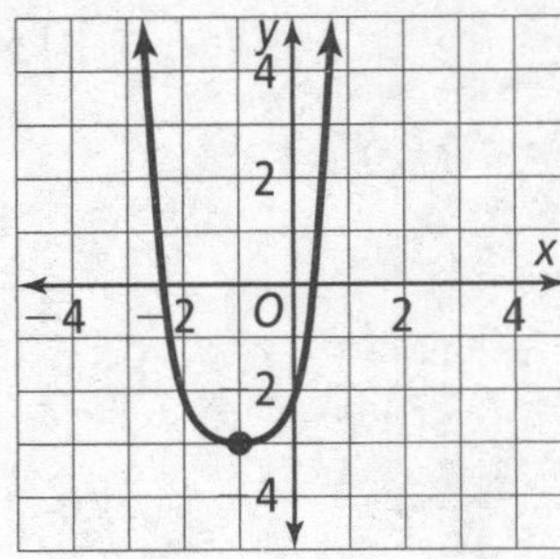

5. Use the equation to classify the function as odd, even, or neither.

$g(x) = 4x^3 - x$

6. The volume of cardboard box is given by the function $V(x) = x(x - 2)(x) = x^3 - 2x^2$. Write a new function for the volume of a cardboard box that is 2 units longer in every dimension.

3-1 Inverse Variation and the Reciprocal Function

PearsonRealize.com

MODEL & DISCUSS

The two rectangles shown both have an area of 144 square units.

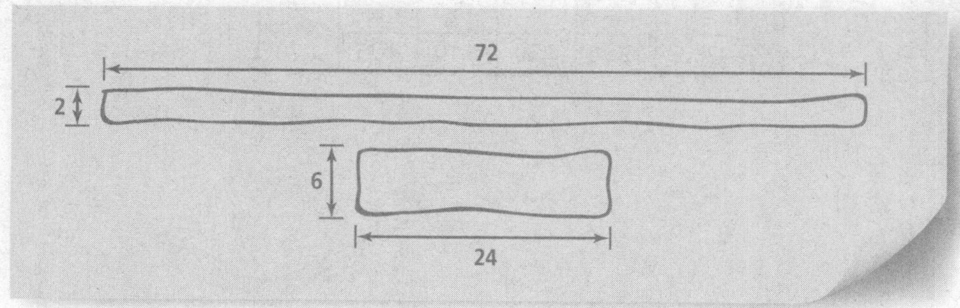

A. Sketch as many other rectangles as you can that have the same area. Organize and record your data for the lengths and widths of the rectangles.

B. Use Structure Considering rectangles with an area of 144 square units, what happens to the width of the rectangle as the length increases?

C. Examine at least five other pairs of rectangles, each pair sharing the same area. How would you describe the relationship between the lengths and widths?

HABITS OF MIND

Use Structure How does the formula for the area of a rectangle make sense with the relationships you found?

Notes

EXAMPLE 1

Try It! Identify Inverse Variation

1. Determine if each table of values represents an inverse variation.

a.

x	1	2	3	5	6	15
y	25.5	12.75	8.50	5.10	4.25	1.70

b.

x	6.6	5.5	4.4	3.3	2.2	1.1
y	3	5	7	9	11	13

EXAMPLE 2

Try It! Use Inverse Variation

2. In an inverse variation, $x = 6$ and $y = \frac{1}{2}$

   a. What is the equation that represents the inverse variation?

   b. What is the value of y when $x = 15$?

HABITS OF MIND

Construct Arguments For rectangles that have a constant perimeter, the length increases as the width decreases. Is the relationship between the length and width an inverse variation? Explain.

Notes

EXAMPLE 3 **Try It!** **Use an Inverse Variation Model**

3. The amount of time it takes for an ice cube to melt varies inversely to the air temperature, in degrees. At 70°F, the ice will melt in 20 min. How long will it take the ice to melt if the temperature is 85°F?

EXAMPLE 4 **Try It!** **Graph the Reciprocal Function**

4. Graph the function $y = \frac{10}{x}$. What are the domain, range, and asymptotes of the function?

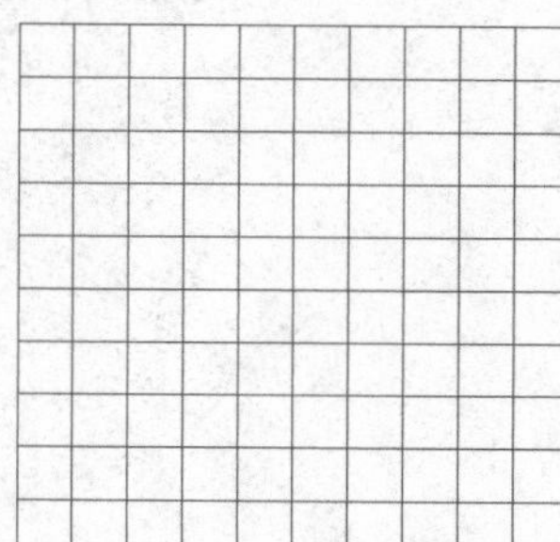

EXAMPLE 5 **Try It!** **Graph Translations of the Reciprocal Function**

5. Graph $g(x) = \frac{1}{x + 2} - 4$. What are the equations of the asymptotes? What are the domain and range?

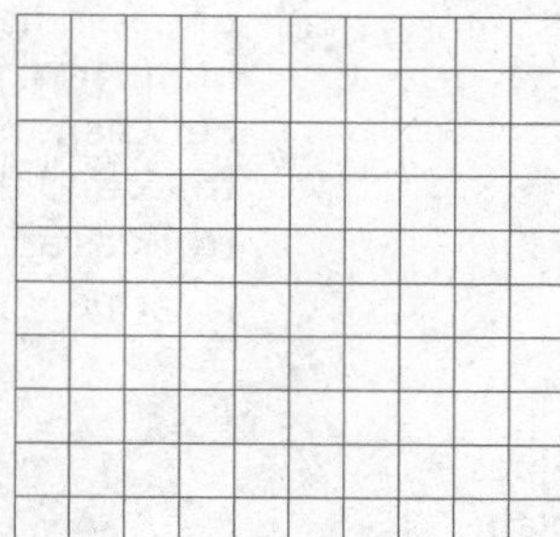

HABITS OF MIND

Communicate Precisely A translation of the reciprocal function has a vertical asymptote at $x = 5$. What is a possible equation for the function?

Do You UNDERSTAND?

1. ESSENTIAL QUESTION How are inverse variations related to the reciprocal function?

2. **Construct Arguments** Explain why the amount of propane in a grill's tank and the time spent grilling could represent an inverse variation.

3. **Vocabulary** Why is it impossible for the graph of the function $y = \frac{1}{x}$ to intersect the horizontal asymptote at the x-axis?

4. **Error Analysis** Carmen said the table of values shown represents an inverse variation. Explain why Carmen is mistaken.

x	1	2	3	4	8	16
y	24	12	8	6	3	2

Do You KNOW HOW?

5. In an inverse variation, $x = -8$ when $y = -\frac{1}{4}$. What is the value of y when $x = 4$?

6. What are the equations of the asymptotes of the function $f(x) = \frac{1}{x-5} + 3$? What are the domain and range?

7. Until the truck runs out of gas, the amount of gas in its fuel tank varies inversely with the number of miles traveled. Model a relationship between the amount of gas in a fuel tank of a truck and the number of miles traveled by the truck as an inverse variation.

Activity

3-2 Graphing Rational Functions

PearsonRealize.com

EXPLORE & REASON

Look at the three functions shown.

$$f(x) = x - 1$$

$$g(x) = \frac{x-1}{2}$$

$$h(x) = \frac{x-1}{x-2}$$

A. Look for Relationships Graph each function. Determine which of the functions are linear. Find the *y*-intercept of each function and the slope, if appropriate.

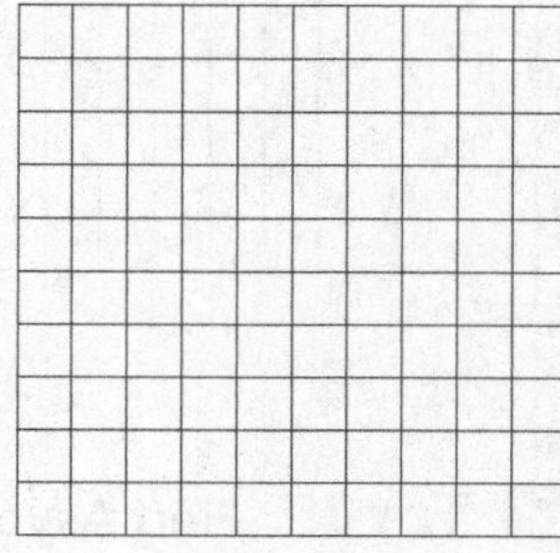

B. What is the effect on the graph of *f* when dividing $x - 1$ by 2?

C. What happens to the graph of *h* as *x* approaches 2?

D. Communicate Precisely What is the effect on the graph of $f(x)$ when dividing $x - 1$ by $x - 2$? (Hint: Compare it to what you found in part (b).)

HABITS OF MIND

Look for Relationships What similarities do you notice between the graph of $h(x) = \frac{x-1}{x-2}$ and the graph of a reciprocal function?

Assess

EXAMPLE 1 **Try It! Rewrite a Rational Function to Identify Asymptotes**

1. Use long division to rewrite each rational function. Find the asymptotes of f and sketch the graph.

   a. $f(x) = \frac{6x}{2x + 1}$

   b. $\frac{x}{x - 6}$

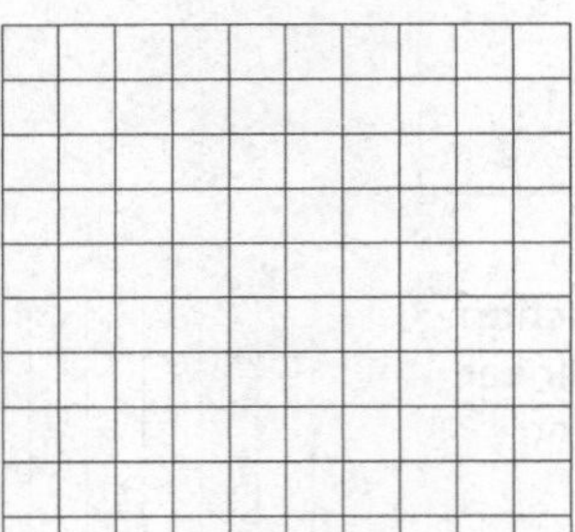

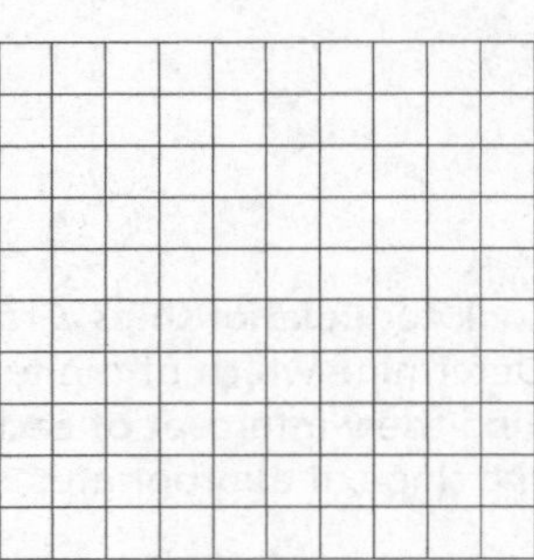

EXAMPLE 2 **Try It! Find Asymptotes of a Rational Function**

2. What are the vertical and horizontal asymptotes of the graph of each function?

   a. $g(x) = \frac{2x^2 + x - 9}{x^2 - 2x - 8}$

   b. $f(x) = \frac{x^2 + 5x + 4}{3x^2 - 12}$

HABITS OF MIND

Model With Mathematics Under what conditions could there be a horizontal asymptote at $y = -2$? Give an example.

EXAMPLE 3 **Try It! Graph a Function of the Form $\frac{ax + b}{cx + d}$**

3. Graph each function.

   a. $f(x) = \frac{4x - 3}{x + 8}$

   b. $g(x) = \frac{3x + 2}{x - 1}$

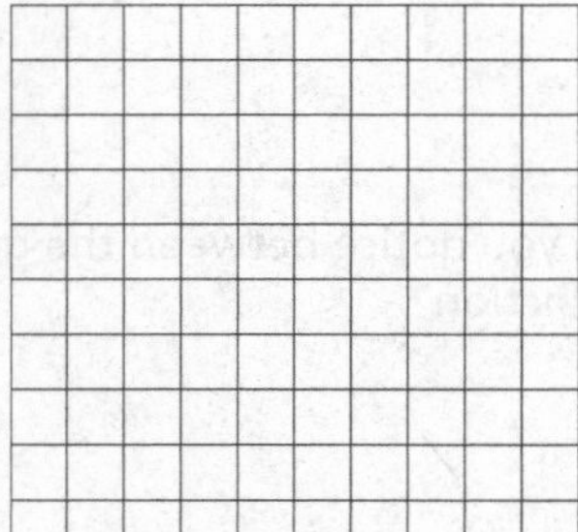

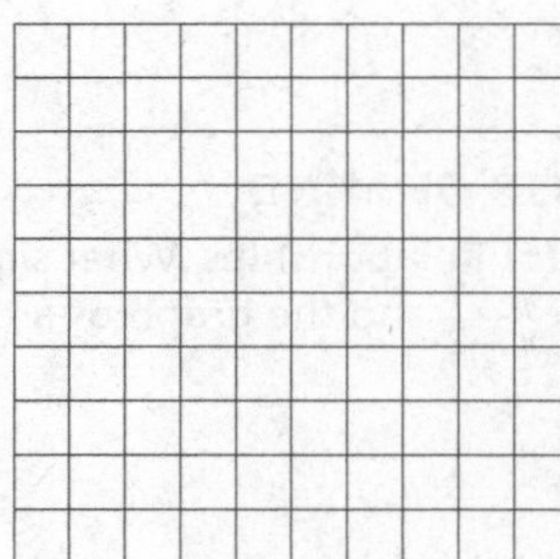

Notes

EXAMPLE 4 **Try It! Use a Rational Function Model**

4. New techniques have changed the cost function. For the new function $g(p) = \frac{3.2p + 1}{100 - p}$, what percent of the pollutant can be removed for \$50 million?

HABITS OF MIND

Make Sense and Persevere What are the asymptotes for the function $g(p) = \frac{3.2p + 1}{100 - p}$?

EXAMPLE 5 **Try It! Graph a Rational Function**

5. Identify the asymptotes and sketch the graph of $g(x) = \frac{x^2 - 5x + 6}{2x^2 - 10}$.

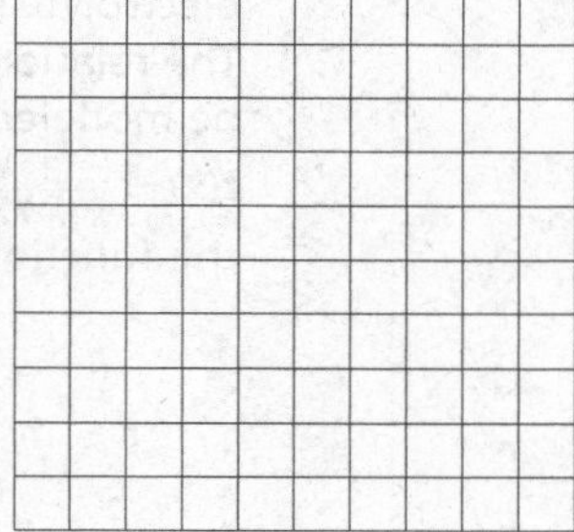

HABITS OF MIND

Reason When will the graph of a rational function have two vertical asymptotes?

Do You UNDERSTAND?

1. 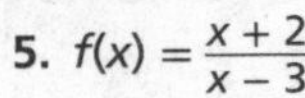

How can you graph a rational function?

2. **Vocabulary** Why does it make sense to call the expressions in this lesson *rational* functions?

3. **Error Analysis** Ashton said the graph of $f(x) = \frac{x+2}{2x^2+4x-6}$ has a horizontal asymptote at $y = \frac{1}{2}$. Describe and correct Ashton's error.

4. **Reason** When will the graph of a rational function have no vertical asymptotes? Give an example of such a function.

Do You KNOW HOW?

Find the vertical asymptote(s) and horizontal asymptote(s) of the rational function. Then graph the function.

5. $f(x) = \frac{x+2}{x-3}$

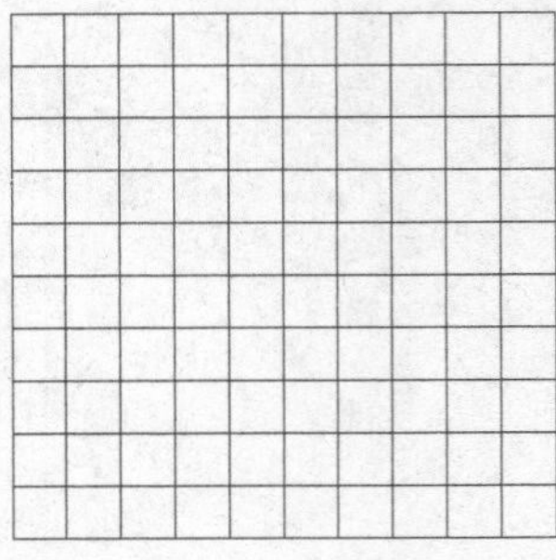

6. $f(x) = \frac{x-1}{2x+1}$

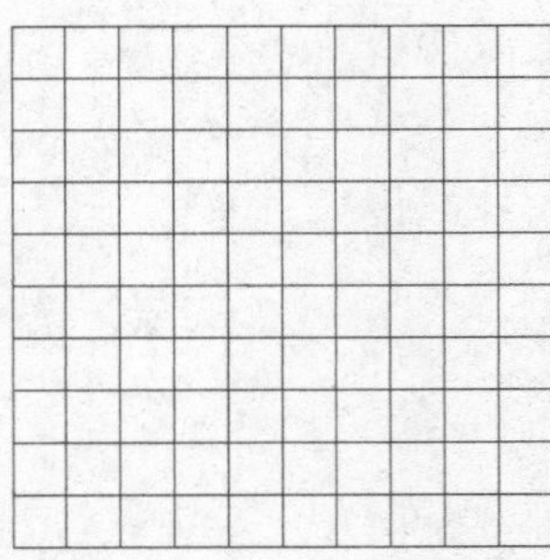

7. A trainer mixed water with an electrolyte solution. The relationship can be modeled by $f(x) = \frac{3}{x+12}$. Graph the function.

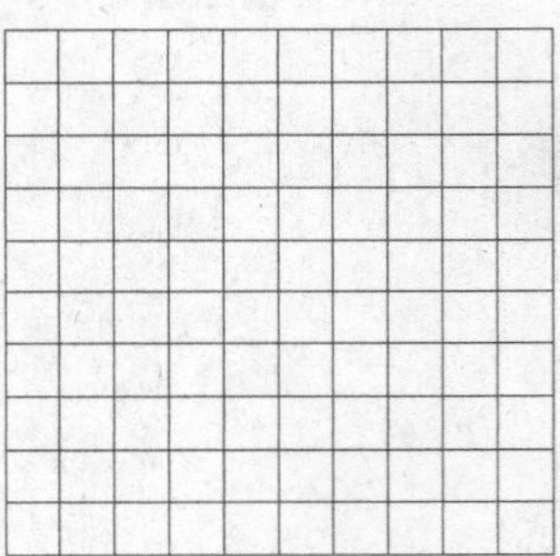

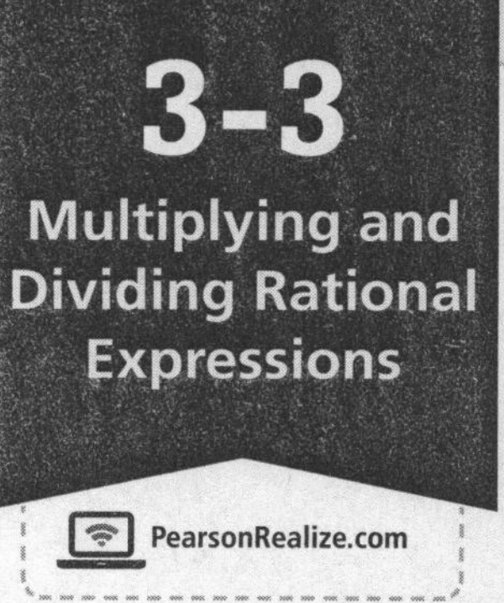

EXPLORE & REASON

Consider the following graph of the function $y = x + 2$.

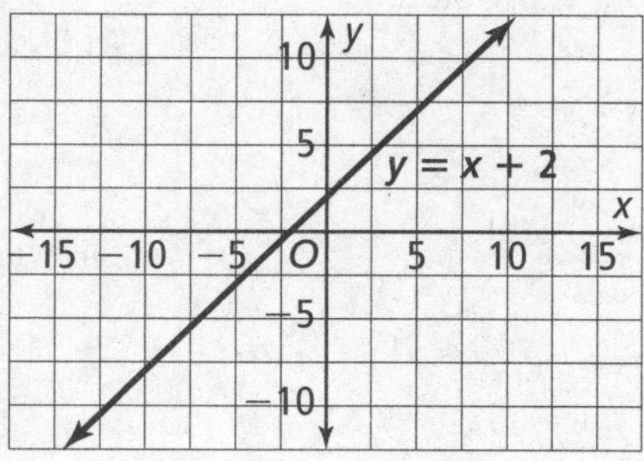

A. What is the domain of this function?

B. Sketch a function that resembles the graph, but restrict its domain to exclude 2.

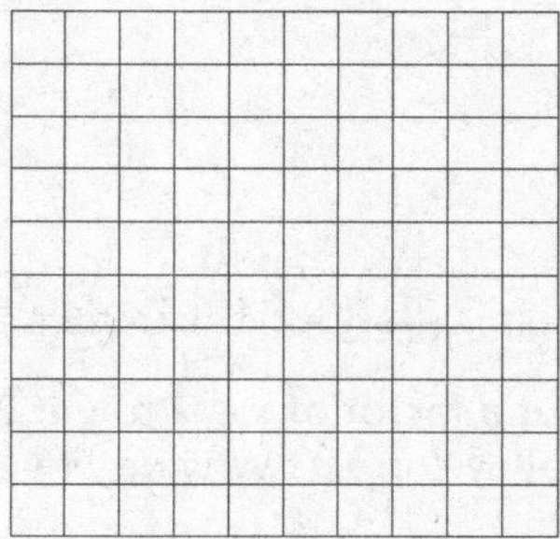

C. Use Structure Consider the function you have sketched. What kind of function might have a graph like this? Explain.

HABITS OF MIND

Reason Does the graph of $y = \frac{2x + 6}{x + 3}$ have a vertical asymptote at $x = -3$? Explain.

Notes

EXAMPLE 1  **Try It! Write Equivalent Rational Expressions**

1. Write an expression equivalent to $\frac{3x^5 - 18x^4 - 21x^3}{2x^6 - 98x^4}$. Remember to give the domain for your expression.

EXAMPLE 2  **Try It! Simplify a Rational Expression**

2. Simplify each expression and show the domain for which the identity with the two expressions is valid.

a. $\frac{x^2 + 2x + 1}{x^3 - 2x^2 - 3x}$

b. $\frac{x^3 + 4x^2 - x - 4}{x^2 + 3x - 4}$

HABITS OF MIND

Critique Reasoning Bailey simplified the rational expression $\frac{x^2 + 2x + 4}{x^2 + x + 2}$ by dividing out the x^2-terms, and then dividing out a factor of $x + 2$ to get 2 as the simplified form of the rational expression. Is Bailey correct? Why or why not?

EXAMPLE 3  **Try It! Multiply Rational Expressions**

3. Find the simplified form of each product, and give the domain.

a. $\frac{x^2 - 16}{9 - x} \cdot \frac{x^2 + x - 90}{x^2 + 14x + 40}$

b. $\frac{x + 3}{4x} \cdot \frac{3x - 18}{6x + 18} \cdot \frac{x^2}{4x + 12}$

Notes

EXAMPLE 4

Try It! Multiply a Rational Expression by a Polynomial

4. Find the simplified form of each product and the domain.

a. $\frac{x^3 - 4x}{6x^2 - 13x - 5} \cdot (2x^3 - 3x^2 - 5x)$ **b.** $\frac{3x^2 + 6x}{x^2 - 49} \cdot (x^2 + 9x + 14)$

HABITS OF MIND

Generalize Why is it important to identify the domain of a rational expression before you simplify it rather than after?

EXAMPLE 5

Try It! Divide Rational Expressions

5. Find the simplified quotient and the domain of each expression.

a. $\frac{1}{x^2 + 9x} \div \left(\frac{6 - x}{3x^2 - 18x}\right)$ **b.** $\frac{2x^2 - 12x}{x + 5} \div \left(\frac{x - 6}{x + 5}\right)$

EXAMPLE 6

Try It! Use Division of Rational Expressions

6. The company compares the ratios of surface area to volume for two more containers. One is a rectangular prism with a square base. The other is a rectangular prism with a rectangular base. One side of the base is equal to the side-length of the first container, and the other side is twice as long. The surface area of this second container is $4x^2 + 6xh$. The heights of the two containers are equal. Which has the smaller surface area-to-volume ratio?

HABITS OF MIND

Use Structure Is the domain of the quotient $\frac{2x^2 - 12x}{x + 5} \div \left(\frac{x - 6}{x + 5}\right)$ different from the domain of the product $\left(\frac{2x^2 - 12x}{x + 5}\right)\left(\frac{x - 6}{x + 5}\right)$? Explain.

Do You UNDERSTAND?

1. ESSENTIAL QUESTION How does understanding operations with fractions help you multiply and divide rational expressions?

2. **Vocabulary** In your own words, define rational expression and provide an example of a rational expression.

3. **Error Analysis** A student divided the rational expressions as follows:
$\frac{4x}{5y} \div \frac{20x^2}{25y^2} = \frac{4x}{\cancel{5}y} \div \frac{{}^{4}\cancel{20}x^2}{25y^2} = \frac{16x^3}{25y^3}$.
Describe and correct the errors the student made.

4. **Communicate Precisely** Why do you have to state the domain when simplifying rational expressions?

Do You KNOW HOW?

5. What is the simplified form of the rational expression $\frac{x^2 - 36}{x^2 + 3x - 18}$? What is the domain?

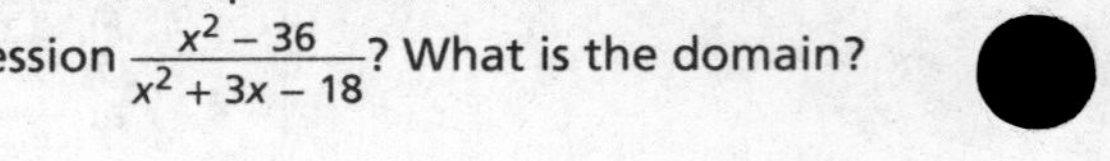

6. Find the product and give the domain of $\frac{y+3}{y+2} \cdot \frac{y^2 + 4y + 4}{y^2 - 9}$.

7. Find and simplify the ratio of the volume of Figure A to the volume of Figure B.

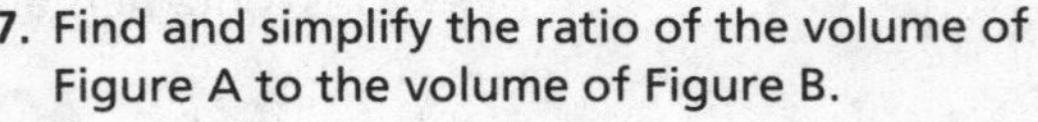

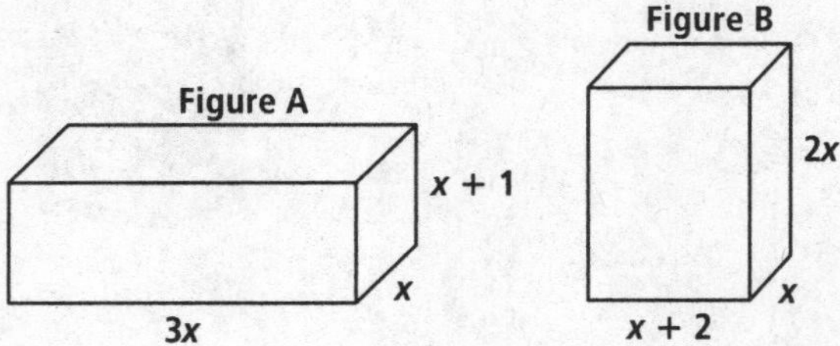

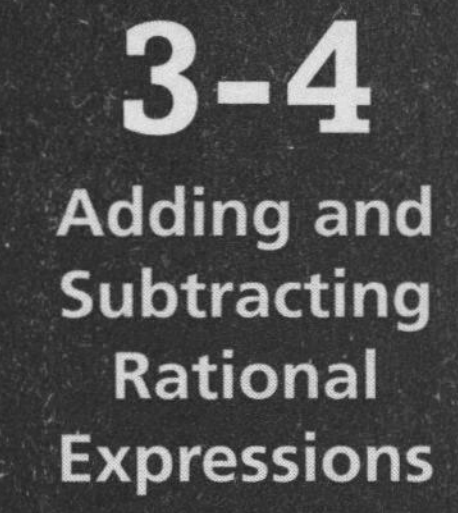

CRITIQUE & EXPLAIN

Teo and Shannon find the following exercise in their homework:

$$\frac{1}{2} + \frac{1}{3} + \frac{1}{9}$$

A. Teo claims that a common denominator of the sum is 2 + 3 + 9 = 14. Shannon claims that it is 2 • 3 • 9 = 54. Is either student correct? Explain why or why not.

B. Find the sum, explaining the method you use.

C. Construct Arguments Timothy states that the quickest way to find the sum of any two fractions with unlike denominators is to multiply their denominators to find a common denominator, and then rewrite each fraction with that denominator. Do you agree?

HABITS OF MIND

Look for Relationships For two fractions with denominators 10 and x, when is $10x$ the least common multiple? When is $10x$ NOT the least common multiple?

 Notes

 Assess

EXAMPLE 1 

Try It! Add Rational Expressions With Like Denominators

1. Find the sum.

a. $\frac{10x-5}{2x+3}+\frac{8-4x}{2x+3}$

b. $\frac{x-5}{x+5}+\frac{3x-21}{x+5}$

HABITS OF MIND

Make Sense and Persevere Explain why it does not make sense to add the denominators when adding rational numbers. Use numerical fractions to support your thinking.

EXAMPLE 2 

Try It! Identify the Least Common Multiple of Polynomials

2. Find the LCM for each set of expressions.

a. $x^3+9x^2+27x+27,\ x^2-4x-21$

b. $10x^2-10y^2,\ 15x^2-30xy+15y^2,\ x^2+3xy+2y^2$

EXAMPLE 3 

Try It! Add Rational Expressions With Unlike Denominators

3. Find the sum.

a. $\frac{x+6}{x^2-4}+\frac{2}{x^2-5x+6}$

b. $\frac{2x}{3x+4}+\frac{4x^2-11x-12}{6x^2+5x-4}$

Notes

Assess

EXAMPLE 4  **Try It! Subtract Rational Expressions**

4. Simplify.

a. $\frac{1}{3x} + \frac{1}{6x} - \frac{1}{x^2}$

b. $\frac{3x-5}{x^2-25} - \frac{2}{x+5}$

HABITS OF MIND

Communicate Precisely How does finding the LCM of two or more polynomials help you to add and subtract rational expressions?

EXAMPLE 5  **Try It! Find a Rate**

5. On the way to work Juan carpools with a fellow co-worker, and then takes the city bus back home in the evening. The average speed of the 20-mi trip is 5 mph faster in the carpool. Write an expression that represents Juan's total travel time.

HABITS OF MIND

Construct Arguments Does Juan spend more time in the carpool or riding the bus? How do you know?

EXAMPLE 6  **Try It! Simplify a Compound Fraction**

6. Simplify.

a. $\dfrac{\frac{1}{x-1}}{\frac{x+1}{3} + \frac{4}{x-1}}$

b. $\dfrac{\frac{2-1}{x}}{\frac{x+2}{x}}$

HABITS OF MIND

Reason Edwin multiplied the top and bottom of the fraction in problem 6 part (a) by $\frac{3}{x+1} + \frac{x-1}{4}$. Will this technique work to simplify the compound fraction? Explain.

Do You UNDERSTAND?

1. ESSENTIAL QUESTION How do you rewrite rational expressions to find sums and differences?

2. **Vocabulary** In your own words, define **compound fraction** and provide an example of one.

3. **Error Analysis** A student added the rational expressions as follows:
$\frac{5x}{x+7} + \frac{7}{x} = \frac{5x}{x+7} + \frac{7(7)}{x+7} = \frac{5x+49}{x+7}$.
Describe and correct the error the student made.

4. **Construct Arguments** Explain why, when stating the domain of a sum or difference of rational expressions, not only should the simplified sum or difference be considered but the original expression should also be considered.

5. **Make Sense and Persevere** In adding or subtracting rational expressions, why is the L in LCD significant?

Do You KNOW HOW?

6. Find the sum of $\frac{3}{x+1} + \frac{11}{x+1}$.

Find the LCM of the polynomials.

7. $x^2 - y^2$ and $x^2 - 2xy + y^2$

8. $5x^3y$ and $15x^2y^2$

Find the sum or difference.

9. $\frac{3x}{4y^2} - \frac{y}{10x}$

10. $\frac{9y+2}{3y^2-2y-8} + \frac{7}{3y^2+y-4}$

11. Find the perimeter of the quadrilateral in simplest form.

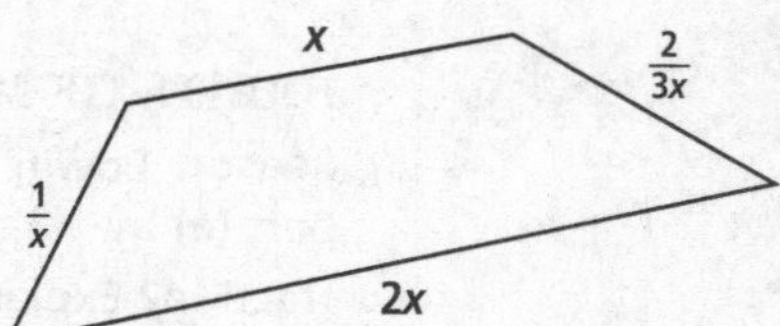

Activity

3-5 Solving Rational Equations

PearsonRealize.com

CRITIQUE & EXPLAIN

Nicky and Tavon used different methods to solve the equation $\frac{1}{2}x + \frac{2}{5} = \frac{9}{10}$.

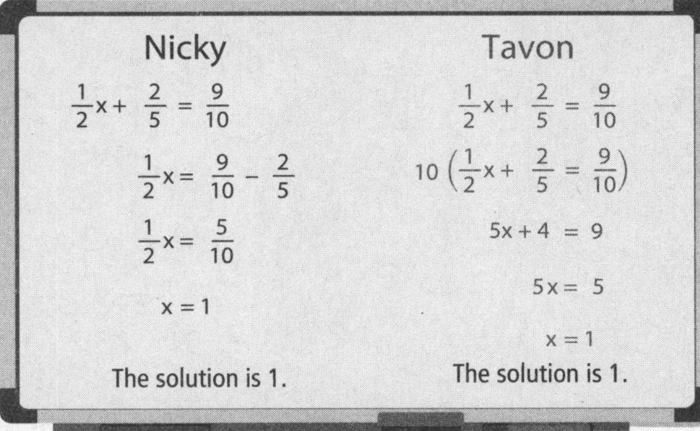

A. Explain the different strategies that Nicky and Tavon used and the advantages or disadvantages of each.

B. Did Nicky use a correct method to solve the equation? Did Tavon?

C. Use Structure Why might Tavon have chosen to multiply both sides of the equation by 10? Could he have used another number? Explain.

HABITS OF MIND

Reason If Tavon had multiplied both sides of the equation by 100, would his answer have been 10 times as much? Explain.

Notes

Assess

EXAMPLE 1  **Try It!** Solve a Rational Equation

1. What is the solution to each equation?

a. $\frac{2}{x+5} = 4$ b. $\frac{1}{x-7} = 2$

HABITS OF MIND

Critique Reasoning For part (b), Kaitlyn wrote $1 = 2x - 7$, then $8 = 2x$, and $4 = x$. Is she correct? Explain.

EXAMPLE 2  **Try It!** Solve a Work-Rate Problem

2. It takes 12 hours to fill a pool with two pipes, where the water in one pipe flows three times as fast as the other pipe. How long will it take the slower pipe to fill the pool by itself?

HABITS OF MIND

Reason In a Work-Rate problem, explain why you can't average the individual rates to determine how long it will take to complete a job together.

Notes 

EXAMPLE 3 

Try It! Identify an Extraneous Solution

3. What is the solution to the equation $\frac{1}{x+2} + \frac{1}{x-2} = \frac{4}{(x+2)(x-2)}$?

EXAMPLE 4

Try It! Solve Problems With Extraneous Solutions

4. What are the solutions to the following equations?

a. $x + \frac{6}{x-3} = \frac{2x}{x-3}$

b. $\frac{x^2}{x+5} = \frac{25}{x+5}$

HABITS OF MIND

Communicate Precisely What is an extraneous solution?

EXAMPLE 5 

Try It! Solve a Rate Problem

5. Three people are planting tomatoes in a community garden. Marta takes 50 minutes to plant the garden alone, Benito takes x minutes and Tyler takes $x + 15$ minutes. If the three of them take 20 minutes to finish the garden, how long would it have taken Tyler alone?

HABITS OF MIND

Make Sense and Persevere What does the fraction $\frac{1}{50}$ mean with regards to Marta?

Do You UNDERSTAND?

1. **ESSENTIAL QUESTION** How can you solve rational equations and identify extraneous solutions?

2. **Vocabulary** Write your own example of a rational equation that, when solved, has at least one **extraneous solution.**

3. **Error Analysis** A student solved the rational equation as follows:

   $\frac{1}{2x} - \frac{2}{5x} = \frac{1}{10x} - 3; x = 0$

   Describe and correct the error the student made.

4. **Construct Arguments** Yuki says, *"You can check the solution(s) of rational equations in any of the steps of the solution process."* Explain why her reasoning is incorrect.

Do You KNOW HOW?

Solve.

5. $\frac{4}{x+6} = 2$

6. 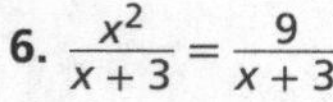 $\frac{x^2}{x+3} = \frac{9}{x+3}$

7. Organizing given information into a table can be helpful when solving rate problems. Use this table to solve the following problem.

	Distance	Rate	Time
Upstream			
Downstream			

The speed of a stream is 4 km/h. A boat can travel 6 km upstream in the same time it takes to travel 12 km downstream. Find the speed of the boat in still water.

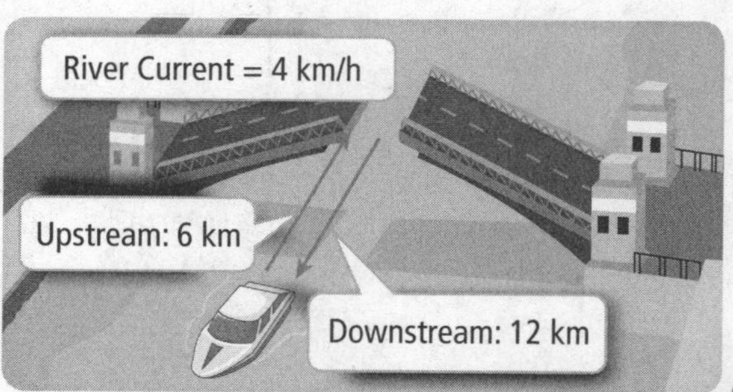

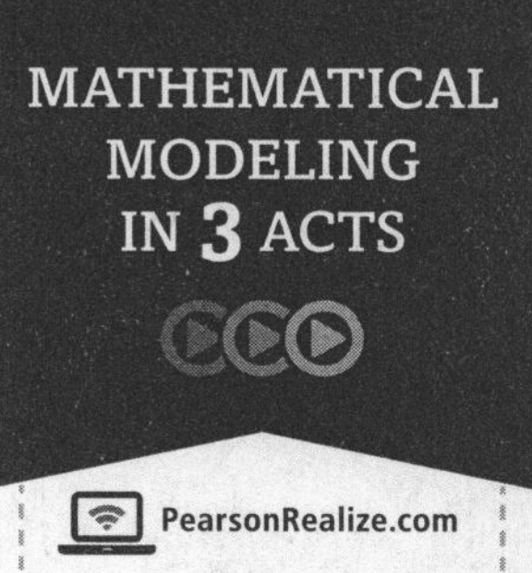

Real Cool Waters

Nothing feels better on a hot day than jumping into a pool! Many cities have swimming pools that people can go to for a small fee. Some people have swimming pools in their backyards that they can enjoy any time.

If neither of these options are available, you can always create your own beach paradise! Get a kiddie pool, a lawn chair, and a beach umbrella. Think about your beach paradise as during the Mathematical Modeling in 3 Acts lesson.

ACT 1 Identify the Problem

1. What is the first question that comes to mind after watching the video?

2. Write down the main question you will answer about what you saw in the video.

3. Make an initial conjecture that answers this main question.

4. Explain how you arrived at your conjecture.

5. Write a number that you know is too small.

6. Write a number that you know is too large.

7. What information will be useful to know to answer the main question? How can you get it? How will you use that information?

ACT 2 Develop a Model

8. Use the math that you have learned in this Topic to refine your conjecture.

ACT 3 Interpret the Results

9. Is your refined conjecture between the highs and lows you set up earlier?

10. Did your refined conjecture match the actual answer exactly? If not, what might explain the difference?

4-1 nth Roots, Radicals, and Rational Exponents

EXPLORE & REASON

The graph shows $y = x^2$.

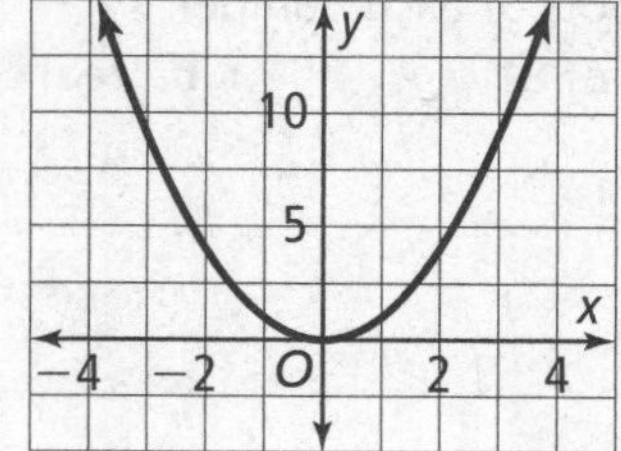

A. Find *all* possible values of x or y so that the point is on the graph.

(a) (2, ______) (b) (3, ______) (c) (−3, ______) (d) (5, ______)

(e) (______, 4) (f) (______, −16) (g) (______, 7) (h) (______, 5)

B. Communicate Precisely Write a precise set of instructions that show how to find an approximate value of $\sqrt{13}$ using the graph.

C. Draw a graph of $y = x^3$. Use the graph to approximate each value.

(a) $\sqrt[3]{5}$ (b) $\sqrt[3]{-5}$ (c) $\sqrt[3]{8}$

(d) A solution to $x^3 = 5$ (e) A solution to $x^3 = -5$ (f) A solution to $x^3 = 8$

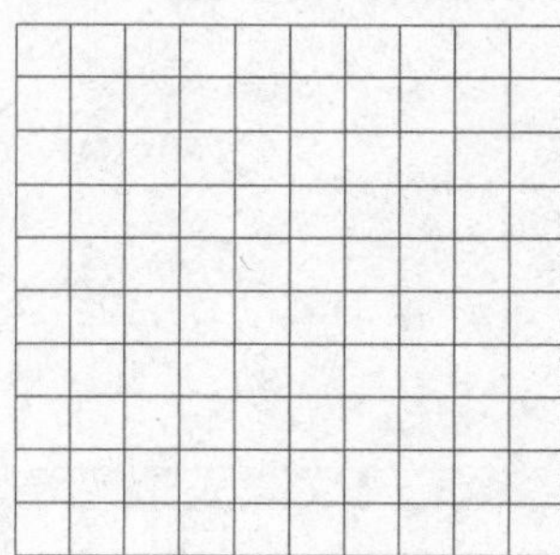

HABITS OF MIND

Look for Relationships How is $\sqrt[6]{5}$ related to $\sqrt[3]{5}$?

Notes

EXAMPLE 1 **Try It! Find All Real *n*th Roots**

1. Find the specified roots of each number.
   a. real fourth roots of 81
   b. real cube roots of 64

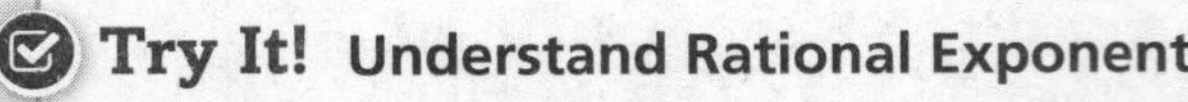

EXAMPLE 2 **Try It! Understand Rational Exponents**

2. Explain what each fractional exponent means, then evaluate.
   a. $25^{\frac{1}{2}}$
   b. $32^{\frac{2}{5}}$

HABITS OF MIND

Generalize What is true about the denominators of fractional exponents in which absolute value must be considered?

EXAMPLE 3 **Try It! Evaluate Expressions With Rational Exponents**

3. What is the value of each expression? Round to the nearest hundredth if necessary.
   a. $-\left(16^{\frac{3}{4}}\right)$
   b. $\sqrt[5]{3.5^4}$

Notes

Assess

EXAMPLE 4

Try It! Simplify *n*th Roots

4. Simplify each expression.

a. $\sqrt[3]{-8a^3b^9}$

b. $\sqrt[4]{256x^{12}y^{24}}$

HABITS OF MIND

Make Sense and Persevere What is an example of a variable expression that has both a cube root and a fourth root which can be simplified to an expression without a radical?

EXAMPLE 5

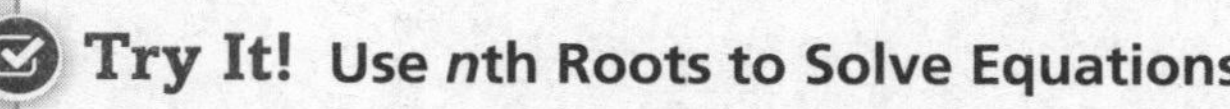

Try It! Use *n*th Roots to Solve Equations

5. a. Solve the equation $5x^3 = 320$.

b. Solve the equation $2p^4 = 162$.

EXAMPLE 6

Try It! Use *n*th Roots to Solve Problems

6. One cube has an edge length 3 cm shorter than the edge length of a second cube. The volume of the smaller cube is 200 cm^3. What is the volume of the larger cube?

HABITS OF MIND

Communicate Precisely What are the steps necessary to solve the equation $ax^n = b$?

Do You UNDERSTAND?

1. ESSENTIAL QUESTION How are exponents and radicals used to represent roots of real numbers?

2. **Error Analysis** Kaitlyn said $\sqrt[3]{10} = 10^3$. Explain Kaitlyn's error.

3. **Vocabulary** In the radical expression $\sqrt[5]{125}$, what is the index? What is the radicand?

4. **Use Structure** Why is $75^{\frac{3}{5}}$ equal to $\left(75^{\frac{1}{5}}\right)^3$?

5. **Construct Arguments** Anastasia said that $(x^8)^{\frac{1}{4}} = \frac{x^8}{x^4} = x^4$. Is Anastasia correct? Explain.

6. **Make Sense and Persevere** Is it possible for a rational exponent to be an improper fraction? Explain how $27^{\frac{4}{3}}$ is evaluated or why it cannot be evaluated.

Do You KNOW HOW?

Write each expression in radical form.

7. $a^{\frac{1}{5}}$

8. $7^{\frac{2}{3}}$

Write each expression in exponential form.

9. $\sqrt[3]{b}$

10. $\sqrt[4]{p^7}$

11. How many real third roots does 1,728 have?

12. How many real sixth roots does 15,625 have?

13. Solve the equation $4x^3 = 324$.

14. Solve the equation $2x^4 = 2{,}500$.

Simplify each expression.

15. $\sqrt[3]{27x^{12}y^6}$

16. $\sqrt[5]{-32x^5y^{30}}$

17. A snow globe is packaged in a cubic container that has volume 64 in.^{3} A large shipping container is also a cube, and its edge length is 8 inches longer than the edge length of the snow globe container. How many snow globes can fit into the larger shipping container?

Activity

4-2
Properties of Exponents and Radicals

PearsonRealize.com

CRITIQUE & EXPLAIN

Olivia was practicing evaluating and simplifying expressions. Her work for three expressions is shown.

1. $24^2 = 400 + 16 = 416$
2. $3^6 = 9(27) = 270 - 27 = 243$
3. $\sqrt{625} = \sqrt{400} + \sqrt{225} = 20 + 15 = 35$

A. Is Olivia's work in the first example correct? Explain your thinking.

B. Is Olivia's work in the second example correct? Explain your thinking.

C. Is Olivia's work in the third example correct? Explain your thinking.

D. **Make Sense and Persevere** What advice would you give Olivia on simplifying expressions?

HABITS OF MIND

Construct Arguments You know that $3^2 + 4^2 = 5^2$. Does $\sqrt{3^2} + \sqrt{4^2} = \sqrt{5^2}$? If not, how could you rewrite the equation using radicals so that it is true?

Notes

Assess

EXAMPLE 1  **Try It! Use Properties of Exponents**

1. How can you rewrite each expression using the properties of exponents?

a. $\left(\frac{3}{32^{\frac{2}{5}}}\right)^{\frac{1}{2}}$

b. $2a^{\frac{1}{3}}\left(ab^{\frac{1}{2}}\right)^{\frac{2}{3}}$

EXAMPLE 2  **Try It! Use Properties of Exponents to Rewrite Radicals**

2. How can you rewrite each expression?

a. $\sqrt[4]{81a^8b^5}$

b. $\sqrt[3]{\frac{x^4y^2}{125x}}$

HABITS OF MIND

Make Sense and Persevere What do you have to check to be sure that an expression is in simplest radical form?

EXAMPLE 3  **Try It! Rewrite the Product or Quotient of a Radical**

3. What is the reduced radical form of each expression?

a. $\sqrt[5]{\frac{7}{16x^3}}$

b. $\sqrt[4]{27x^2} \cdot \sqrt{3x}$

EXAMPLE 4  **Try It!** **Add and Subtract Radical Expressions**

4. How can you rewrite each expression in a simpler form?

a. $\sqrt[3]{2{,}000} + \sqrt{2} - \sqrt[3]{128}$

b. $\sqrt{20} - \sqrt{600} - \sqrt{125}$

HABITS OF MIND

Critique Reasoning Divit says that you can simplify the product of any two radical expressions, but not necessarily the sum. Is he correct? Give an example.

EXAMPLE 5  **Try It!** **Multiply Binomial Radical Expressions**

5. Multiply.

a. $(x - \sqrt{10})(x + \sqrt{10})$

b. $\sqrt{6}(5 + \sqrt{3})$

EXAMPLE 6  **Try It!** **Rationalize a Binomial Denominator**

6. What is the reduced radical form of each expression?

a. $\dfrac{5 - \sqrt{2}}{2 - \sqrt{3}}$

b. $\dfrac{-4x}{1 - \sqrt{x}}$

HABITS OF MIND

Reason Is the product of two irrational binomials always irrational? Explain.

Do You UNDERSTAND?

1. **ESSENTIAL QUESTION** How can properties of exponents and radicals be used to rewrite radical expressions?

2. **Vocabulary** How can you determine if a radical expression is in reduced form?

3. **Use Structure** Explain why $(-64)^{\frac{1}{3}}$ equals $-64^{\frac{1}{3}}$ but $(-64)^{\frac{1}{2}}$ does not equal $-64^{\frac{1}{2}}$.

4. **Error Analysis** Explain the error in Julie's work in rewriting the radical expression.

$$\sqrt{-3} \cdot \sqrt{-12} = \sqrt{-3(-12)} = \sqrt{36} = 6$$

Do You KNOW HOW?

What is the reduced radical form of each expression?

5. $49^{\frac{3}{4}} \cdot 49^{\frac{-1}{4}}$

6. $\left(\frac{a^2b^8}{a^{\frac{1}{3}}}\right)^{\frac{3}{4}}$

7. $\sqrt[4]{1{,}024x^9y^{12}}$

8. $\sqrt[3]{\frac{4}{9m^2}}$

9. $\sqrt{63} - \sqrt{700} - \sqrt{112}$

10. $\sqrt{5}(6 + \sqrt{2})$

11. $\frac{3}{\sqrt{6}}$

12. $\frac{\sqrt{7}}{\sqrt{5} + 3}$

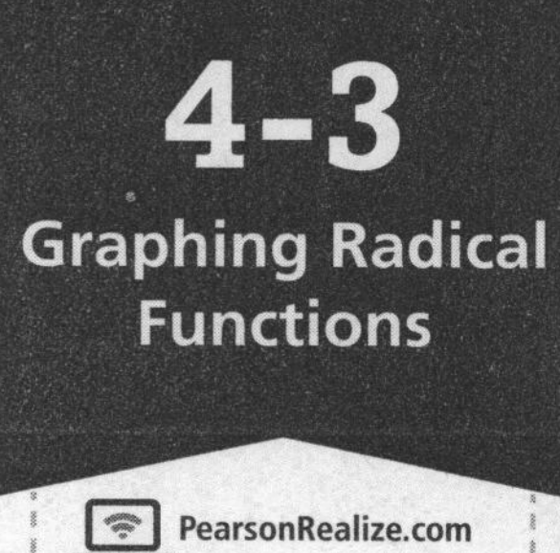

EXPLORE & REASON

Consider the formula for the area of a square: $A = s^2$.

A. Graph the function that represents area as a function of side length.

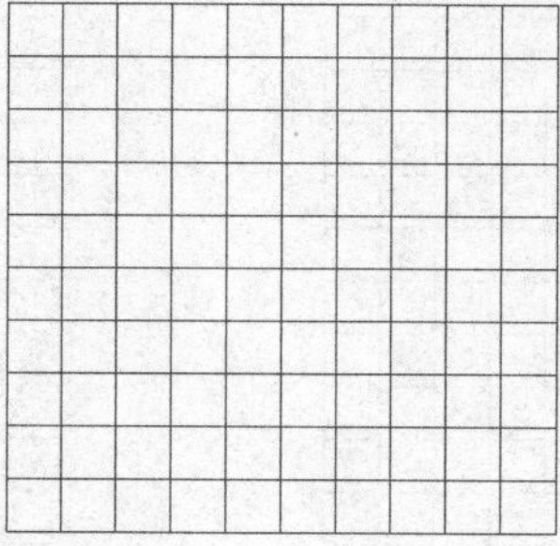

B. On the same set of axes, graph the function that represents side length as a function of area.

C. Look for Relationships How are the two graphs related?

HABITS OF MIND

Communicate Precisely What is the domain and range of each function?

Notes

EXAMPLE 1

Try It! Graph Square Root and Cube Root Functions

1. Graph the following functions. What are the domain and range of each function? Is the function increasing or decreasing?

   a. $f(x) = \sqrt{x - 5}$

   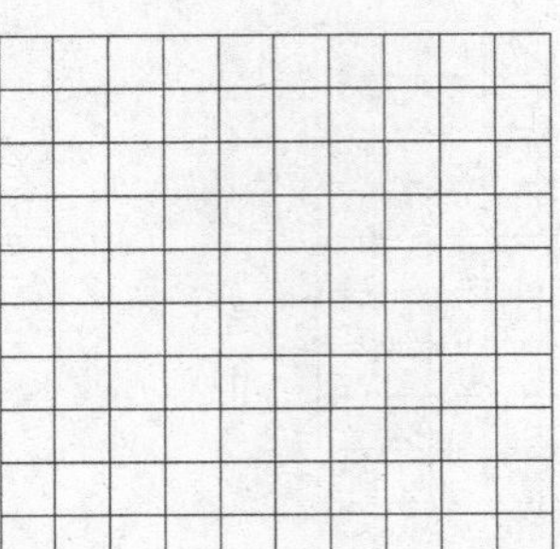

   b. $g(x) = \sqrt[3]{x + 1}$

   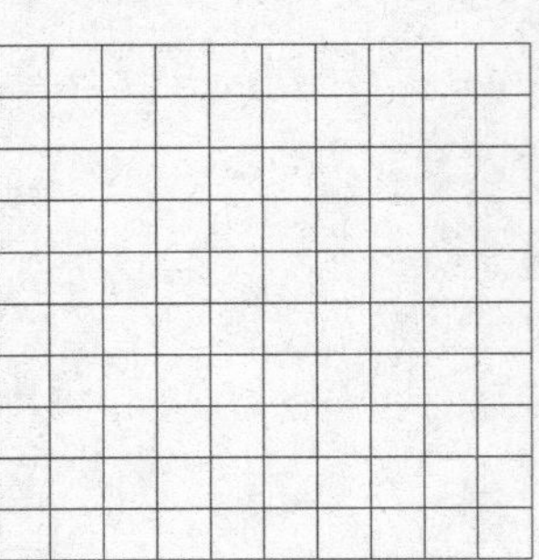

EXAMPLE 2

Try It! Graph a Transformation of a Radical Function

2. Graph $g(x) = \frac{1}{2}\sqrt{x - 1} - 3$. What transformations of the graph of $f(x) = \sqrt{x}$ produce the graph of g? What is the effect of the transformations on the domain and range of g?

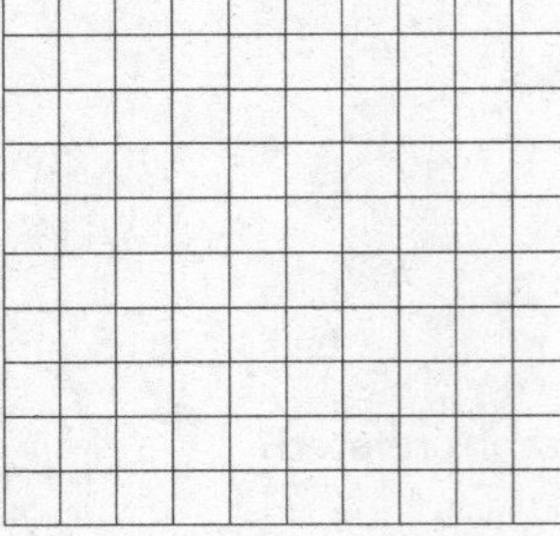

HABITS OF MIND

Use Structure How does the graph of $y = \sqrt{x - a} + b$ compare to the graph of $y = \sqrt{x}$?

Notes

Assess

EXAMPLE 3  **Try It! Rewrite Radical Functions to Identify Transformations**

3. What transformations of the parent graph of $f(x) = \sqrt{x}$ produce the graphs of the following functions?

   a. $m(x) = \sqrt{7x - 3.5} - 10$

   b. $j(x) = -2\sqrt{12x} + 4$

EXAMPLE 4  **Try It! Write an Equation of a Transformation**

4. What radical function is represented in each graph below?

   a.

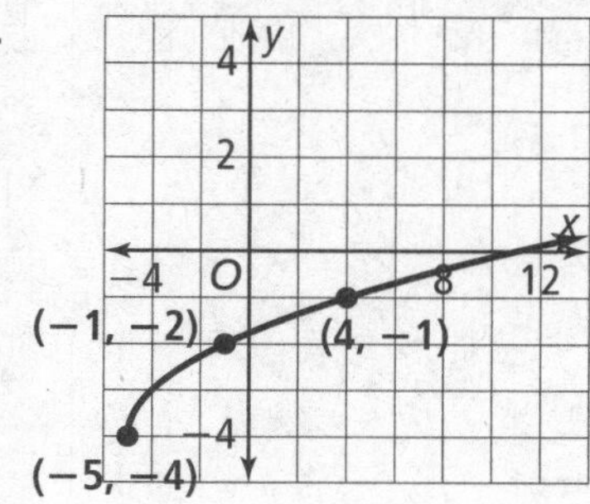

   b.

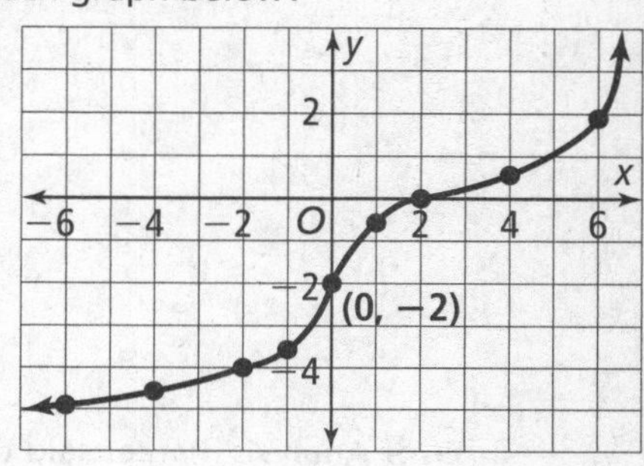

HABITS OF MIND

Model With Mathematics What is an example of a radical function whose domain is $x \geq -3$ and range is $y \geq 2$?

EXAMPLE 5  **Try It! Interpret a Radical Function Model**

5. Use the same function as in Example 5. Suppose Sasha's brother walks through elevations ranging from 8 ft to 48 ft. What are the minimum and maximum distances that he can see?

HABITS OF MIND

Generalize What transformations result in a cube root function being an odd function?

Do You UNDERSTAND?

1. ESSENTIAL QUESTION How can you use what you know about transformations of functions to graph radical functions?

2. **Error Analysis** Parker said the graph of the radical function $g(x) = -\sqrt{x+2} - 1$ is a translation 2 units left and 1 unit down from the parent function $f(x) = \sqrt{x}$. Describe and correct the error.

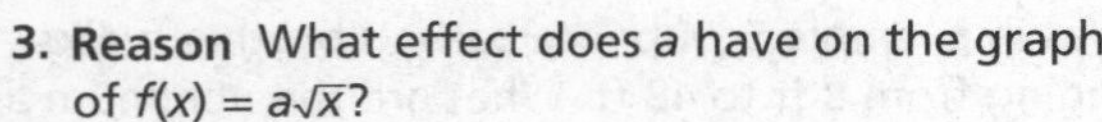

3. **Reason** What effect does a have on the graph of $f(x) = a\sqrt{x}$?

Do You KNOW HOW?

Graph each function. Then identify its domain and range.

4. $f(x) = \sqrt{x-2}$

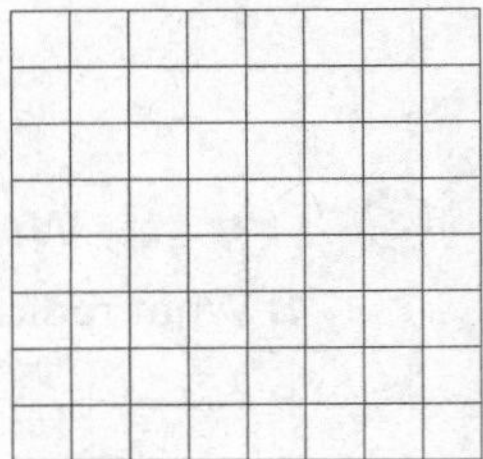

5. $f(x) = \sqrt[3]{x+2}$

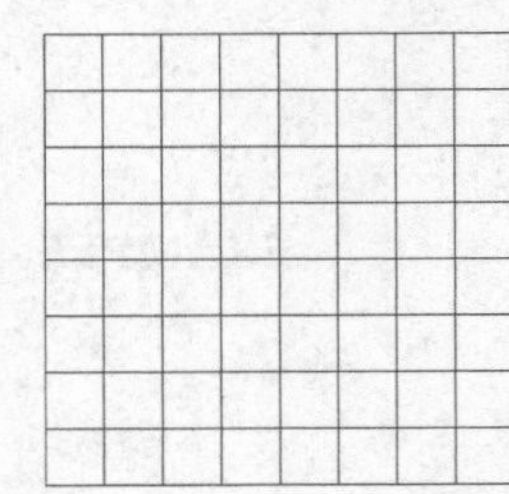

6. $f(x) = \sqrt{x+1} - 2$

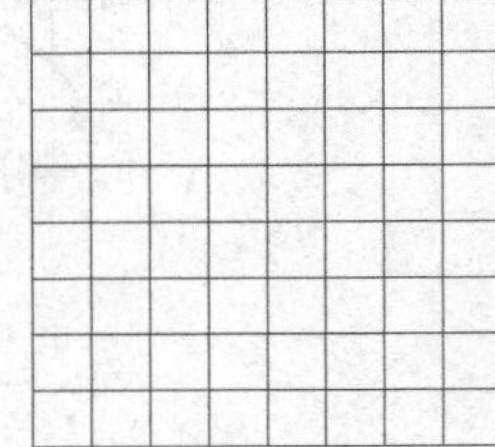

7. $f(x) = \sqrt[3]{x-3} + 2$

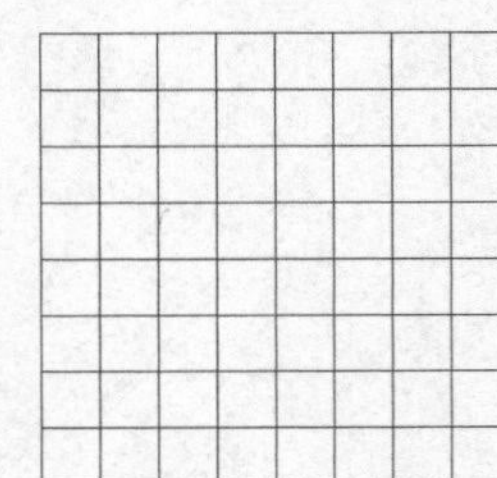

8. $f(x) = 3\sqrt{x-5}$

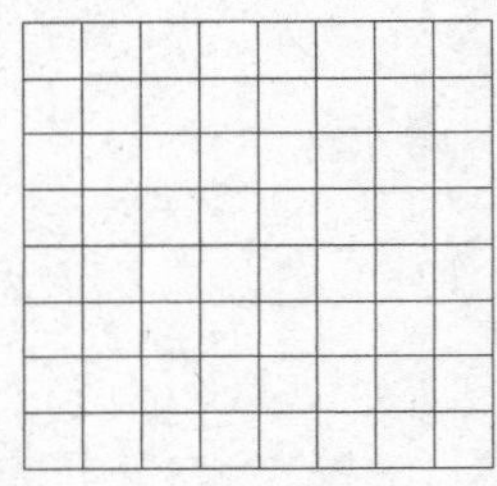

9. $f(x) = \frac{1}{2}\sqrt[3]{x} + 1$

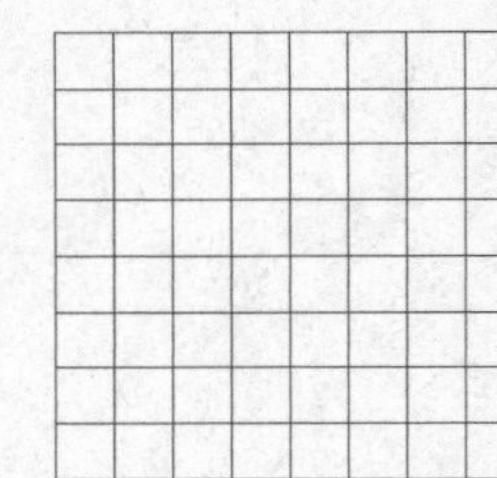

10. The volume of a cube is a function of the cube's side length. The function can be written as $V(s) = s^3$, where s is the side length and V is the volume.

 a. Express a cube's side length as a function of its volume, $s(V)$.

 b. Graph $V(s)$ and $s(V)$. What are the domain and range of the functions? Explain.

Activity

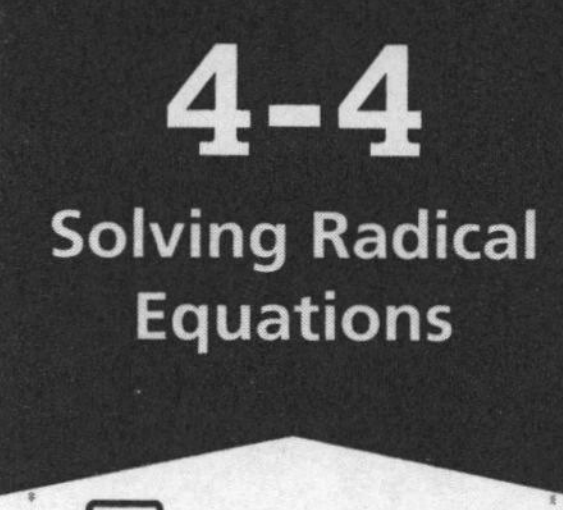

EXPLORE & REASON

A. Solve $3(a + 1)^2 + 2 = 11$. Use at least two different methods.

B. Try each of the methods you used in part (a) to solve $\sqrt[3]{(a + 1)} + 2 = 11$.

C. **Generalize** Which of the methods is better suited for solving an equation with a radical? What problems arise when using the other method?

HABITS OF MIND

Construct Arguments The squares of two numbers are equal. Does that mean that the two numbers themselves must also be equal? Explain.

Notes

Assess

EXAMPLE 1  **Try It! Solve an Equation With One Radical**

1. Solve each radical equation.

   a. $\sqrt{x-2}+3=5$

   b. $\sqrt[3]{x-1}=2$

EXAMPLE 2 **Try It! Rewrite a Formula**

2. The speed, v, of a vehicle in relation to its stopping distance, d, is represented by the equation $v = 3.57\sqrt{d}$. What is the equation for the stopping distance in terms of the vehicle's speed?

HABITS OF MIND

Reason Reese solved the equation in **1(a)** by first squaring both sides. Is this an appropriate first step? Why or why not?

EXAMPLE 3  **Try It! Identify an Extraneous Solution**

3. Solve each radical equation. Identify any extraneous solutions.

   a. $x=\sqrt{7x+8}$

   b. $x+2=\sqrt{x+2}$

Notes

Assess

EXAMPLE 4  **Try It! Solve Equations With Rational Exponents**

4. Solve each equation.

a. $(x^2 - 3x - 6)^{\frac{3}{2}} - 14 = -6$

b. $(x + 8)^2 = (x - 10)^{\frac{5}{2}}$

EXAMPLE 5 **Try It! Solve an Equation With Two Radicals**

5. Solve each radical equation. Check for extraneous solutions.

a. $\sqrt{x + 4} - \sqrt{3x} = -2$

b. $\sqrt{15 - x} - \sqrt{6x} = -3$

HABITS OF MIND

Reason Why are extraneous solutions a possibility for radical equations?

EXAMPLE 6  **Try It! Solve a Radical Inequality**

6. A doctor calculates that a particular dose of medicine is appropriate for an individual whose BSA is less than 1.8. If the mass of the individual is 75 kg, how many centimeters tall can he or she be for the dose to be appropriate?

HABITS OF MIND

Make Sense and Persevere How are the steps for solving a radical inequality different from the steps for solving a radical equation?

Do You UNDERSTAND?

1. ESSENTIAL QUESTION How can you solve equations that include radicals or rational exponents?

2. **Construct Arguments** How can you use a graph to show that the solution to $\sqrt[3]{84x+8} = 8$ is 6?

3. **Vocabulary** Why does solving a radical equation sometimes result in an extraneous solution?

4. **Error Analysis** Neil said that −3 and 6 are the solutions to $\sqrt{3x+18} = x$. What error did Neil make?

5. **Communicate Precisely** Describe how you would solve the equation $x^{\frac{2}{3}} = n$. How is this solution method to be interpreted if the equation had been written in radical form instead?

Do You KNOW HOW?

Solve for *x*.

6. $3\sqrt{x+22} = 21$

7. $\sqrt[3]{5x} = 25$

In exercises 8 and 9, find the extraneous solution.

8. $\sqrt{8x+9} = x$

9. $x = \sqrt{24-2x}$

10. Rewrite the equation $y = \sqrt{\frac{x-48}{6}}$ to isolate x.

11. Use a graph to find the solution to the equation $9 = \sqrt{3x+11}$.

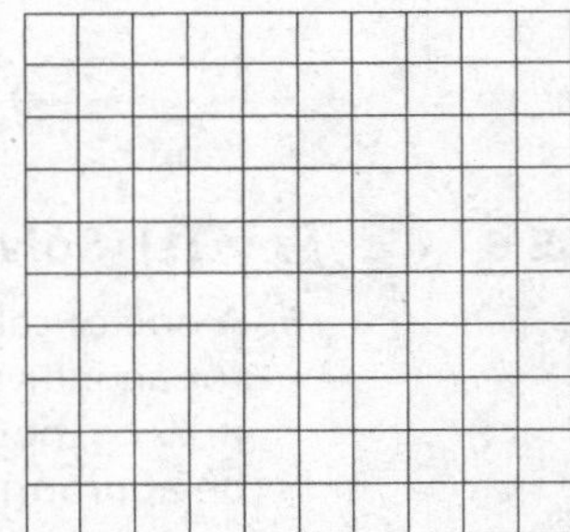

Solve each equation.

12. $(3x+2)^{\frac{2}{5}} = 4$

13. $\sqrt{2x-5} - \sqrt{x-3} = 1$

14. $\sqrt{x+2} + \sqrt{3x+4} = 2$

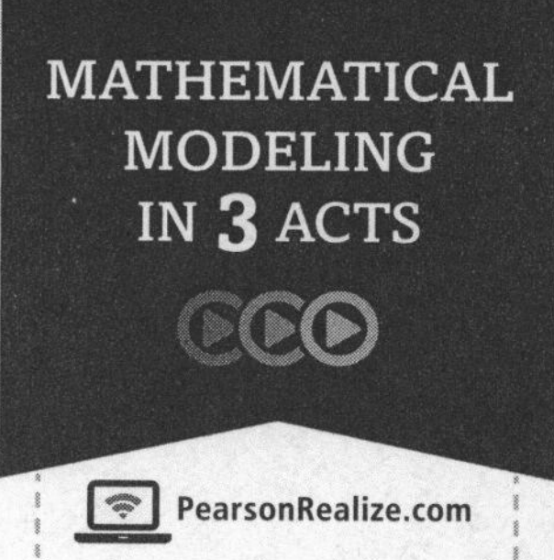

The Snack Shack

Americans seem to love the beach! When the weather is warm, people flock to the beach. Some people bring coolers packed with food and drinks. Others prefer to take advantage of snack bars and shops set up along the beach.

Some beachside communities have built long wooden walkways, or boardwalks, to make it easier for beachgoers to walk to the snack bars and stores. How easy do you find walking in the sand? Think about this during the Mathematical Modeling in 3 Acts lesson.

ACT 1 Identify the Problem

1. What is the first question that comes to mind after watching the video?

2. Write down the main question you will answer about what you saw in the video.

3. Make an initial conjecture that answers this main question.

4. Explain how you arrived at your conjecture.

5. What information will be useful to know to answer the main question? How can you get it? How will you use that information?

Video

ACT 2 Develop a Model

6. Use the math that you have learned in this Topic to refine your conjecture.

ACT 3 Interpret the Results

7. Did your refined conjecture match the actual answer exactly? If not, what might explain the difference?

4-5
Function Operations

PearsonRealize.com

MODEL & DISCUSS

In business, the term *profit* is used to describe the difference between the money the business earns (revenue) and the money the business spends (cost).

A. Grooming USA charges $25 for every pet that is groomed. Let x represent the number of pets groomed in a month. Define a revenue function for the business.

B. Materials and labor for each pet groomed costs $15. The business also has fixed costs of $1,000 each month. Define a cost function for this business.

C. Last month, Grooming USA groomed 95 pets. Did they earn a profit? What would the profit be if the business groomed 110 pets in a month?

D. Generalize Explain your procedure for calculating the profit for Grooming USA. Suppose you wanted to calculate the profit for several different scenarios. How could you simplify your process?

HABITS OF MIND

Make Sense and Persevere A business "breaks even" when its revenue equals its costs. How many pets would Grooming USA have to groom in order to break even?

 Notes

Assess

EXAMPLE 1

Try It! Add and Subtract Functions

1. Let $f(x) = 2x^2 + 7x - 1$ and $g(x) = 3 - 2x$. Identify rules for the following functions.

   a. $f + g$

   b. $f - g$

EXAMPLE 2

Try It! Multiply Functions

2. Suppose demand, d, for a company's product at cost, x, is predicted by the function $d(x) = -0.25x^2 + 1{,}000$, and the price, p, that the company can charge for the product is given by $p(x) = x + 16$. Find the company's revenue function.

EXAMPLE 3

Try It! Divide Functions

3. Identify the rule and domain for $\frac{f}{g}$ for each pair of functions.

   a. $f(x) = x^2 - 3x - 18$, $g(x) = x + 3$

   b. $f(x) = x - 3$, $g(x) = x^2 - x - 6$

HABITS OF MIND

Communicate Precisely How are the domains of $f + g$, $f - g$, $f \cdot g$, and $\frac{f}{g}$ related to the domains of f and g?

Notes

EXAMPLE 4 **Try It!** **Compose Functions**

4. Let $f(x) = 2x - 1$ and $g(x) = 3x$. Identify the rules for the following functions.

a. $f(g(2))$

b. $f(g(x))$

EXAMPLE 5 **Try It!** **Write a Rule for a Composite Function**

5. Identify the rules for $f \circ g$ and $g \circ f$.

a. $f(x) = x^3$, $g(x) = x + 1$

b. $f(x) = x^2 + 1$, $g(x) = x - 5$

EXAMPLE 6 **Try It!** **Use a Composite Function Model**

6. As a member of the Games Shop rewards program, you get a 20% discount on purchases. All sales are subject to a 6% sales tax. Write functions to model the discount and the sales tax, then identify the rule for the composition function that calculates the final price you would pay at the Games Shop.

HABITS OF MIND

Reason Let $f(x) = \frac{1}{3}(x - 2)$ and $g(x) = 3x + 2$. Find the rules for $f \circ g$ and $g \circ f$. Are they equivalent? If so, does this prove that the composition of two functions is commutative?

Assess

Do You UNDERSTAND?

1. ESSENTIAL QUESTION How do you combine, multiply, divide, and compose functions, and how do you find the domain of the resulting function?

2. **Vocabulary** In your own words, define and provide an example of a composite function.

3. **Error Analysis** Reagan said the domain of $\frac{f}{g}$ when $f(x) = 5x^2$ and $g(x) = x + 3$ is the set of real numbers. Explain why Reagan is incorrect.

4. **Use Structure** Explain why changing the order in which two functions occur affects the result when subtracting and dividing the functions.

Do You KNOW HOW?

Let $f(x) = 3x^2 + 5x + 1$ and $g(x) = 2x - 1$.

5. Identify the rule for $f + g$.

6. Identify the rule for $f - g$.

7. Identify the rule for $g - f$.

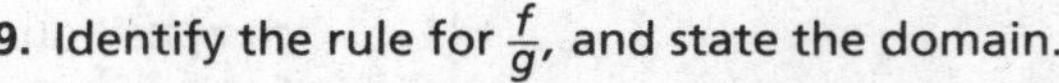

Let $f(x) = x^2 + 2x + 1$ and $g(x) = x - 4$.

8. Identify the rule for $f \bullet g$.

9. Identify the rule for $\frac{f}{g}$, and state the domain.

10. Identify the rule for $\frac{g}{f}$, and state the domain.

11. If $f(x) = 2x^2 + 5$ and $g(x) = -3x$, what is $f(g(x))$?

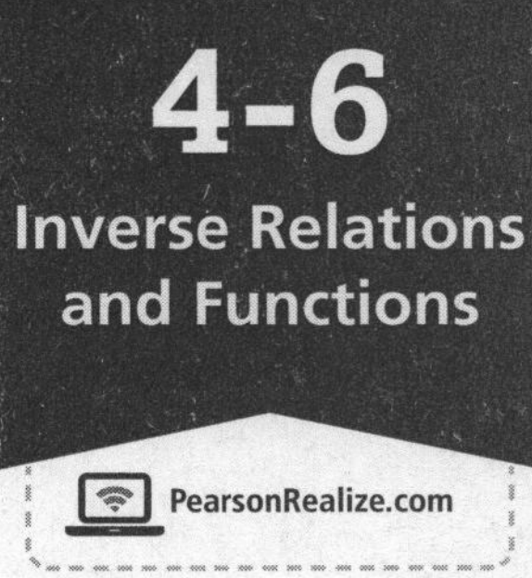

4-6 Inverse Relations and Functions

EXPLORE & REASON

Each number path will lead you from a number in the domain, the set of all real numbers, to a number in the range.

Number Path $f: x \rightarrow f(x)$
- Start with x.
- Subtract 3.
- Multiply by -2.
- Add 5.

Number Path $g: x \rightarrow g(x)$
- Start with x.
- Add 1.
- Square the value.
- Subtract 2.

A. Follow the number paths to find $f(1)$ and $g(1)$.

B. Identify all possible values of x that lead to $f(x) = 7$ and all values that lead to $g(x) = 7$.

C. Communicate Precisely Based on the two number paths, under what conditions can you follow a path back to a unique value in the domain?

HABITS OF MIND

Model With Mathematics Write a rule for Number Path f. Write a rule for the process of following the number path backward. How do the two rules compare?

EXAMPLE 1 Try It! Represent the Inverse of a Relation

1. Identify the inverse relation. Is it a function?

x	−1	0	1	2	3	4
y	9	7	5	3	1	−1

EXAMPLE 2 Try It! Find an Equation of an Inverse Relation

2. Let $f(x) = 2x + 1$.

a. Write an equation to represent the inverse of f.

b. How can you use the graph of f to determine if the inverse of f is a function? Explain your answer.

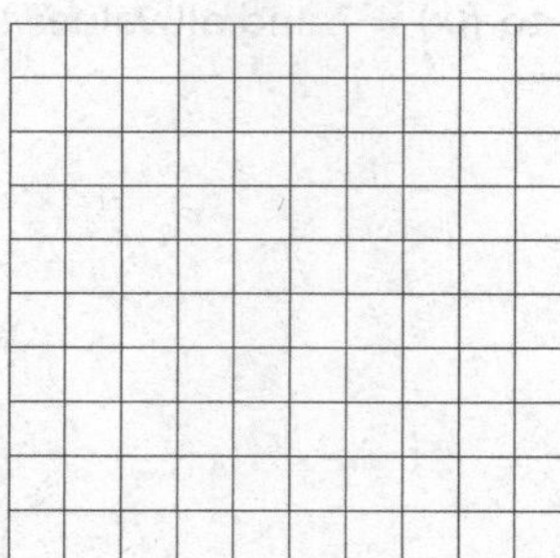

HABITS OF MIND

Communicate Precisely Think of $f(x) = 2x + 1$ as a number path: start with x, multiply by 2, and add 1. How could you describe the path from the result back to x?

EXAMPLE 3 Try It! Restrict a Domain to Produce an Inverse Function

3. Find the inverse of each function by identifying an appropriate restriction of its domain.

a. $f(x) = x^2 + 8x + 16$

b. $f(x) = x^2 - 9$

Notes

Assess

EXAMPLE 4

Try It! Find an Equation of an Inverse Function

4. Let $f(x) = 2 - \sqrt[3]{x + 1}$.

a. Sketch the graph of f.

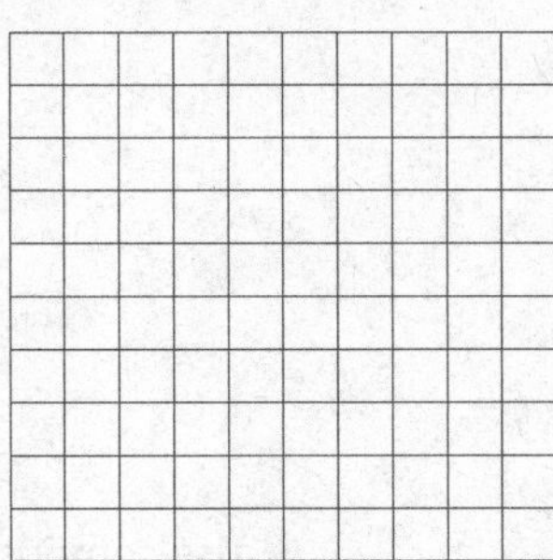

b. Verify that the inverse will be a function and write an equation for $f^{-1}(x)$.

EXAMPLE 5

Try It! Use Composition to Verify Inverse Functions

5. Use composition to determine whether f and g are inverse functions.

a. $f(x) = \frac{1}{4}x + 7$, $g(x) = 4x - 7$

b. $f(x) = \sqrt[3]{x - 1}$, $g(x) = x^3 + 1$

HABITS OF MIND

Construct Arguments Dana says that the functions $f(x) = (x - 2)^2 + 5$ and $g(x) = \sqrt{x - 5} + 2$ are inverses. Keegan says that the functions are inverses only if the domain is restricted. Is either person correct? Explain.

EXAMPLE 6

Try It! Rewrite a Formula

6. The manufacturer of a gift box designs a box with length and width each twice as long as its height. Find a formula that gives the height h of the box in terms of its volume V. Then give the length of the box if the volume is 640 cm^3.

HABITS OF MIND

Make Sense and Persevere In the formula $V = \frac{4}{3}\pi r^3$, which variable is the dependent variable? In the formula $r = \sqrt[3]{\frac{3}{4\pi}V}$, which variable is the dependent variable?

Do You UNDERSTAND?

1. ESSENTIAL QUESTION How can you find the inverse of a function and verify the two functions are inverses?

2. **Error Analysis** Abi said the inverse of $f(x) = 3x + 1$ is $f^{-1}(x) = \frac{1}{3}x - 1$. Is she correct? Explain.

3. **Construct Arguments** Is the inverse of a function always a function? Explain.

Do You KNOW HOW?

Consider the function $f(x) = -\frac{1}{2}x + 5$.

4. Write an equation for the inverse of $f(x)$.

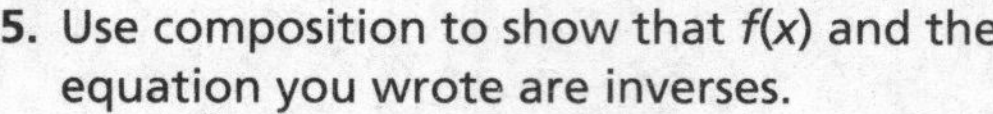

5. Use composition to show that $f(x)$ and the equation you wrote are inverses.

6. Sketch a graph of f and its inverse.

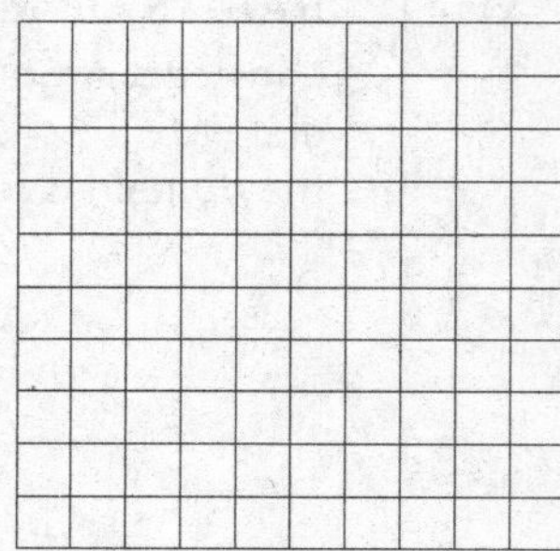

7. How can you verify by the graph of f and its inverse that they are indeed inverses?

8. Is the inverse of $f(x)$ a function? Explain.

5-1 Key Features of Exponential Functions

PearsonRealize.com

EXPLORE & REASON

Margaret investigates three functions: $y = 3x$, $y = x^3$, and $y = 3^x$. She is interested in the differences and ratios between consecutive y-values. Here is the table she started for $y = 3x$.

Investigating $y = 3x$			
x	y	Difference between y-values	Ratio between y-values
1	3		
2	6	$6 - 3 = 3$	$\frac{6}{3} = 2$
3	9	$9 - 6 = 3$	$\frac{9}{6} = 1.5$
4	12	$12 - 9 = 3$	$\frac{12}{9} \approx 1.33$

A. Create tables like Margaret's for all three functions and fill in more rows.

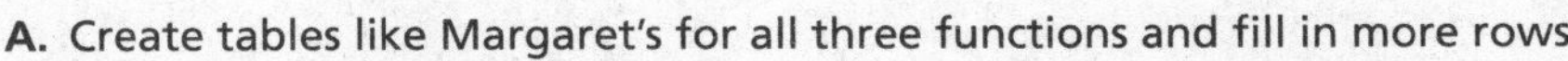

B. Which functions have a constant difference between consecutive y-values? Constant ratio?

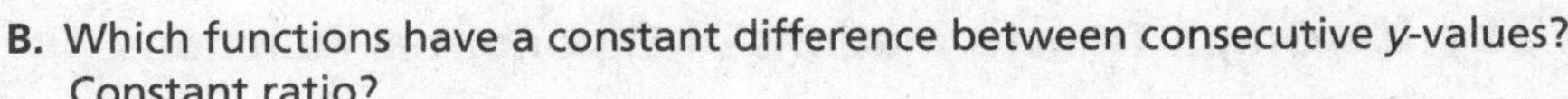

C. Use Structure Which of these three functions will have y-values that increase the fastest as x increases? Why?

HABITS OF MIND

Generalize Let b represent a whole number. For $b > 1$, which function do you think will increase at a faster rate as x increases, $f(x) = b^x$ or $g(x) = x^b$? Explain.

✎ Notes

Assess

EXAMPLE 1

Try It! Identify Key Features of Exponential Functions

1. Graph $f(x) = 4(0.5)^x$. What are the domain, range, intercepts, asymptote, and the end behavior for this function?

EXAMPLE 2

Try It! Graph Transformations of Exponential Functions

2. How do the asymptote and intercept of the given function compare to the asymptote and intercept of the function $f(x) = 5^x$?

a. $g(x) = 5^{x+3}$

b. $h(x) = 5^{-x}$

HABITS OF MIND

Reason What kinds of transformations will affect the asymptote or the intercept(s) of an exponential function? Explain.

 Notes

EXAMPLE 3

Try It! Model with Exponential Functions

3. A factory purchased a 3D Printer on January 2, 2010. The value of the printer is modeled by the function $f(x) = 30(0.93)^x$, where x is the number of years since 2010.

   a. What is the value of the printer after 10 years?

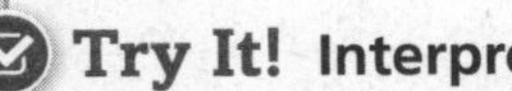

   b. Does the printer lose more of its value in the first 10 years or in the second?

EXAMPLE 4

Try It! Interpret an Exponential Function

4. Two-hundred twenty hawks were released into a region in 2016. The function $f(x) = 220(1.05)^x$ can be used to model the number of red-tailed hawks in the region x years after 2016.

   a. Is the population increasing or decreasing? Explain.

   b. In what year will the number of hawks reach 280?

HABITS OF MIND

Use Structure How can you determine the growth or decay factor by looking at an exponential function? The growth or decay rate?

EXAMPLE 5

Try It! Compare Two Exponential Functions

5. In Example 5, will the value of the painting ever surpass the value of the sculpture according to the models? Explain.

HABITS OF MIND

Reason For two functions $f(x) = b^x$ and $g(x) = b^{x+n}$, where $n > 0$, is it possible that the two graphs will intersect? Explain.

Assess

Do You UNDERSTAND?

1. **ESSENTIAL QUESTION** How do graphs and equations reveal key features of exponential growth and decay functions?

2. **Vocabulary** How do *exponential functions* differ from polynomial and rational functions?

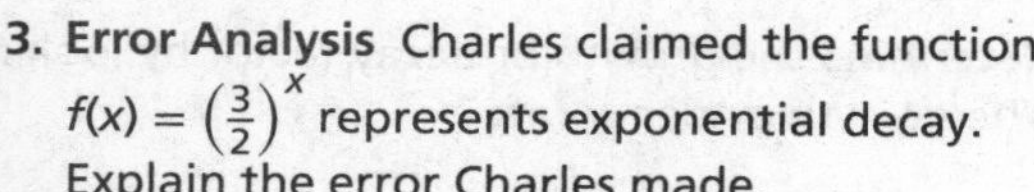

3. **Error Analysis** Charles claimed the function $f(x) = \left(\frac{3}{2}\right)^x$ represents exponential decay. Explain the error Charles made.

4. **Communicate Precisely** How are exponential growth functions similar to exponential decay functions? How are they different?

Do You KNOW HOW?

5. Graph the function $f(x) = 4 \times 3^x$. Identify the domain, range, intercept, asymptote, and describe the end behavior.

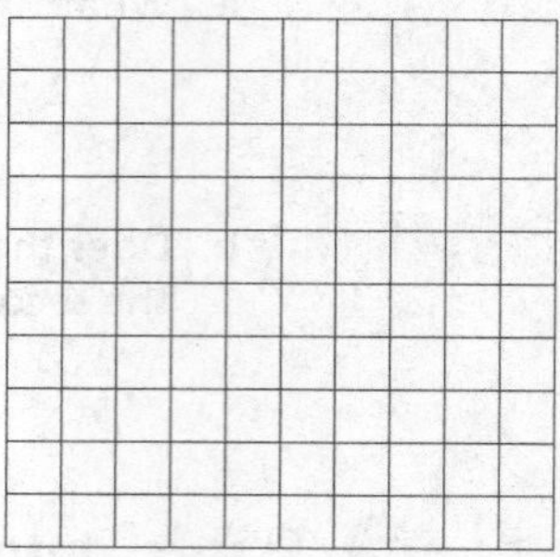

6. The exponential function $f(x) = 2500(0.4)^x$ models the amount of money in Zachary's savings account over the last 10 years. Is Zachary's account balance increasing or decreasing? Write the base in terms of the rate of growth or decay.

7. Describe how the graph of $g(x) = 4(0.5)^{x-3}$ compares to the graph of $f(x) = 4(0.5)^x$.

8. Two trucks were purchased by a landscaping company in 2016. Their values are modeled by the functions $f(x) = 35(0.85)^x$ and $g(x) = 46(0.75)^x$ where x is the number of years since 2016. Which function models the truck that is worth the most after 5 years? Explain.

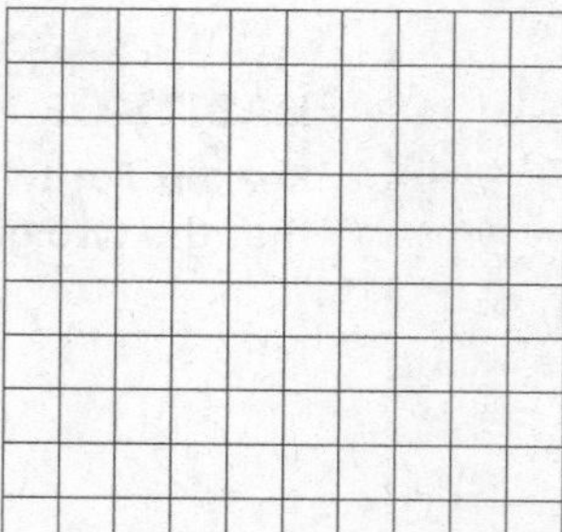

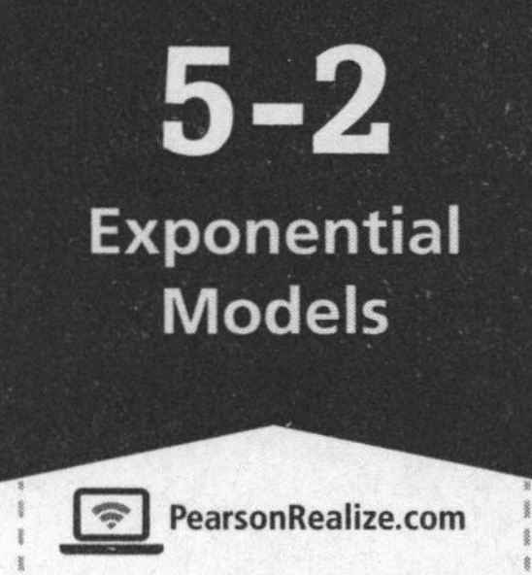

EXPLORE & REASON

Juan is studying exponential growth of bacteria cultures. Each is carefully controlled to maintain a specific growth rate. Copy and complete the table to find the number of bacteria cells in each culture.

Culture	Initial Number of Bacteria	Growth Rate per Day	Time (days)	Final Number of Bacteria
A	10,000	8%	1	
B	10,000	4%	2	
C	10,000	2%	4	
D	10,000	1%	8	

A. What is the relationship between the daily growth rate and the time in days for each culture?

B. Look for Relationships Would you expect a culture with a growth rate of $\frac{1}{2}$% and a time of 16 days to have more or fewer cells than the others in the table? Explain.

HABITS OF MIND

Model With Mathematics Describe another situation that you could represent using an exponential function.

 Notes

 Assess

EXAMPLE 1 

Try It! Rewrite an Exponential Function to Identify a Rate

1. The population in a small town is increasing annually at 1.8%. What is the quarterly rate of population increase?

HABITS OF MIND

Generalize Why can't you just divide an annual interest rate by 4 to obtain a quarterly interest rate?

EXAMPLE 2 

Try It! Understand Continuously Compounded Interest

2. \$3,000 is invested in an account that earns 3% annual interest, compounded monthly.
   a. What is the value of the account after 10 years?
   b. What is the value of the account after 100 years?

EXAMPLE 3 

Try It! Understanding Continuously Compounded Interest

3. If you continued the table for $n = 1{,}000{,}000$, would the value in the account increase or decrease? How do you know?

HABITS OF MIND

Generalize Which yields the greatest return on investment: compounding quarterly, hourly, or continuously? Explain.

Notes

EXAMPLE 4 **Try It!** **Find Continuously Compounded Interest**

4. You invest $125,000 in an account that earns 4.75% annual interest, compounded continuously.

   a. What is the value of the account after 15 years?

   b. What is the value of the account after 30 years?

EXAMPLE 5 **Try It!** **Use Two Points to Find an Exponential Model**

5. A surveyor determined the value of an area of land over a period of several years since 1950. The land was worth $31,000 in 1954 and $35,000 in 1955. Use the data to determine an exponential model that describes the value of the land.

EXAMPLE 6 **Try It!** **Use Regression to Find an Exponential Model**

6. According to the model in Example 6, what was the approximate temperature 35 minutes after cooling started?

HABITS OF MIND

Generalize How can a graph help you determine whether an exponential model is appropriate for a data set? Explain.

Do You UNDERSTAND?

1. ESSENTIAL QUESTION Why do you develop exponential models to represent and interpret situations?

2. **Error Analysis** The exponential model $y = 5{,}000(1.05)^t$ represents the amount Yori earns in an account after t years when \$5,000 is invested. Yori said the monthly interest rate of the exponential model is 5%. Explain Yori's error.

3. **Vocabulary** Explain the similarities and differences between compound interest and continuously compounded interest.

4. **Communicate Precisely** Kylee is using a calculator to find an exponential regression model. How would you explain to Kylee what the variables in the model $y = ab^x$ represent?

Do You KNOW HOW?

The exponential function models the annual rate of increase. Find the monthly and quarterly rates.

5. $f(t) = 2{,}000(1.03)^t$

6. $f(t) = 500(1.055)^t$

Find the total amount of money invested in an account at the end of the given time period.

7. compounded monthly, $P = \$2{,}000$, $r = 3\%$, $t = 5$ years

8. continuously compounded, $P = \$1{,}500$, $r = 1.5\%$, $t = 6$ years

Write an exponential model given two points.

9. (3, 55) and (4, 70)

10. (7, 12) and (8, 25)

11. Paul invests \$6,450 in an account that earns continuously compounded interest at an annual rate of 2.8%. What is the value of the account after 8 years?

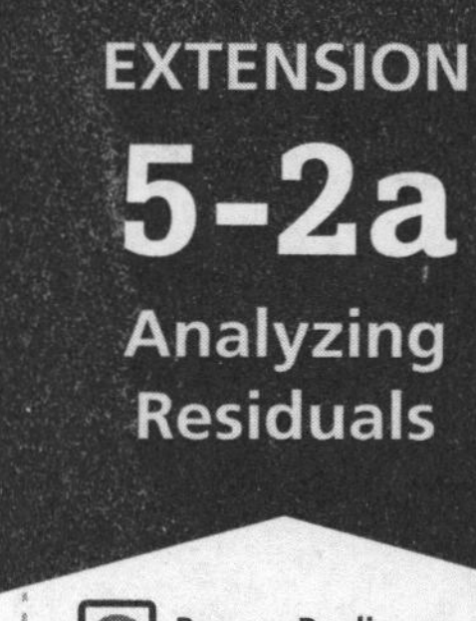

Notes

Assess

EXAMPLE 1

Try It! Analyze Residuals

1. A biologist is tracking the population of raccoons in a forest since 2010 as shown in the table. She creates the exponential model $y = 638 \cdot 0.99^x$, where x is the number of years since 2010, to model the population. Use a residual plot to analyze how well the model fits the data.

Year (x)	0	1	2	3	4	5	6	7
Population (y)	635	622	618	615	612	601	597	593

HABITS OF MIND

Communicate Precisely How would you explain the process of using residuals to analyze the goodness of fit of a model?

Do You UNDERSTAND?

1. ESSENTIAL QUESTION How can you use residuals to determine the goodness of fit off a function model?

2. **Reason** When a model is a good fit for the data, what would you expect to see in the sum of the residuals? Explain.

3. **Error Analysis** A student calculated the residuals for a model and found that they were all between 0 and 3, so the student concluded that the model was a good fit for the data. Explain the error the student made.

Do You KNOW HOW?

Use the table for Exercises 4–6.

x	0	1	2	3	4	5	6
y	118	129	145	156	178	185	210

4. Use technology to perform an exponential regression on the data.

5. Make a residual plot for the exponential model and the data in the table. How well does the model fit the data? Explain.

6. Use the model to predict the y-value when $x = 12$.

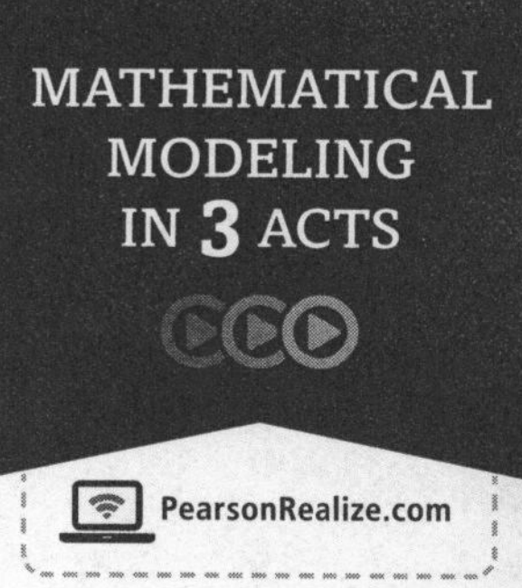

The Crazy Conditioning

Like all sports, soccer requires its players to be well trained. That is why players often have to run sprints in practice.

To make sprint drills more interesting, many coaches set up competitions. Coaches might split the players into teams and have them run relay races against each other. Or they might have the players sprint around cones and over barriers. What other ways would make doing sprints more fun? Think about this during this Mathematical Modeling in 3 Acts lesson.

ACT 1 Identify the Problem

1. What is the first question that comes to mind after watching the video?

2. Write down the main question you will answer about the video.

3. Make an initial conjecture that answers this main question.

4. Explain how you arrived at your conjecture.

5. Write a number that you know is too small.

Video

6. What information will be useful to know to answer the main question? How can you get it? How will you use that information?

ACT 2 Develop a Model

7. Use the math that you have learned in the topic to refine your conjecture.

8. Is your refined conjecture between the high and low estimates you came up with earlier?

ACT 3 Interpret the Results

9. Did your refined conjecture match the actual answer exactly? If not, what might explain the difference?

5-3 Linear, Exponential, and Quadratic Models

PearsonRealize.com

MODEL & DISCUSS

Jacy and Emma use different functions to model the value of a bike x years after it is purchased. Each function models the data in the table.

Jacy's function: $f(x) = -14.20x + 500$

Emma's function: $f(x) = 500(0.85)^x$

Time (yr)	Value ($)
0	500.00
1	485.20
2	472.13
3	461.00
4	452.10

A. Make Sense and Persevere Why did Jacy and Emma not choose a quadratic function to model the data?

B. Whose function do you think is a better model? Explain.

C. Do you agree with this statement? Explain why or why not.

To ensure that you are finding the best model for a table of data, you need to find the values of the functions for the same values of x.

HABITS OF MIND

Communicate Precisely How is finding the best model for data in a real-world situation similar to finding the best model in a mathematical situation? How is it different?

EXAMPLE 1

Try It! Determine Which Function Type Represents Data

1. Does a linear, quadratic, or exponential function best model the data? Explain.

a.

x	0	1	2	3	4
y	−2	−5	−14	−29	−50

b.

x	−2	−1	0	1	2
y	4	12	36	108	324

EXAMPLE 2

Try It! Choose a Function Type for Real-World Data

2. Determine whether a linear, quadratic, or exponential function best models the data. Then, use regression to find the function that models the data.

x	0	1	2	3	4
y	100	89.5	78.9	68.4	57.8

HABITS OF MIND

Reason If a table of data does not have common differences or a common ratio, can you still make predictions about other data points in the data set? Explain.

 Notes

Assess

EXAMPLE 3 **Try It! Compare Linear, Exponential, and Quadratic Growth**

3. Compare the functions $f(x) = 3x + 2$, $g(x) = 2x^2 + 3$, and $h(x) = 2^x$. Show that as x increases, $h(x)$ will eventually exceed $f(x)$ and $g(x)$.

HABITS OF MIND

Generalize How can the rate of change help determine the type of function that best fits the data?

Do You UNDERSTAND?

1. 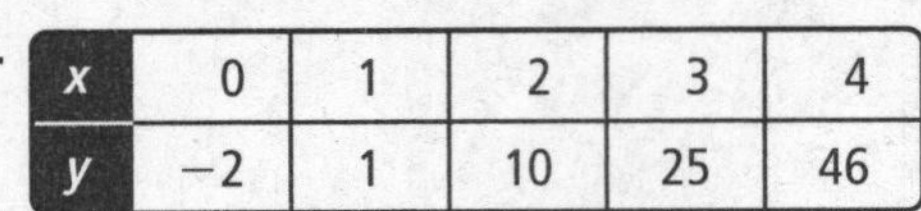 ESSENTIAL QUESTION How can you determine whether a linear, exponential, or quadratic function best models data?

2. **Reason** The growth of a function is less from $x = 1$ to $x = 4$ than from $x = 5$ to $x = 8$. What type of function could it be? Explain.

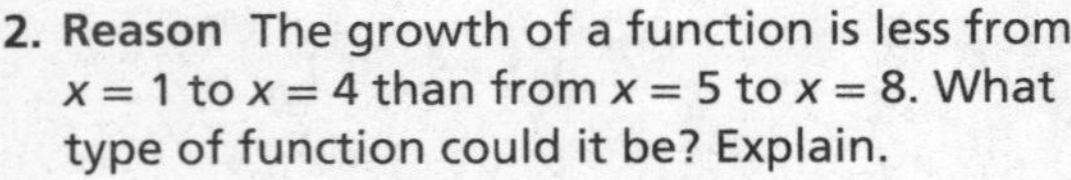

3. **Error Analysis** Kiyo used a quadratic function to model data with constant first differences. Explain the error Kiyo made.

Do You KNOW HOW?

Determine whether the data are best modeled by a linear, quadratic, or exponential function.

4.

x	0	1	2	3	4
y	−2	1	10	25	46

5.

x	−2	−1	0	1	2
y	2	7	12	17	22

6. A company's profit from a certain product is represented by $P(x) = -5x^2 + 1{,}125x - 5{,}000$, where x is the price of the product. Compare the growth in profits from $x = 120$ to $x = 140$ and from $x = 140$ to $x = 160$. What do you notice?

PearsonRealize.com

CRITIQUE & EXPLAIN

Earthquakes make seismic waves through the ground. The equation $y = 10^x$ relates the height, or amplitude, in microns, of a seismic wave, y, and the power, or magnitude, x, of the ground-shaking it can cause.

Taylor and Chen used different methods to find the magnitude of the earthquake with amplitude 5,500.

Magnitude, x	Amplitude, y
2	100
3	1,000
?	4,500
4	10,000

Taylor

5,500 is halfway between 1,000 and 10,000.

3.5 is halfway between 3 and 4.

The magnitude is about 3.5.

Chen

$y = 10^x$

$10^3 = 1{,}000$
$10^4 = 10{,}000$
$10^{3.5} \approx 3{,}162$
$10^{3.7} \approx 5{,}012$
$10^{3.8} \approx 6{,}310$
$10^{3.74} \approx 5{,}500$

The magnitude is about 3.74.

A. What is the magnitude of an earthquake with amplitude 100,000? How do you know?

B. Construct Arguments Critique Taylor's and Chen's work. Is each method valid? Could either method be improved?

C. Describe how to express the exact value of the desired magnitude.

HABITS OF MIND

Reason Taylor reasoned that since 5,500 was halfway between 1,000 and 10,000, that the magnitude had to be halfway between 3 and 4. What is incorrect about Taylor's reasoning?

Notes

Assess

EXAMPLE 1 **Try It!** **Understand Logarithms**

1. Write the logarithmic form of $y = 8^x$.

EXAMPLE 2 **Try It!** **Convert Between Exponential and Logarithmic Forms**

2. a. What is the logarithmic form of $7^3 = 343$?

b. What is the exponential form of $\log_4 16 = 2$?

HABITS OF MIND

Communicate Precisely Write a sentence to describe what the equation $\log_a b = c$ means.

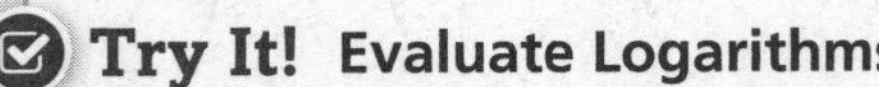

EXAMPLE 3 **Try It!** **Evaluate Logarithms**

3. What is the value of each logarithmic expression?

a. $\log_3\left(\frac{1}{81}\right)$ **b.** $\log_7(-7)$ **c.** $\log_5 5^9$

Notes

Assess

EXAMPLE 4

Try It! Evaluate Common and Natural Logarithms

4. What is the value of each logarithmic expression to the nearest ten-thousandth?

a. log 321 **b.** ln 1,215 **c.** log 0.17

HABITS OF MIND

Reason In order for log x or ln x to be defined, what must be true about x?

EXAMPLE 5

Try It! Solve Equations With Logarithms

5. Solve each equation. Round to the nearest thousandth.

a. $\log(3x - 2) = 2$ **b.** $e^{x+2} = 8$

EXAMPLE 6

Try It! Use Logarithms to Solve Equations

6. What is the magnitude of an earthquake with a seismic energy of 1.8×10^{23} joules?

HABITS OF MIND

Make Sense and Persevere How do logarithms help you to solve an equation in which the variable is an exponent?

Do You UNDERSTAND?

1. ESSENTIAL QUESTION What are logarithms and how are they evaluated?

2. **Error Analysis** Amir said the expression $\log_5(-25)$ simplifies to –2. Explain Amir's possible error.

3. **Vocabulary** Explain the difference between the common logarithm and the natural logarithm.

4. **Make Sense and Persevere** How can logarithms help to solve an equation such as $10^t = 656$?

Do You KNOW HOW?

Write each equation in logarithmic form.

5. $2^{-6} = \frac{1}{64}$

6. $e^4 \approx 54.6$

Write each equation in exponential form.

7. $\log 200 \approx 2.301$

8. $\ln 25 \approx 3.22$

Evaluate the expression.

9. $\log_4 64$

10. $\log \frac{1}{100}$

11. $\ln e^5$

12. Solve for x. $4e^x = 7$.

5-5
Logarithmic Functions

PearsonRealize.com

EXPLORE & REASON

Compare the graphs.

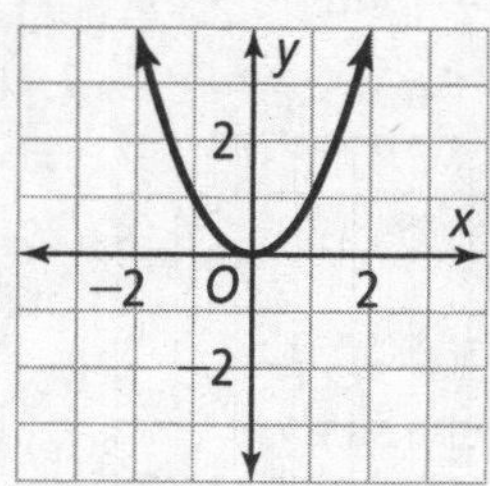
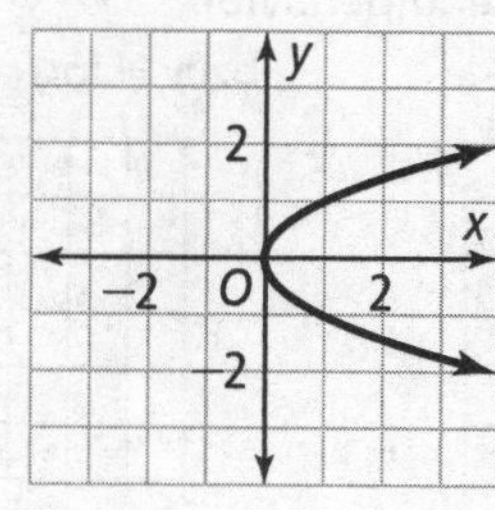
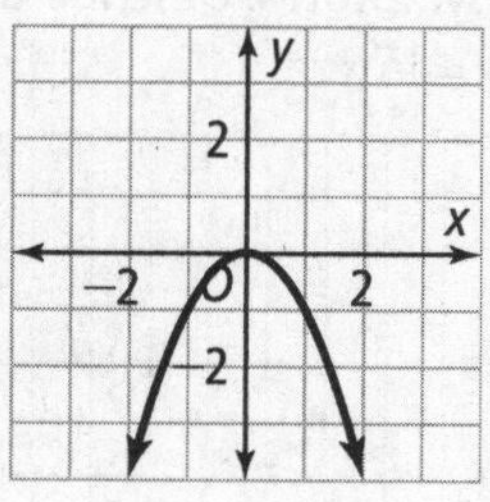

A. Which two graphs represent the inverse of each other? Explain.

B. Look for Relationships What is the relationship between the domain and the range of the two inverse relations?

HABITS OF MIND

Communicate Precisely How are the points on graphs of functions that are inverses of each other related?

 Notes

Assess

EXAMPLE 1 **Try It!** **Identify Key Features of Logarithmic Functions**

1. Graph each function and identify the domain and range. List any intercepts or asymptotes. Describe the end behavior.

a. $y = \ln x$

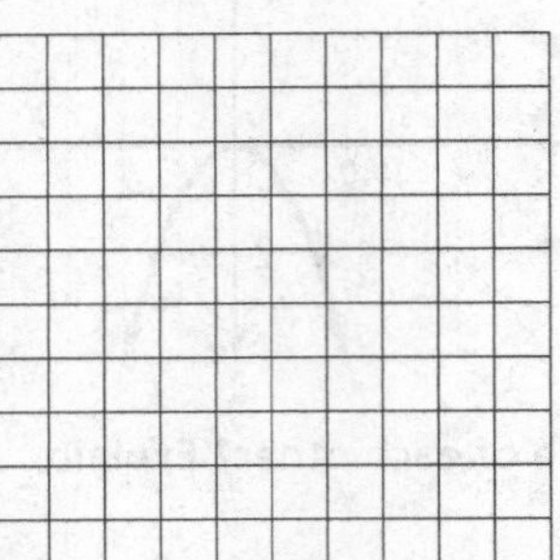

b. $y = \log_{\frac{1}{2}} x$

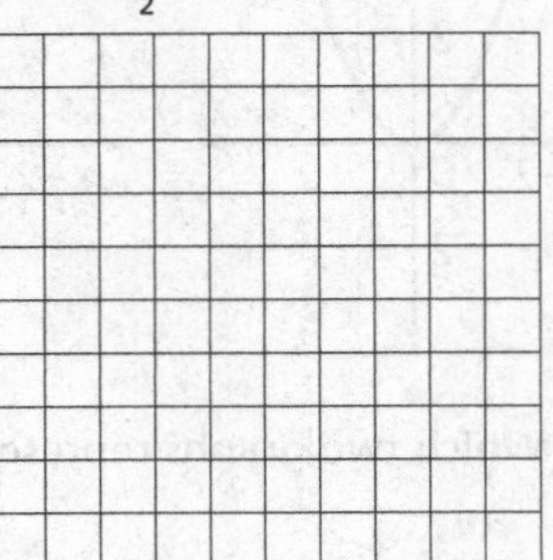

EXAMPLE 2 **Try It!** **Graph Transformations of Logarithmic Functions**

2. Describe how each graph compares to the graph of $f(x) = \ln x$.

a. $g(x) = \ln x + 4$

b. $h(x) = 5 \ln x$

HABITS OF MIND

Use Structure Does the graph of either $y = \ln x + 4$ or $y = \ln (x + 4)$ have an intercept that is different from the intercept of $y = \ln x$? Explain.

Notes

Assess

EXAMPLE 3  **Try It! Inverses of Exponential and Logarithmic Functions**

3. Find the inverse of each function.

   a. $f(x) = 3^{x+2}$

   b. $g(x) = \log_7 x - 2$

EXAMPLE 4  **Try It! Interpret the Inverse of a Formula Involving Logarithms**

4. Describe what happens to the amount of monthly revenue as the amount of advertising increases. How might you determine the optimal advertising budget? Explain.

HABITS OF MIND

Generalize How would you explain, in your own words, how to find the inverse of a logarithmic function?

EXAMPLE 5  **Try It! Compare Two Logarithmic Functions**

5. For which plane do you think the altitude will change more quickly over the interval $15 \leq t \leq 20$? Explain your reasoning.

HABITS OF MIND

Look for Relationships How does the average rate of change of the function $f(x) = \log x$ change as x increases?

Do You UNDERSTAND?

1. ESSENTIAL QUESTION How is the relationship between logarithmic and exponential functions revealed in the key features of their graphs?

2. **Error Analysis** Raynard claims the domain of the function $y = \log_3 x$ is all real numbers. Explain the error Raynard made.

3. **Communicate Precisely** How are the graphs of $f(x) = \log_5 x$ and $g(x) = -\log_5 x$ related?

Do You KNOW HOW?

4. Graph the function $y = \log_4 x$ and identify the domain and range. List any intercepts or asymptotes. Describe the end behavior.

5. Write the equation for the function $g(x)$, which can be described as a vertical shift $1\frac{1}{2}$ units up from the function $f(x) = \ln x - 1$.

6. The function $y = 5 \ln(x + 1)$ gives y, the number of downloads, in hundreds, x minutes after the release of a song. Find the equation of the inverse and interpret its meaning.

5-6

Properties of Logarithms

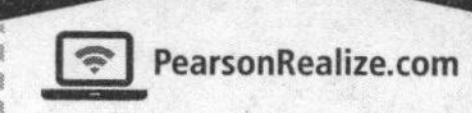

EXPLORE & REASON

Look at the graph of $y = \log x$ and the ordered pairs shown.

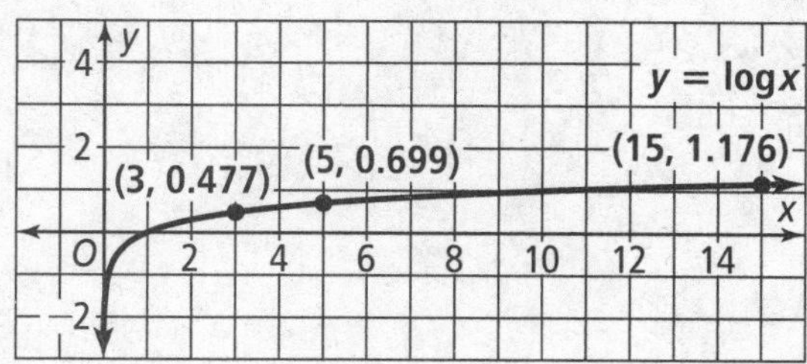

A. Complete the table shown.

x	3	5	15
$\log x$			

B. Look for Relationships What is the relationship between the numbers 3, 5, and 15? What is the relationship between the logarithms of 3, 5, and 15?

C. What is your prediction for the value of log 45? log 75? Explain.

HABITS OF MIND

Generalize Do you think that the relationships you found in the Explore & Reason activity would also hold for natural logarithms? Give an example.

Notes

EXAMPLE 1  **Try It! Prove a Property of Logarithms**

1. Prove the Quotient Property of Logarithms.

EXAMPLE 2  **Try It! Expand Logarithmic Expressions**

2. Use the properties of logarithms to expand each expression.

a. $\log_7\left(\frac{r^3t^4}{v}\right)$

b. $\ln\left(\frac{7}{225}\right)$

EXAMPLE 3  **Try It! Write Expressions as Single Logarithms**

3. Write each expression written as a single logarithm.

a. $5\log_2 c - 7\log_2 n$

b. $2\ln 7 + \ln 2$

HABITS OF MIND

Make Sense and Persevere Using the fact that $\log 2 \approx 0.3010$ and $\log 3 \approx 0.4771$, what is log 18? Show how you know.

Notes

EXAMPLE 4 **Try It! Apply Properties of Logarithms**

4. What is the concentration of hydrogen ions in a liter of orange juice?

HABITS OF MIND

Generalize What types of numbers have logarithms that are negative? Explain.

EXAMPLE 5 **Try It! Evaluate Logarithmic Expressions by Changing the Base**

5. Estimate the value of each logarithm. Then use a calculator to find the value of each logarithm to the nearest thousandth.

a. $\log_2 7$

b. $\log_5 3$

EXAMPLE 6 **Try It! Use the Change of Base Formula**

6. What is the solution to the equation $3^x = 15$? Express the solution as a logarithm and then evaluate. Round to the nearest thousandth.

HABITS OF MIND

Use Appropriate Tools Why is the Change of Base Formula useful when evaluating a logarithm with a calculator?

Do You UNDERSTAND?

1. ESSENTIAL QUESTION How are the properties of logarithms used to simplify expressions and solve logarithmic equations?

2. **Vocabulary** While it is not necessary to change to base 10 when applying the Change of Base Formula, why is it common to do so?

3. **Error Analysis** Amanda claimed the expanded form of the expression $\log_4(c^2d^5)$ is $5\log_4 c + 5\log_4 d$. Explain the error Amanda made.

Do You KNOW HOW?

4. Use the properties of logarithms to expand the expression $\log_6\left(\frac{49}{5}\right)$.

5. Use the properties of logarithms to write the expression $5 \ln s + 6 \ln t$ as a single logarithm.

6. Use the formula $\text{pH} = \log\frac{1}{[H^+]}$ to write an expression for the concentration of hydrogen ions, $[H^+]$, in a container of baking soda with a pH of 8.9.

5-7 Exponential and Logarithmic Equations

PearsonRealize.com

MODEL & DISCUSS

A store introduces two new models of fitness trackers to its product line. A glance at the data is enough to see that sales of both types of fitness trackers are increasing. Unfortunately, the store has limited space for the merchandise. The manager decides that the store will sell both models until sales of TrackSmart exceed those of FitTracker.

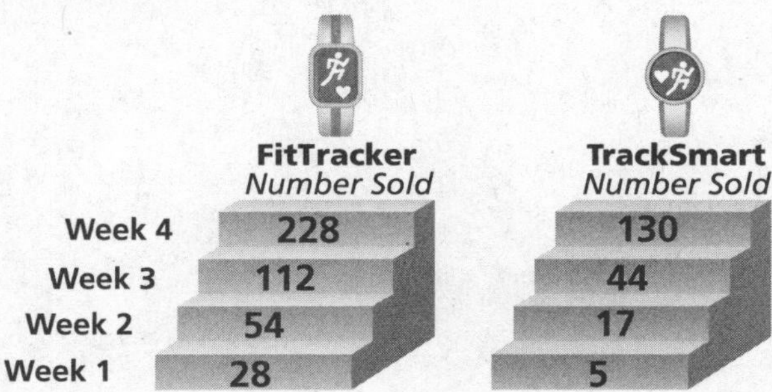

A. Model With Mathematics Find an equation of an exponential that models the sales for each fitness tracker. Describe your method.

B. Based on the equations that you wrote, determine when the store will stop selling FitTracker.

HABITS OF MIND

Look for Relationships How do you know that the sales data is modeled by an exponential function?

Notes

Assess

EXAMPLE 1 **Try It! Solve Exponential Equations Using a Common Base**

1. Solve each equation using a common base.

a. $25^{3x} = 125^{x+2}$

b. $0.001 = 10^{6x}$

EXAMPLE 2 **Try It! Rewrite Exponential Equations Using Logarithms**

2. Rewrite the equation $5^x = 12$ using logarithms.

HABITS OF MIND

Communicate Precisely In order to set the exponents of two exponential expressions equal to each other, what must be true about the exponential expressions?

Notes

Assess

EXAMPLE 3 **Try It!** **Solve Exponential Equations Using Logarithms**

3. What is the solution to $2^{3x} = 7^{x+1}$?

EXAMPLE 4 **Try It!** **Use an Exponential Model**

4. About how many minutes does it take the fire to spread to cover 100 acres?

HABITS OF MIND

Use Structure Why is it useful to use logarithms to solve an exponential equation?

EXAMPLE 5 **Try It!** **Solve Logarithmic Equations**

5. Solve each equation.

a. $\log_5 (x^2 - 45) = \log_5 (4x)$

b. $\ln (-4x - 1) = \ln (4x^2)$

EXAMPLE 6 **Try It!** **Solve Logarithmic and Exponential Equations by Graphing**

6. Solve each equation by graphing. Round to the nearest thousandth.

a. $3(2)^{x+2} - 1 = 3 - x$

b. $\ln (3x - 1) = x - 5$

HABITS OF MIND

Generalize Summarize the procedure for solving a logarithmic equation.

Assess

Do You UNDERSTAND?

1. ESSENTIAL QUESTION How do properties of exponents and logarithms help you solve equations?

2. **Vocabulary** Jordan claims that $x^2 + 3 = 12$ is an exponential equation. Is Jordan correct? Explain your thinking.

3. **Communicate Precisely** How can properties of logarithms help to solve an equation such as $\log_6 (8x - 2)^3 = 12$?

Do You KNOW HOW?

Solve. Round to the nearest hundredth, if necessary. List any extraneous solutions.

4. $16^{3x} = 256^{x+1}$

5. $6^{x+2} = 4^x$

6. $\log_5 (x^2 - 44) = \log_5 (7x)$

7. $\log_2 (3x - 2) = 4$

8. $4^{2x} = 9^{x-1}$

9. A rabbit farm had 200 rabbits in 2015. The number of rabbits increases by 30% every year. How many rabbits are on the farm in 2031?

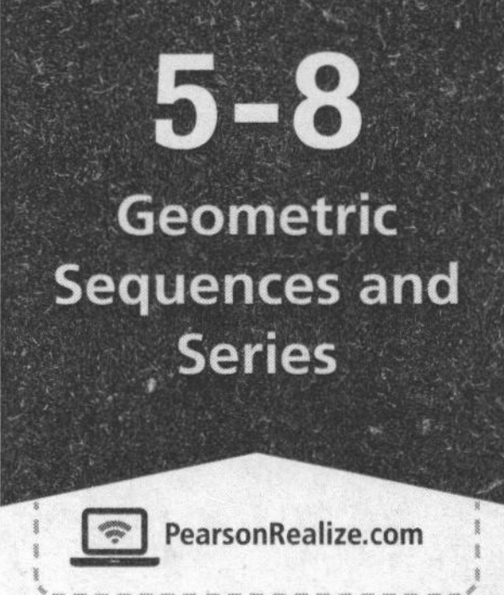

EXPLORE & REASON

A store offered customers two plans for getting bonus points:

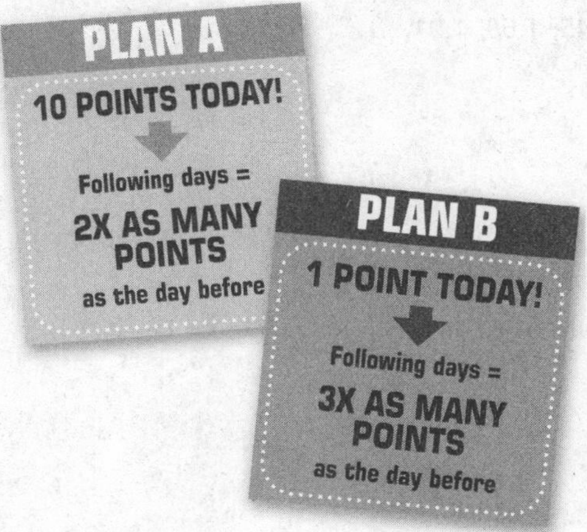

A. What expression represents the number of points received each day for Plan A?

B. What expression represents the number of points received each day for Plan B?

C. **Reason** On the 7th day, which plan would offer the most bonus points? Explain.

HABITS OF MIND

Reason Does Plan B always offer more points than Plan A? Explain.

EXAMPLE 1  **Try It!** **Identify Geometric Sequences**

1. Is the sequence a geometric sequence? If so, write a recursive definition for the sequence.

   a. 1.22, 1.45, 1.68, 1.91, ...

   b. −1.5, 0.75, −0.375, 0.1875, ...

EXAMPLE 2 **Try It!** **Translate Between Recursive and Explicit Definitions**

2. a. Given the recursive definition $a_n = \begin{cases} 12, & n = 1 \\ \frac{1}{3}a_{n-1}, & n > 1 \end{cases}$;
   what is the explicit definition for the sequence?

   b. Given the explicit definition $a_n = 6(1.2)^{n-1}$;
   what is the recursive definition?

EXAMPLE 3 **Try It!** **Solve Problems with Geometric Sequences**

3. A geometric sequence can be used to describe the growth of bacteria in an experiment. On the first day of the experiment there were 9 bacteria in a Petri dish. On the 10th day, there are 3^{20} bacteria in the dish. How many bacteria were in the dish on the 7th day of the experiment?

HABITS OF MIND

Use Appropriate Tools How can you use the recursive definition for a geometric sequence to find the 19th term?

Notes

EXAMPLE 4  **Try It! Formula for the Sum of a Finite Geometric Series**

4. a. Write the expanded form of the series $\sum_{n=1}^{5} \frac{1}{2}(3)^{n-1}$. What is the sum?

b. Write the series $-2 + \left(\frac{-2}{3}\right) + \ldots + \left(\frac{-2}{243}\right)$ using sigma notation. What is the sum?

EXAMPLE 5  **Try It! Find the Number of Terms in a Finite Geometric Series**

5. a. How many terms are in the geometric series $3 + 6 + 12 + \ldots + 768$?

b. The sum of a geometric series is 155. The first term of the series is 5, and its common ratio is 2. How many terms are in the series?

EXAMPLE 6  **Try It! Use a Finite Geometric Series**

6. What is the monthly payment for a $40,000 loan for 4 years with an annual interest rate of 4.8%?

HABITS OF MIND

Make Sense and Persevere Why is using a formula easier than calculating and adding all 10 terms?

Assess

Do You UNDERSTAND?

1. ESSENTIAL QUESTION How can you represent and use geometric sequences and series?

2. **Error Analysis** Denzel claims the sequence 0, 7, 49, 343, ... is a geometric sequence and the next number is 2,401. What error did he make?

3. **Vocabulary** Describe the similarities and differences between a common difference and a common ratio.

4. **Use Structure** What happens to the terms of a sequence if a_1 is positive and $r > 1$? What happens if $0 < r < 1$? Explain.

Do You KNOW HOW?

Find the common ratio and the next three terms of each geometric sequence.

5. 2, −4, 8, −16, ...

6. −64, −16, −4, −1, ...

7. 0.8, 2.4, 7.2, 21.6, ...

8. 2, −10, 50, −250, ...

9. 100, 50, 25, 12.5, ...

10. In a video game, players earn 10 points for finishing the first level and twice as many points for each additional level. How many points does a player earn for finishing the fifth level? How many points will the player have earned in the game up to that point?

6-1 Trigonometric Functions and Acute Functions

EXPLORE & REASON

In the figure below, $\triangle ABC \sim \triangle DEF$.

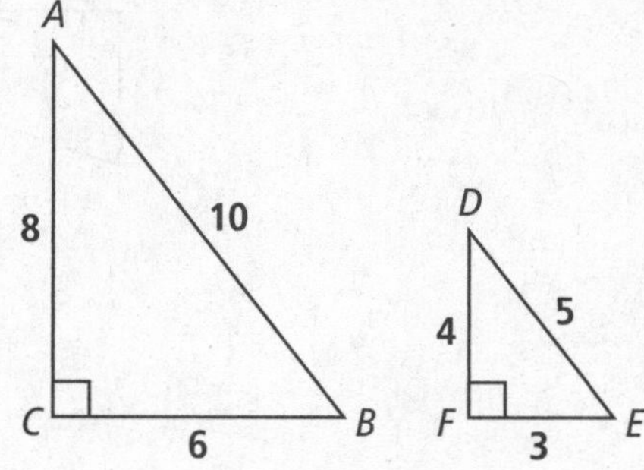

A. Write as many ratios as you can using two side lengths from $\triangle ABC$.

B. Write as many ratios as you can using two side lengths from $\triangle DEF$.

C. Look for Relationships What do the results from parts (a) and (b) suggest about the ratios of side lengths in similar right triangles?

HABITS OF MIND

Look for Relationships Find the side lengths of two right triangles, one that is similar to the triangles above and one that is not. How do the ratios in these triangles compare to the ones above?

 Notes

Assess

EXAMPLE 1

Try It! Write Trigonometric Ratios

1. Write the six trigonometric ratios for θ.

a.

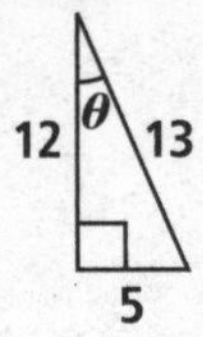

b.

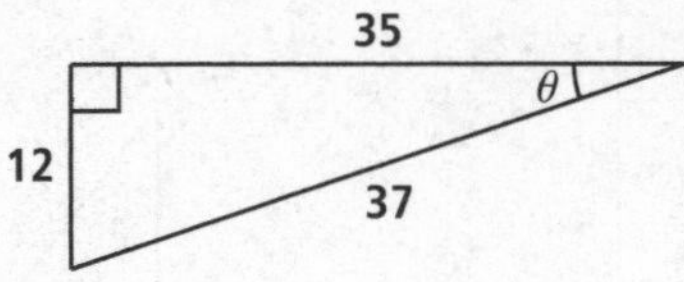

EXAMPLE 2

Try It! Use One Trigonometric Ratio to Find Another

2. What are the trigonometric ratios of an angle with measure θ in a right triangle in which $\sin\theta = \frac{24}{25}$?

HABITS OF MIND

Reason What are the side lengths for two different right triangles that have $\tan\theta = \frac{12}{5}$?

EXAMPLE 3

Try It! Find a Missing Side Length

3. The sun shines at a 60° angle to the ground. How long is the shadow cast by a 20 ft tall flagpole?

Notes

Assess

EXAMPLE 4  **Try It! Evaluate Trigonometric Ratios in Special Triangles**

4. The length of the hypotenuse in a 45° –45° –90° triangle is $5\sqrt{2}$. What are the sine and secant ratios for a 45° angle?

HABITS OF MIND

Construct Arguments Is it true that if $\sec\theta = \sqrt{2}$ for θ in a right triangle that the triangle must be isosceles? Explain.

EXAMPLE 5  **Try It! Explain Trigonometric Identities**

5. What are the cofunction identities for tangent and cotangent?

HABITS OF MIND

Communicate Precisely What is an equation that relates the three functions cosecant, secant, and cotangent?

Do You UNDERSTAND?

1. **ESSENTIAL QUESTION** How can ratios of lengths of sides within right triangles help determine other lengths and angle measures in the triangles?

2. **Error Analysis** Terrell said that cos θ is the reciprocal of sin θ. Explain and correct Terrell's error.

3. **Vocabulary** Explain what it means to say that $\tan\theta = \frac{1}{\cot\theta}$ is an identity.

4. **Construct Arguments** Why are the cofunction identities true for all right triangles?

5. **Generalize** How does knowing one trigonometric ratio allow you to find the other five trigonometric ratios?

6. **Look for Relationships** Why do secant and cosecant always have to be greater than 1 or less than −1?

Do You KNOW HOW?

Find sin θ using the given trigonometric ratio.

7. $\csc\theta = \frac{7}{3}$

8. $\tan\theta = \frac{5}{12}$

Use the trigonometric ratio given to write the other five trigonometric ratios for θ.

9. $\cos\theta = \frac{5}{13}$

10. $\tan\theta = \frac{3}{4}$

Write the reciprocal identity of the given trigonometric ratio.

11. $\cos\theta$

12. $\sec\theta$

Write the cofunction identity of the given trigonometric ratio.

13. $\csc\theta$

14. $\sec\theta$

15. A right triangle has a side of 16 m adjacent to an angle of 37°. What is the length of the hypotenuse rounded to the nearest whole meter?

16. A flagpole is 24 ft tall. A support wire runs from the top of the flagpole to an anchor in the ground. The wire makes a 73° angle with the ground. To the nearest tenth of a foot, how far from the base of the flagpole is the anchor?

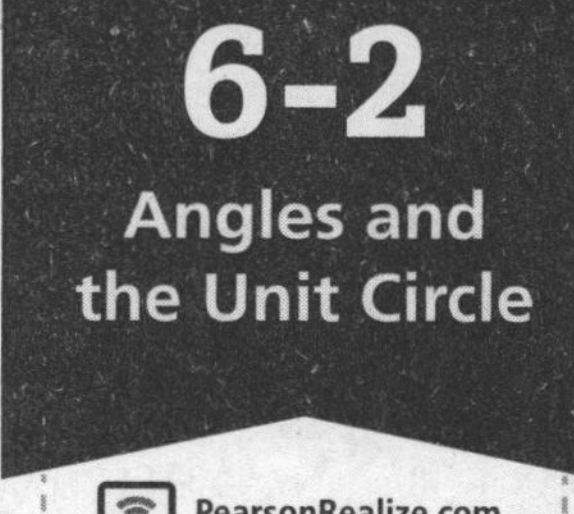

EXPLORE & REASON

A bug is placed at the point (1, 0) of the coordinate plane as shown. It starts walking counterclockwise along a circle with radius 1.

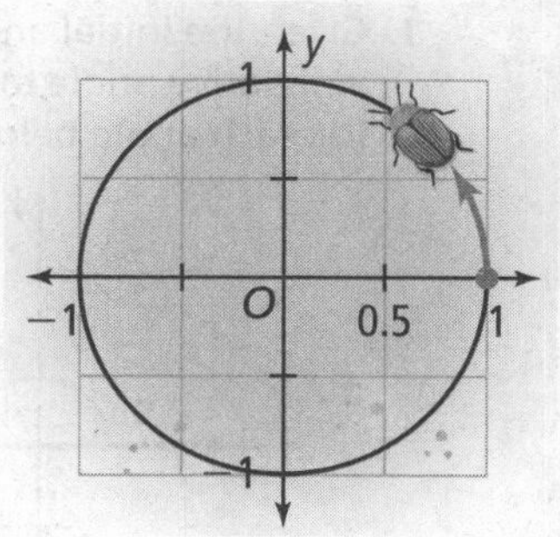

A. **Model With Mathematics** How can you calculate the distance along the circle the bug has traveled? How can you determine the measure of the central angle?

B. When the bug has traveled $\frac{1}{8}$ of the way along the circle, how far has it traveled? What central angle does its path travel through?

C. What are the distances traveled and the central angles when the bug has traveled $\frac{1}{6}$ of the way around the circle and $\frac{4}{5}$ of the way around the circle?

HABITS OF MIND

Look for Relationships A second bug is placed on a circle with radius 2. After it has traveled $\frac{4}{5}$ of the way along this new circle, how far has it traveled compared to the first bug? How do the central angles of the two bugs' paths compare?

Notes

Assess

EXAMPLE 1  **Try It!** **Find the Measure of an Angle in Standard Position**

1. Given the initial and terminal sides, find a positive angle measure, a negative angle measure, and an angle measure greater than 360° for each angle below.

a.

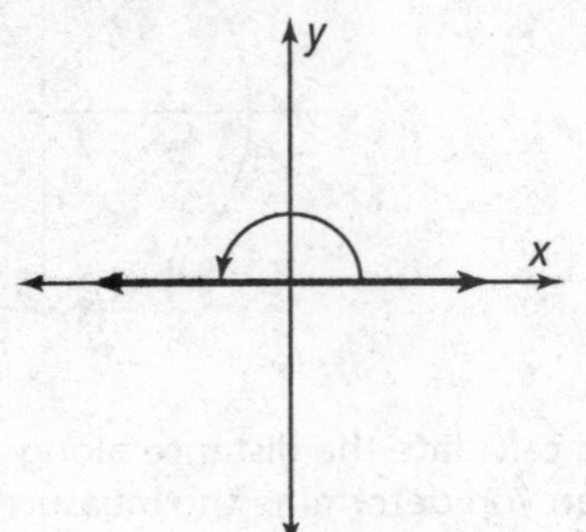

b.

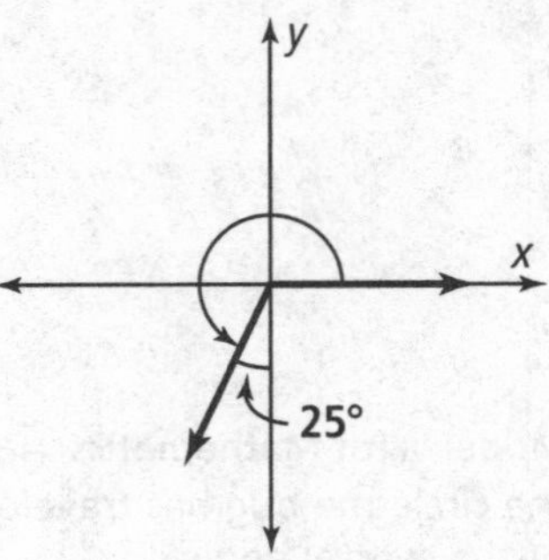

EXAMPLE 2 **Try It!** 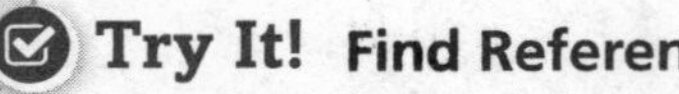 **Find Reference Angles**

2. Give a possible positive angle measure and a possible negative angle measure for each reference angle.

a. 10° in Quadrant III

b. 15° in Quadrant I

EXAMPLE 3  **Try It!** **Find the Coordinates of a Point on the Unit Circle**

3. An angle, θ, has a measure of 45° and a terminal side that intercepts the unit circle at (x, y). What are the values of x and y?

HABITS OF MIND

Make Sense and Persevere Why is the reference angle the angle between the terminal side and the x-axis instead of the y-axis?

Notes

EXAMPLE 4  **Try It! Understand Radian Measure on the Unit Circle**

4. Sketch the graph of an angle that measures $-\frac{5\pi}{6}$ in standard position.

EXAMPLE 5  **Try It! Convert Between Degrees and Radians**

5. Convert the angle measures.

a. 112° to radians

b. $\frac{\pi}{6}$ radians to degrees

EXAMPLE 6  **Try It! Use Radians to Find Arc Length**

6. If the satellite could be tracked for 5,000 km, what angle in radians would it pass through?

HABITS OF MIND

Reason Which angle is larger, an angle measuring 180° or an angle measuring 3 radians? Explain.

Do You UNDERSTAND?

1. ESSENTIAL QUESTION How can we extend the trigonometric ratios to angles greater than 90°?

2. **Error Analysis** Camilla said that θ and its reference angle are always supplementary angles. Explain and correct Camilla's error.

3. **Vocabulary** What two features distinguish a circle as the unit circle?

4. **Reason** If given an angle measure in radians, how can you determine in which quadrant its terminal side will be, without converting to degrees?

5. **Make Sense and Persevere** If you are using a calculator to find the measure of an angle in degrees, what type of measure might make you question whether your calculator is actually in radian mode? Explain.

Do You KNOW HOW?

The angles given are in standard position. What is the reference angle for each given angle?

6. 65°

7. 145°

In what quadrant does the angle, given in radians, lie?

8. $\frac{\pi}{6}$

9. $\frac{5\pi}{3}$

What is the negative angle of rotation for the angle with given positive angle of rotation?

10. 270°

11. 110°

Convert each radian measure to a degree measure.

12. $\frac{\pi}{3}$

13. $\frac{7\pi}{4}$

Convert each degree measure to a radian measure.

14. −30°

15. 480°

6-3 Trigonometric Functions and Real Numbers

EXPLORE & REASON

The graph shows the terminal sides of an angle with measure θ and its supplement, $180 - \theta$, on the unit circle.

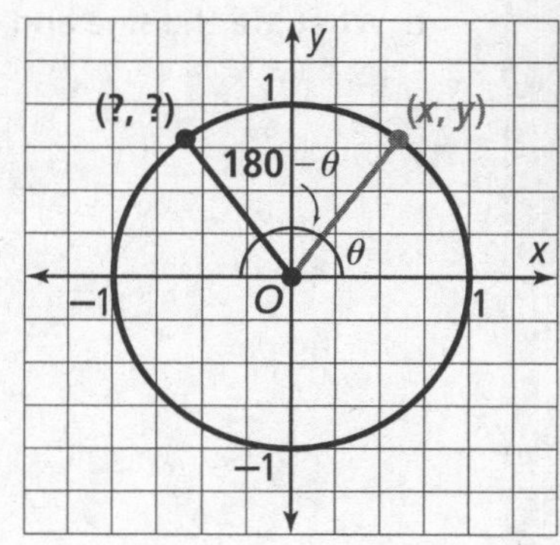

A. How are the coordinates of the intersection of the terminal side of an angle with measure θ and the unit circle related to the sine and cosine of the angle?

B. What do you notice about θ and about the acute angle formed by the terminal side of $180 - \theta$ and the x-axis?

C. Draw the terminal sides of angles in Quadrants III and IV that form the same acute angle with the x-axis as the angles in Quadrants I and II. How are these angles related to θ?

D. Communicate Precisely How are all four terminal sides related geometrically on the coordinate plane?

HABITS OF MIND

Reason When you connect the four points on the unit circle above, the figure is a rectangle. For what angle θ is that rectangle a square?

Notes

EXAMPLE 1 **Try It!** **Use Reference Triangles to Evaluate Sine and Cosine**

1. What are the sine and cosine of each angle?

   a. $\frac{4\pi}{3}$ b. $\frac{3\pi}{4}$

HABITS OF MIND

Use Structure In which quadrants do the coordinates of the terminal point of an angle θ result in a negative value for $\tan\theta$? Explain.

EXAMPLE 2 **Try It!** **Use the Pythagorean Identity $\sin^2\theta + \cos^2\theta = 1$**

2. a. What is $\sin\theta$ if $\cos\theta = \frac{\sqrt{2}}{2}$ and $0 < \theta < \frac{\pi}{2}$?

   b. What is $\cos\theta$ if $\sin\theta = -0.8$ and θ is in Quadrant IV?

Notes

EXAMPLE 3  **Try It! Use the Unit Circle to Evaluate Tangents**

3. What is the tangent of each angle?

a. $-\frac{3\pi}{2}$

a. 675°

EXAMPLE 4  **Try It! Evaluate the Reciprocal Functions**

4. What are the secant, cosecant, and cotangent for each angle?

a. 210°

b. $-\frac{10\pi}{4}$

HABITS OF MIND

Make Sense and Persevere If $\sin\theta = \frac{5}{13}$ and $\tan\theta < 0$, what are all the possible values of $\sec\theta$? Explain.

EXAMPLE 5  **Try It! Use Any Circle Centered at the Origin**

5. What is the final position of a search team relative to the camp if they travel 30° north of due west, or 150°, for 5 mi from their base camp?

HABITS OF MIND

Look for Relationships How does the length of the radius of the circle affect the value of cosine and sine of 150°?

Do You UNDERSTAND?

1. ESSENTIAL QUESTION How is the unit circle related to trigonometric functions?

2. **Error Analysis** Hugo said $\sin \frac{5\pi}{2} = -1$. Explain an error Hugo could have made.

3. **Vocabulary** What is a reference triangle, and how does it help you work with the angles on the unit circle?

4. **Reason** Why is $\cos 30° = \cos(-30°)$?

Do You KNOW HOW?

Find the sine and cosine of each angle.

5. $\frac{5\pi}{4}$

6. 120°

7. What is $\sin \theta$ if $\cos \theta = \frac{4}{5}$ and θ is in Quadrant II?

8. What is $\cos \theta$ if $\sin \theta = -\frac{1}{2}$ and θ is in Quadrant III?

Find the tangent of each angle.

9. $\frac{\pi}{6}$

10. −45°

11. Evaluate the secant, cosecant, and tangent of a 135° angle.

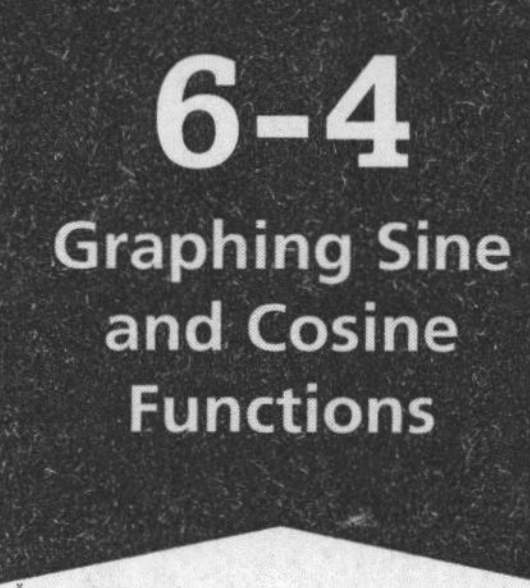

EXPLORE & REASON

The graph shows a rider's height above the platform when riding a Ferris wheel *t* minutes after entering the Ferris wheel car.

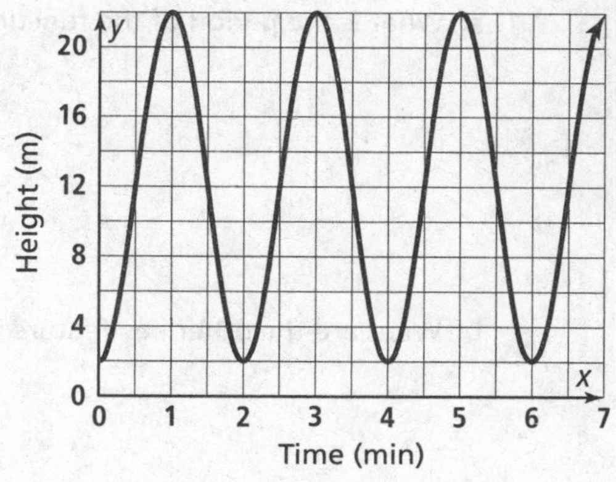

A. Sketch a graph of a rider's height if the Ferris wheel is twice as high. How does the graph represent the change in height?

B. Sketch a graph of a rider's height if the Ferris wheel is the same height as the first but goes twice as fast. How does the graph represent the change in speed?

C. Communicate Precisely How are the three graphs similar? How are they different?

HABITS OF MIND

Reason In the section of the graph shown, how many revolutions did the Ferris wheel make? Explain.

Notes

EXAMPLE 1  **Try It! Understand the Graph of a Periodic Function**

1. a. What is the period of the function $f(x) = \cos x$?

b. What are the other key features of the function?

EXAMPLE 2  **Try It! Identify Amplitude and Period**

2. What are the amplitude and period of each function?

a. $y = \frac{1}{3}\cos\left(\frac{1}{2}x\right)$

b. $y = 2\sin(\pi x)$

EXAMPLE 3  **Try It! Graph $y = a\sin(bx)$ and $y = a\cos(bx)$**

3. Graph $y = \frac{3}{2}\cos(3\pi x)$. What is the frequency?

b. What is the average rate of change over the interval [0,1]?

HABITS OF MIND

Generalize In the equation $y = a\sin(bx)$, how is the frequency affected by the parameters a and b?

Notes

Assess

EXAMPLE 4 Try It! **Develop a Graph and an Equation From a Description**

4. Construct a graph over 3 h for the tip of the minute hand t minutes after noon if the minute hand is 8 in. long. What is the period?

EXAMPLE 5 Try It! **Compare Key Features of Two Periodic Functions**

5. a. How do the frequencies of f and g compare?

b. What else is different about the two functions? Explain.

HABITS OF MIND

Use Structure Suppose you have two graphs, $y = a\sin(bx)$ and $y = c\cos(dx)$. The amplitude of the sine graph is larger than that of the cosine graph. The period of the cosine graph is larger than that of the sine graph. How are the parameters a, b, c, and d related?

Assess

Do You UNDERSTAND?

1. **ESSENTIAL QUESTION** How can you identify, use, and interpret key features of sine and cosine functions?

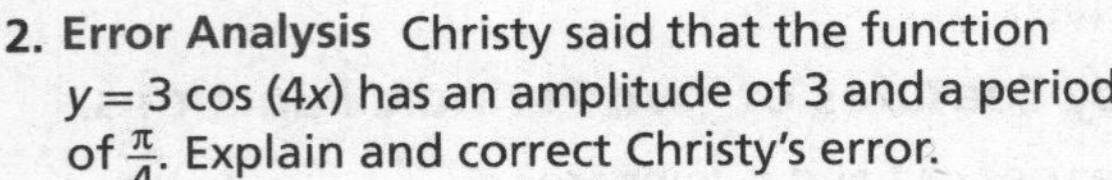

2. **Error Analysis** Christy said that the function $y = 3\cos(4x)$ has an amplitude of 3 and a period of $\frac{\pi}{4}$. Explain and correct Christy's error.

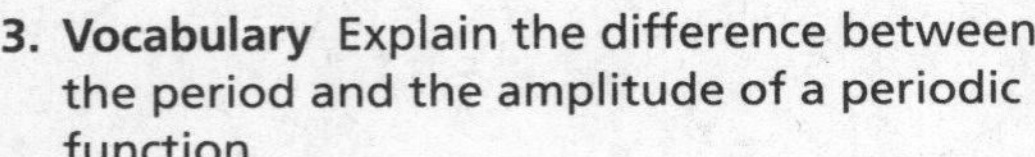

3. **Vocabulary** Explain the difference between the period and the amplitude of a periodic function.

4. **Reason** What is the range of the cosine function? How does the range compare to the amplitude of the function?

Do You KNOW HOW?

Find the period and amplitude of each function.

5.

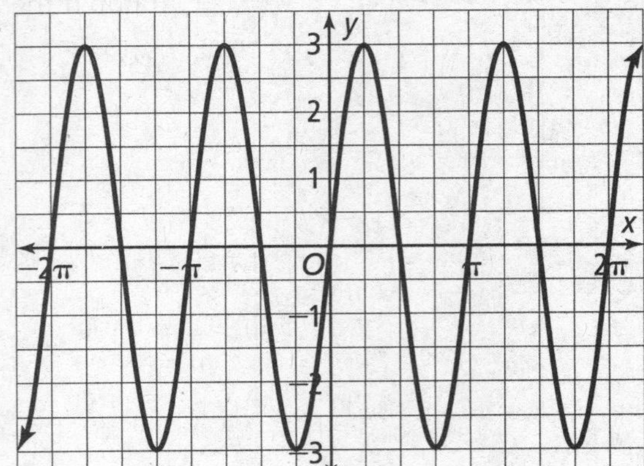

6.

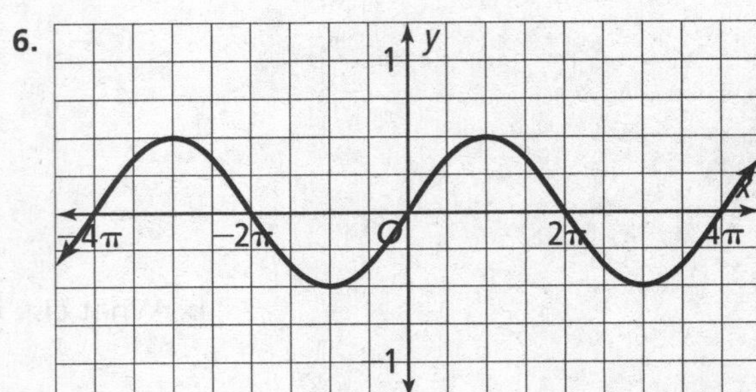

7. Use the graph from Exercise 6. How many cycles does the function have in the interval from 0 to 2π?

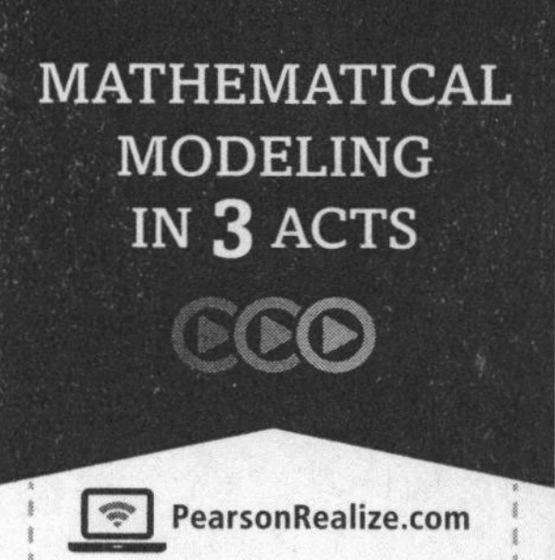

What Note Was That?

Sounds are created by vibrations. As the vibrations travel through the air, they create sound waves. The frequency of a sound is the measurement of the number of cycles of that wave per second, in a unit called hertz (Hz). Music notes can be identified by their frequency.

What information do you need to determine the frequency of a note? How accurate does your data need to be? Think about this during the Mathematical Modeling in 3 Acts lesson.

ACT 1 Identify the Problem

1. What is the first question that comes to mind after watching the video?

2. Write down the Main Question you will answer.

3. Make an initial conjecture that answers this Main Question.

4. Explain how you arrived at your conjecture.

5. What information will be useful to know to answer the main question? How can you get it? How will you use that information?

Video

ACT 2 Develop a Model

6. Use the math that you have learned in the topic to refine your conjecture.

ACT 3 Interpret the Results

7. Did your refined conjecture match the actual answer exactly? If not, what might explain the difference?

6-5

Graphing Other Trigonometric Functions

PearsonRealize.com

EXPLORE & REASON

Use the graphs of $f(x) = x + 3$ and $g(x) = \frac{1}{x+3}$ to compare these reciprocal functions.

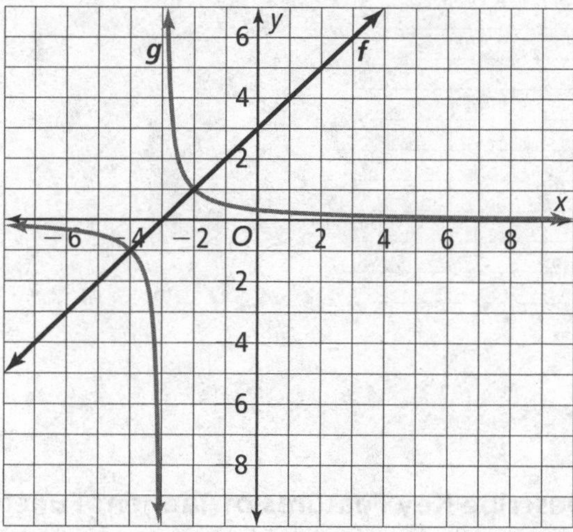

A. Identify the zeros of each function.

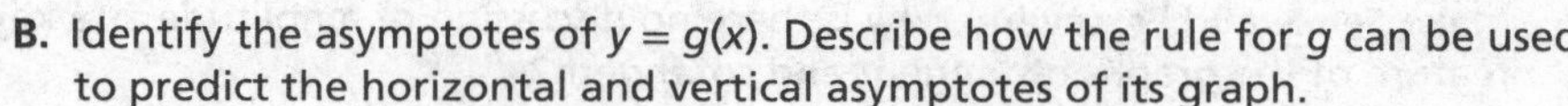

B. Identify the asymptotes of $y = g(x)$. Describe how the rule for g can be used to predict the horizontal and vertical asymptotes of its graph.

C. Look for Relationships How can you use the graph of f to predict a vertical asymptote in the graph of g, the reciprocal of f?

HABITS OF MIND

Reason What is causing the vertical asymptote at $x = -3$ in g? Explain.

Assess

EXAMPLE 1  **Try It! Graph $y = \tan x$**

1. Create a table of values, and use the unit circle to help you sketch the graph of $y = \cot x$. Plot the function's zeros and asymptotes in your sketch.

EXAMPLE 2  **Try It! Describe Key Features of Tangent Functions**

2. Describe the key features of the graph of the function $y = \cot x$. Refer to your graph from Example 1, Try It!

HABITS OF MIND

Make Sense and Persevere Why is there no discussion of amplitude as a key feature of the graphs of tangent and cotangent?

EXAMPLE 3  **Try It! Graph $y = a \tan bx$**

3. Sketch the graph of the function $y = \frac{1}{2} \cot 3x$.

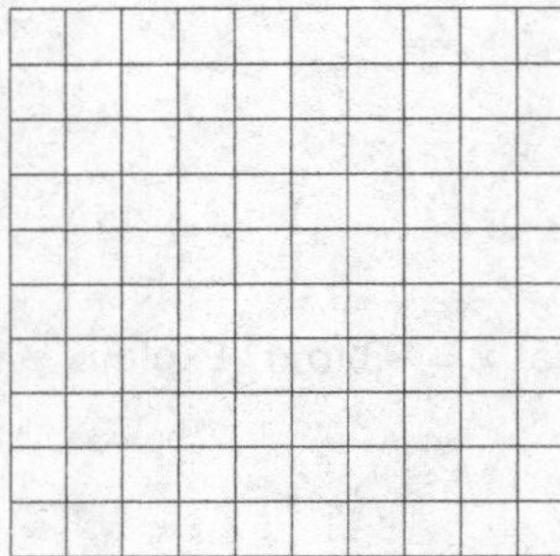

Notes

EXAMPLE 4

Try It! Model With a Trigonometric Function

4. About how high is the rocket when the angle of inclination is $\frac{\pi}{3}$?

HABITS OF MIND

Use Structure Since the tangent function has no amplitude, how can you describe the effect of the parameter a in the equation $y = a \tan x$?

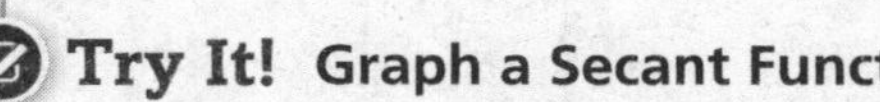

EXAMPLE 5

Try It! Graph a Secant Function

5. How is the graph of $y = \csc x$ related to the graph of $y = \sin x$?

HABITS OF MIND

Communicate Precisely What are the period and amplitude for the graphs of the secant and cosecant functions?

Do You UNDERSTAND?

1. ESSENTIAL QUESTION How do key features of one trigonometric function relate to key features of other trigonometric functions?

2. **Error Analysis** Mia said the period of the tangent function is 2π. Explain an error that Mia could have made.

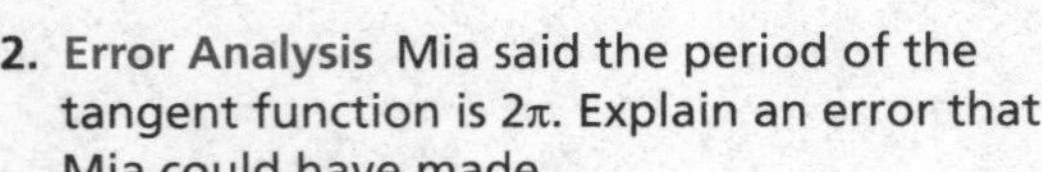

3. **Reason** Explain why the graph of $y = \tan x$ does not have an amplitude.

Do You KNOW HOW?

Solve each equation.

4. Sketch the graph of the function $y = \frac{1}{2}\tan x$ over the interval $-\frac{\pi}{2} < x < \frac{\pi}{2}$. How does this graph differ from the graph of $y = \tan x$?

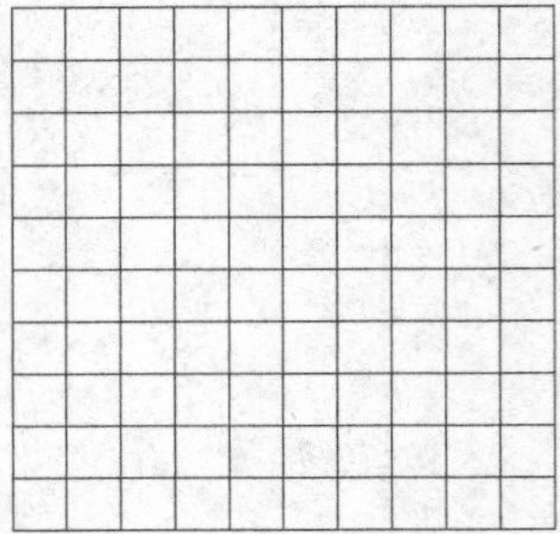

5. Find the period of the function $y = \tan 3x$.

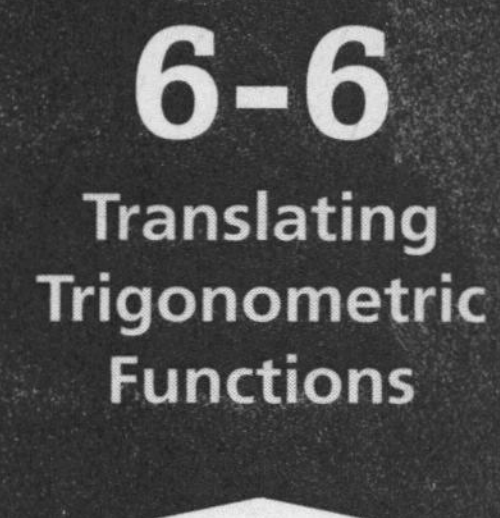

CRITIQUE & EXPLAIN

Sadie and Zhang use translations to relate the graphs of sine and cosine. Sadie claims that $\sin x = \cos\left(x - \frac{\pi}{2}\right)$. Zhang insists that $\cos x = \sin\left(x + \frac{\pi}{2}\right)$.

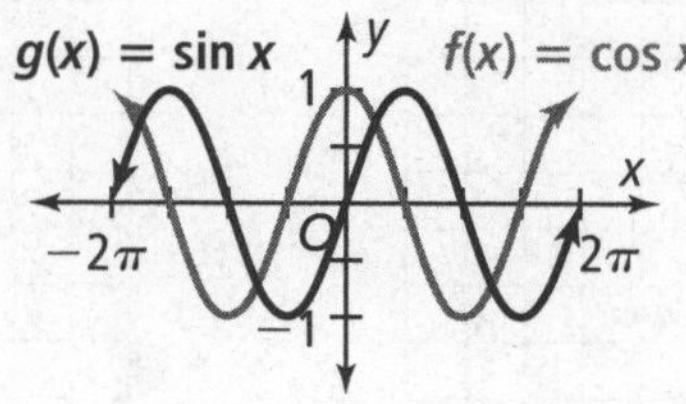

A. Who is correct? How do you know?

B. Communicate Precisely Victor claims that knowing $\sin 0 = \cos \frac{\pi}{2}$ can be used to determine who is correct. Is Victor's suggestion helpful? If so, explain why. If not, explain why not.

HABITS OF MIND

Make Sense and Persevere Do you think there might be a similar relationship between the graphs of tangent and cotangent? Explain.

Notes

Assess

EXAMPLE 1 **Try It!** Understand Phase Shift as a Horizontal Translation

1. Sketch the graph.

a. $y = 3\cos\left(x + \frac{\pi}{4}\right)$

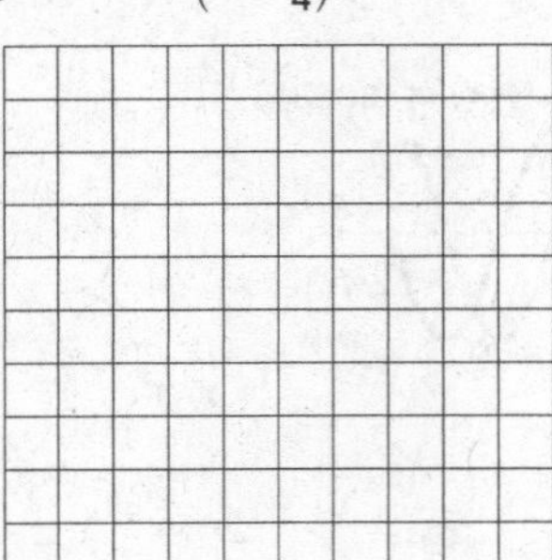

a. $y = \cos\left(3x + \frac{3\pi}{4}\right)$

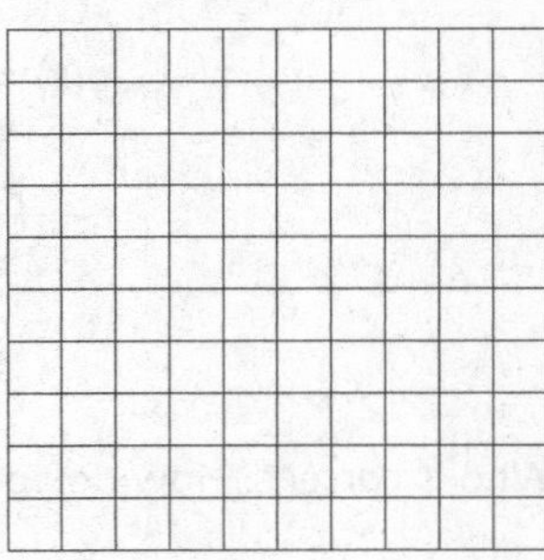

EXAMPLE 2 **Try It!** Graph a Sine or Cosine Function

2. Sketch the graph of the function $y = \frac{2}{3}\cos\left(x - \frac{\pi}{2}\right) + 1$.

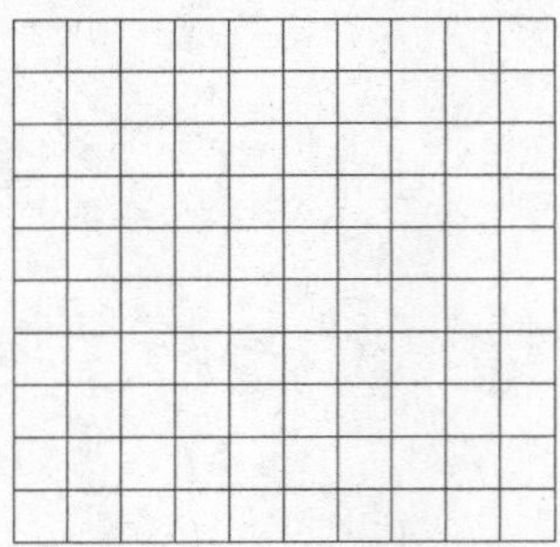

EXAMPLE 3 **Try It!** Analyze a Sine or Cosine Function

3. Identify the amplitude, period, phase shift, vertical shift, and the maximum and minimum values of each function.

a. $y = \frac{1}{2}\sin\left(x - \frac{\pi}{3}\right) - 4$

b. $y = 2\cos\left(2x + \frac{\pi}{4}\right) + 2$

HABITS OF MIND

Look for Relationships For other types of functions $y = f(x - a)$ was always a horizontal translation by a units of the parent function $y = f(x)$. Does that rule hold for trigonometric functions? Explain.

EXAMPLE 4

Try It! Write the Equation of a Translation

4. Write an equation that models the function represented by the graph.

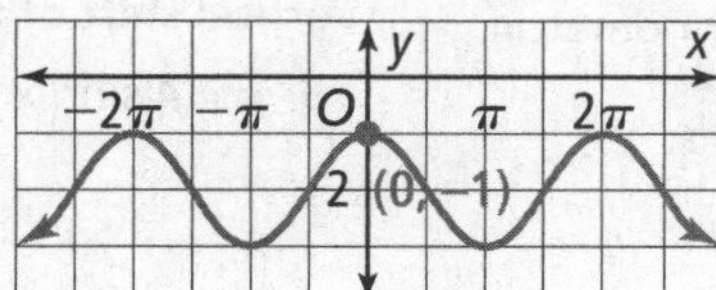

EXAMPLE 5

Try It! Find a Trigonometric Model

5. Write a trigonometric function to model the average high temperatures for Philadelphia, Pennsylvania. How does the midline value compare with the average of the 12 temperatures?

Month	Jan.	Feb.	Mar.	Apr.	May	June	July	Aug.	Sept.	Oct.	Nov.	Dec.
High (°F)	40	44	53	64	74	83	87	85	78	67	56	45

HABITS OF MIND

Model With Mathematics How do you know whether you should use a sine or cosine function to model a periodic graph?

Do You UNDERSTAND?

1. ESSENTIAL QUESTION How can you find and use translations of graphs of trigonometric functions?

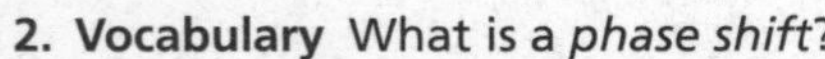

2. **Vocabulary** What is a *phase shift*?

3. **Error Analysis** Felipe said the function $y = \frac{1}{2}\cos\left[3\left(x + \frac{\pi}{4}\right)\right] - 3$ has a phase shift $\frac{\pi}{4}$ units to the right and a vertical shift 3 units down. Describe and correct the error Felipe made.

4. **Use Structure** Write a sine function that has an amplitude of $\frac{1}{6}$, a period of $\frac{8\pi}{3}$, a phase shift of 2π units to the right, and a vertical shift of 5 units up.

Do You KNOW HOW?

Identify the amplitude, period, phase shift, and vertical shift of the function.

5. $y = 4\sin\left(x - \frac{\pi}{6}\right) + 2$

6. $y = \frac{1}{3}\cos\left[2\left(x + \frac{\pi}{2}\right)\right] - 1$

7. Write an equation for the function represented by the graph using the cosine function.

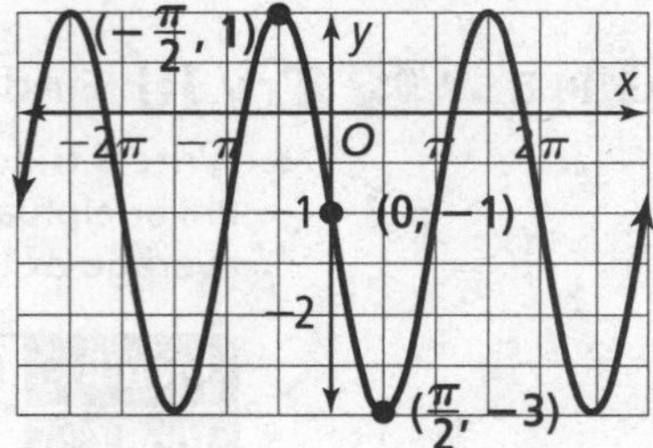

8. Sketch a graph of the function $y = \sin\left[2\left(x + \frac{\pi}{2}\right)\right] + 1$.

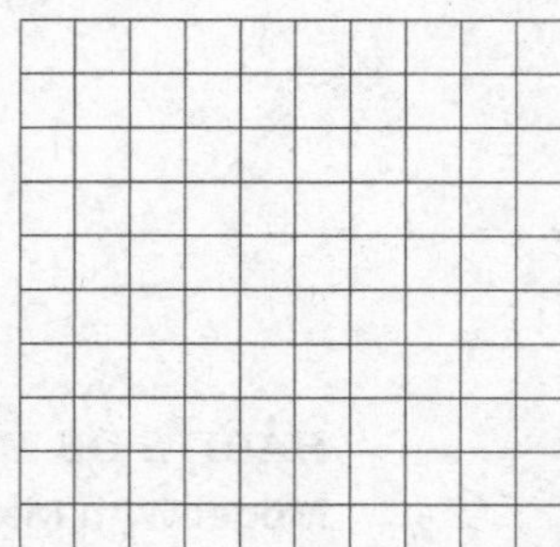

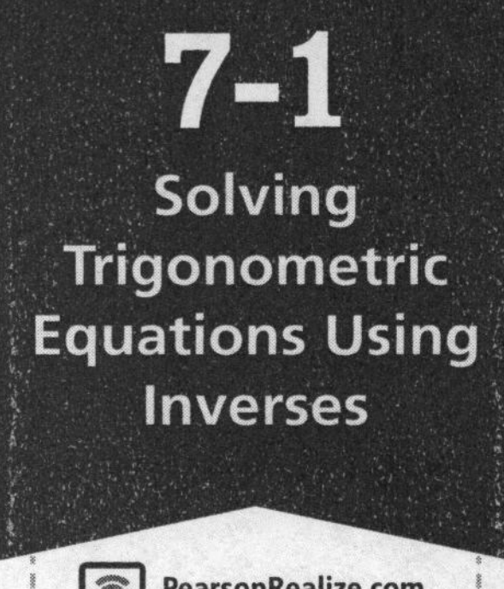

PearsonRealize.com

CRITIQUE & EXPLAIN

Marisol and Nadia are both asked to find θ given $\sin \theta = \frac{\sqrt{3}}{2}$.

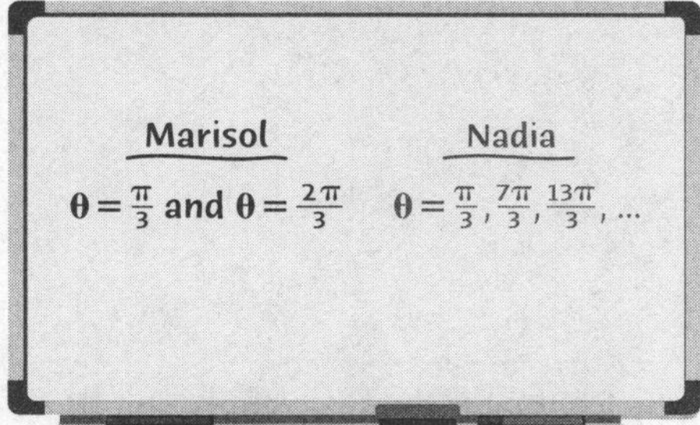

A. Is either student correct? Explain.

B. Make Sense and Persevere What are all of the correct solutions for θ?

HABITS OF MIND

Communicate Precisely Dylan answered the same question by writing $\frac{\pi}{3} + 2k\pi$ and $\frac{2\pi}{3} + 2k\pi$, for integer values of k. Does this show all the possible solutions? Explain.

Notes

Assess

EXAMPLE 1  **Try It! Define Inverse Trigonometric Functions**

1. How should the domain of $y = \cos x$ be restricted to define the inverse cosine function?

HABITS OF MIND

Construct Arguments Does choosing *any* interval for cosine where the function is always increasing (or decreasing) guarantee that the restricted domain includes *all* values in the range? Explain.

EXAMPLE 2  **Try It! Evaluate Inverse Trigonometric Functions**

2. a. What is $\cos^{-1}\left(\frac{\sqrt{2}}{2}\right)$?

   b. What is $\tan^{-1}(-\sqrt{3})$?

EXAMPLE 3  **Try It! Find All Angles With a Given Trigonometric Value**

3. a. What are all of the angles that have a sine value of 0.95?

   b. What are all of the angles that have a cosine value of 0.54?

HABITS OF MIND

Look for Relationships For any valid input into an inverse sine function, there are an infinite number of angles that have that sine value. Why is it important that an inverse sine function returns a single angle?

Go Online | PearsonRealize.com

Notes

EXAMPLE 4 **Try It! Solve a Trigonometric Equation**

4. a. What is the value for θ when $0.25\cos\theta + 1 = 1.5\cos\theta$ for values between 0 and 2π?

b. What is the value for θ when $3\tan\theta - 4 = \tan\theta$ for values between 0 and π?

EXAMPLE 5 **Try It! Use a Trigonometric Model**

5. The average monthly high temperature in a city is modeled by the function $T = 30\sin\left(\frac{\pi}{6}x - 1.8\right) + 61$, where T is the temperature in °F, x is the month, and $x = 1$ corresponds to January. Use this function to determine the months that have a monthly high temperature of 54°.

HABITS OF MIND

Generalize How do the steps for solving the equation $0.25x + 1 = 1.5x$ compare to solving the equation $0.25\cos\theta + 1 = 1.5\cos\theta$?

Assess

Do You UNDERSTAND?

1. ESSENTIAL QUESTION How can you use an inverse function to find all the solutions of a trigonometric equation?

2. **Error Analysis** Luis said that the inverse of $y = \cos x$ is a function. Explain and correct Luis's error.

3. **Use Structure** What are the radian measures of the angles whose sine is 1?

4. **Error Analysis** Describe and correct the error a student made when asked to find the radian measures of the angles whose sine is 1.

Let n be an integer.
$\sin(0 + 2\pi n) = 1$
✗

Do You KNOW HOW?

5. What is $\sin^{-1}\left(\frac{\sqrt{2}}{2}\right)$?

6. What is $\tan^{-1}(\sqrt{3})$?

7. What are all of the angles (in degrees) that have a cosine value of 0.74?

8. What are all of the angles (in degrees) that have a sine value of 0.83?

9. Solve $4\sin\theta - 1 = 0$ for values between 0 and 2π.

10. Solve $2\tan\theta + 3 = 0$ for values from 0° to 360°. Round angle measures to the nearest degree.

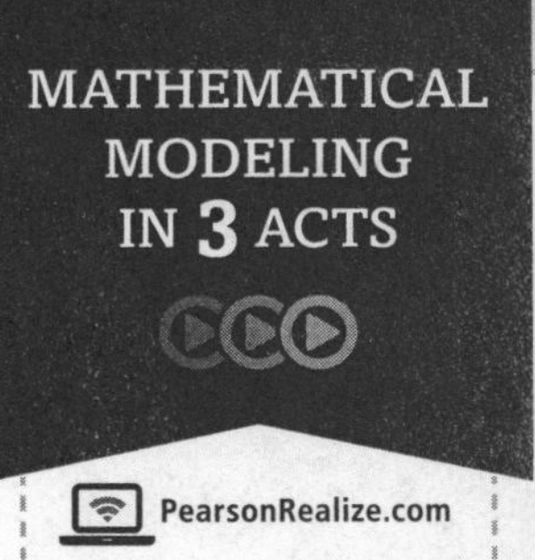

Ramp Up Your Design

Wheelchair users and others with mobility challenges require ramps or elevators to access buildings and other public spaces. Most public buildings are required to have accessible ramps through the Americans with Disabilities Act. However, most homes do not have such ramps. Wheelchair users who move into a home with steps will have to have a new ramp installed.

The construction of accessibility ramps must follow strict guidelines. If ramps are not accurately built to follow these guidelines, they can be dangerous to use. Think about this during the Mathematical Modeling in 3 Acts lesson.

ACT 1 Identify the Problem

1. What is the first question that comes to mind after watching the video?

2. Write down the Main Question you will answer.

3. Make an initial conjecture that answers this Main Question.

4. Explain how you arrived at your conjecture.

5. What information will be useful to know to answer the main question? How can you get it? How will you use that information?

Video

ACT 2 Develop a Model

6. Use the math that you have learned in the topic to refine your conjecture.

ACT 3 Interpret the Results

7. Did your refined conjecture match the actual answer exactly? If not, what might explain the difference?

Go Online | PearsonRealize.com

7-2 Law of Sines and Law of Cosines

PearsonRealize.com

MODEL & DISCUSS

A biologist measures the slant height of a conical termite mound to be about 32 ft. The angle from the ground to the top of the mound is 51°. The base of the mound has a diameter of about 40 ft.

A. Draw a model to help the biologist.

B. Make Sense and Persevere What is the height of the mound?

HABITS OF MIND

Reason How did you decide which trigonometric function to use to solve the problem?

Notes

EXAMPLE 1 **Try It!** **Prove the Law of Sines**

1. How can you derive the Law of Sines for angles B and C?

EXAMPLE 2 **Try It!** **Use the Law of Sines**

2. In $\triangle NPQ$, $m\angle N = 105°$, $n = 12$, and $p = 10$.
   a. To the nearest degree, what is $m\angle Q$?

   b. What is the length of side q? Round to the nearest tenth of a unit.

EXAMPLE 3 **Try It!** **Understand the Ambiguous Case**

3. In $\triangle ABC$, $m\angle A = 30°$, $a = 5$, and $b = 8$. Find $m\angle B$. How many possible triangles are there?

HABITS OF MIND

Use Structure In $\triangle ABC$, $m\angle A = 50°$, $b = 6$, and $c = 3$. Gregory says that the Law of Sines does not allow you to find side length a. Is he correct? If so, what would he need to know in order to be able to find it?

Notes

Assess

EXAMPLE 4 **Try It!** **Prove the Law of Cosines**

4. a. How can you derive the Law of Cosines for an obtuse angle *C*?

b. How does the equation compare to the equation for an acute angle?

EXAMPLE 5 **Try It!** **Use the Law of Cosines**

5. a. In $\triangle JKL$, $j = 15$, $k = 13$, and $l = 12$. What is $m\angle J$?

b. In $\triangle ABC$, $a = 11$, $b = 17$, and $m\angle C = 42°$. What is c?

EXAMPLE 6 **Try It!** **Use the Law of Cosines and the Law of Sines**

6. A bike race follows a triangular path, represented by triangle *ABC*. If *A* is the starting point and the measure of the angle at point *B* is 70°, what is the measure of the angle at point *C*?

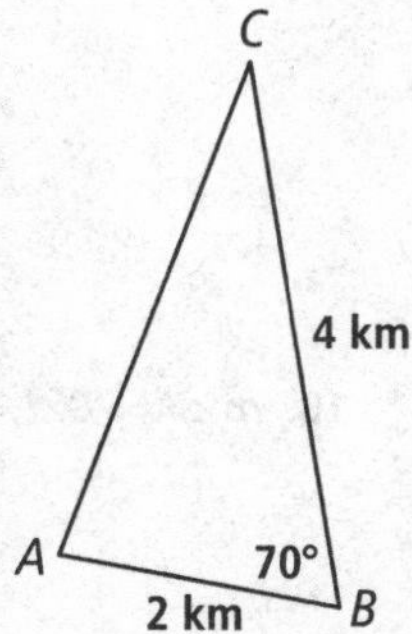

HABITS OF MIND

Use Appropriate Tools Given the lengths of two sides of a triangle, and the measure of one angle, how do you know whether to use the Law of Sines or the Law of Cosines?

Assess

Do You UNDERSTAND?

1. ESSENTIAL QUESTION How can you use the sine and cosine functions with non-right triangles?

2. **Error Analysis** Alejandro said the Law of Sines always gives one answer. Explain and correct Alejandro's error.

3. **Construct Arguments** Consider the Law of Cosines as $a^2 = b^2 + c^2 - 2bc(\cos A)$. Explain why the negative square root of a is not a valid solution.

4. **Reason** In what situations do you use the Law of Sines? Law of Cosines?

Do You KNOW HOW?

Use the Law of Sines or the Law of Cosines to find the indicated measure in $\triangle ABC$.

5. $m\angle A = 50°$, $a = 4.5$, $b = 3.8$; find $m\angle B$.

6. $m\angle A = 72°$, $a = 61$, $c = 58$; find $m\angle C$.

7. $m\angle A = 18°$, $m\angle C = 75°$, $c = 101$; find a.

8. $m\angle B = 112°$, $m\angle C = 20°$, $c = 1.6$; find b.

9. $m\angle C = 45°$, $a = 15$, $b = 8$; find c.

10. $m\angle A = 82°$, $b = 2.5$, $c = 6.8$; find a.

11. $a = 14$, $b = 12$, $c = 5.8$; find $m\angle A$.

7-3 Problem Solving With Trigonometry

MODEL & DISCUSS

A search-and-rescue team is having a nighttime practice drill. Two members of the team are in a helicopter that is hovering at 2,000 feet above ground level.

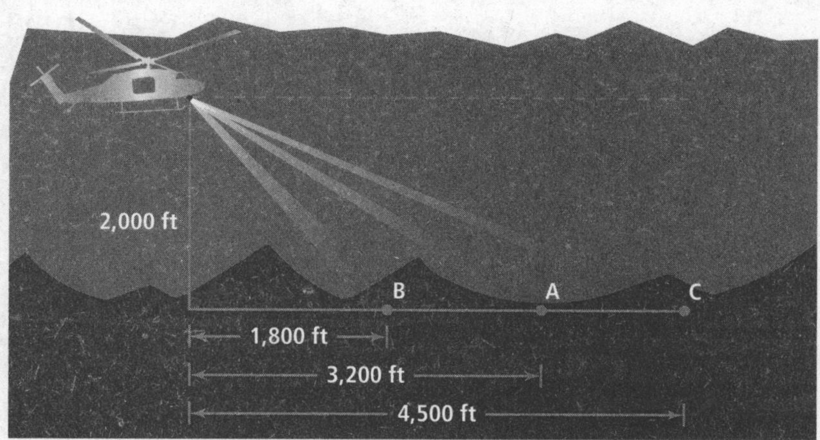

A. The team first tries to locate object A. At what angle from the horizontal line even with the helicopter should they position the spotlight so that it shines on object A?

B. Next, they shine the spotlight on object B. How does the angle of the spotlight from the horizontal line change?

C. **Use Structure** In general, how does the angle of the spotlight from the horizontal change as the light moves from object A to object B? From object A to object C?

HABITS OF MIND

Use Structure What geometric figures are useful in modeling situations where you want to find angle measures? Why are these figures helpful?

Notes

EXAMPLE 1

Try It! Identify Angles of Elevation and Depression

1. In Example 1, how does the angle of depression, ∠1, compare with the angle of elevation, ∠2? Explain your reasoning.

EXAMPLE 2

Try It! Use Angles of Elevation and Depression

2. Nadeem sees the tour bus from the top of the tower. To the nearest foot, how far is the bus from the base of the tower?

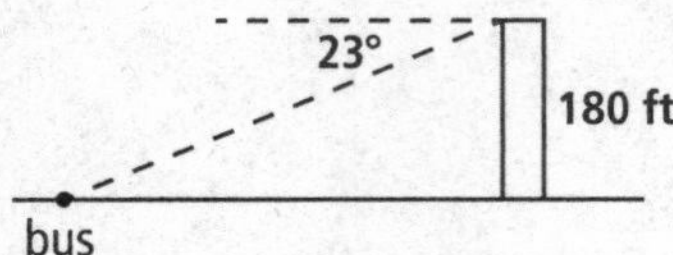

HABITS OF MIND

Communicate Precisely How can you relate angles of elevation and depression to parallel lines intersected by a transversal?

Notes

EXAMPLE 3  **Try It!** **Use Trigonometry to Solve Problems**

3. In Example 3, how far is the student from the instructor at the resting point?

EXAMPLE 4  **Try It!** **Use Trigonometry to Find Triangle Area**

4. a. What is the area of $\triangle JKL$?

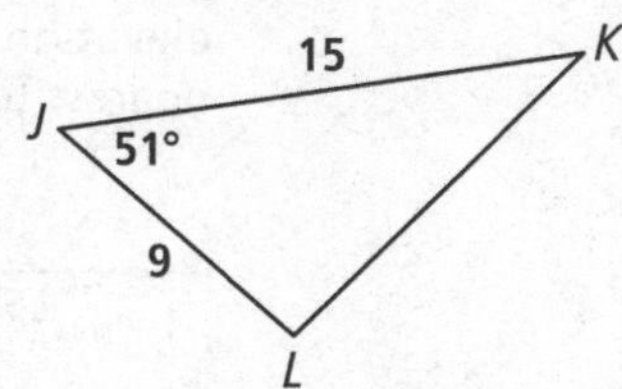

b. What is the area of $\triangle PQR$? *Hint:* First apply the Law of Cosines to find the measure of the angle included between $\overline{PQ}$ and $\overline{PR}$. Then apply the area formula with the sine of the angle measure.

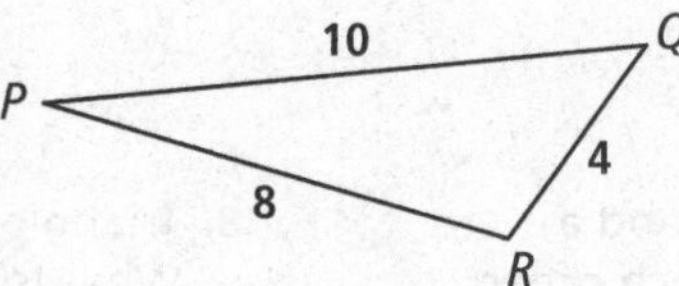

HABITS OF MIND

Reason What quantities do you need to know if you want to apply the Law of Sines or Cosines to solve a problem?

Do You UNDERSTAND?

1. **ESSENTIAL QUESTION** How can trigonometry be used to solve real-world and mathematical problems?

2. **Error Analysis** What error does Jamie make in finding the area?

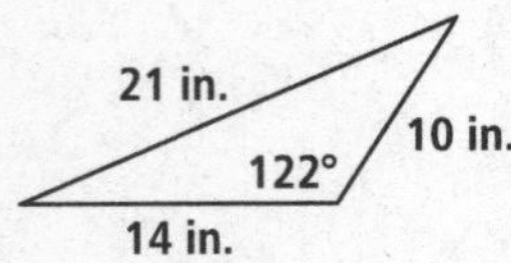

$A = \frac{1}{2}bc \sin A$

$A = \frac{1}{2} \cdot 210 \cdot 0.8480$

Area is about 89 in.^{2}

✗

3. **Vocabulary** A person on a balcony and a person on a street are looking at each other. Draw a diagram to represent the situation and label the angles of elevation and depression.

4. **Make Sense and Persevere** How do you find the area of a triangle when given only the lengths of three sides?

Do You KNOW HOW?

5. A person rides a glass elevator in a hotel lobby. As the elevator goes up, how does the angle of depression to a fixed point on the lobby floor change?

6. A person observes the top of a radio antenna at an angle of elevation of 5°. After getting 1 mile closer to the antenna, the angle of elevation is 10°. How tall is the antenna to the nearest tenth of a foot?

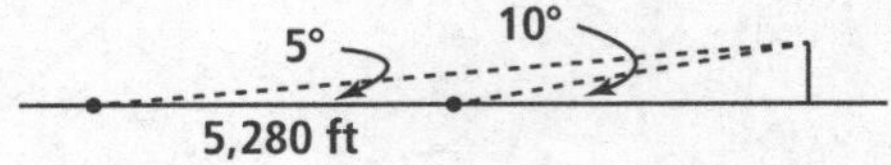

7. Triangle ABC has $AB = 13$, $AC = 15$, and $m\angle A = 59$. What is the area of the triangle to the nearest tenth?

8. Triangle DEF has $DE = 13$, $DF = 15$, and $EF = 14$. What is the area of the triangle to the nearest tenth?

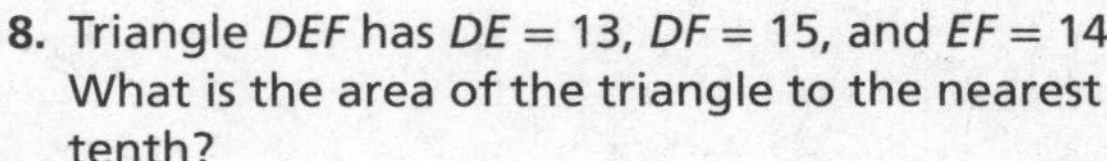

9. A temporary pen for cattle is built using 10-foot sections of fence arranged in a triangle. One side of the pen has 4 sections, one has 5 sections, and the last has 6 sections. What is the area enclosed by the pen?

7-4

Trigonometric Identities

EXPLORE & REASON

Two right triangles share the same base leg length.

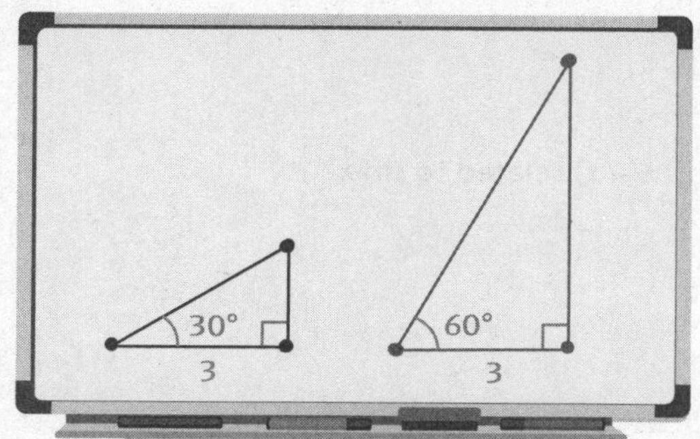

A. Is the ratio between the base angles the same as the ratio between the vertical heights? Explain.

B. How do the values of $\sin(2(30°))$ and $2 \sin 30°$ compare?

C. Look for Relationships Graph $y = \sin 2x$ and $y = 2 \sin x$ on the same coordinate plane. How do the two graphs help explain your answer to part (b)?

HABITS OF MIND

Make Sense and Persevere Are there any functions for which $f(2x) = 2f(x)$ for all x? Investigate three different types of functions. Show your work. What do you conclude?

Notes

EXAMPLE 1

Try It! Use the Unit Circle to Verify Trigonometric Identities

1. a. Verify that for $f(x) = \cos x$, $f(-x) = f(x)$.

b. How are $\sin(x + \pi)$ and $\sin(2\pi - x)$ related to $\sin x$?

HABITS OF MIND

Communicate Precisely Since $\cos(-x) = \cos x$, cosine is an even function. How can you see this by looking at the graph of cosine?

EXAMPLE 2

Try It! Use Identities to Rewrite Expressions

2. What is a simplified form of each expression?

a. $\tan\left(x - \frac{\pi}{2}\right)$

b. $\sin(-x)\tan(-x) + \cos x$

EXAMPLE 3

Try It! Prove Sum and Difference Formulas

3. a. Use the cosine difference formula and the fact that $\sin(\alpha + \beta) = \cos\left(\frac{\pi}{2} - (\alpha + \beta)\right) = \cos\left(\left(\frac{\pi}{2} - \alpha\right) - \beta\right)$ to prove the sine sum formula.

b. Prove the sine difference formula.

HABITS OF MIND

Reason Why might it be useful to know the identity for the sine of a sum?

Notes

Assess

EXAMPLE 4

Try It! Use a Sum or Difference Formula to Find a Value

4. What is the exact value of each expression?

   a. $\tan 15°$

   b. $\sin\left(-\frac{\pi}{12}\right)$

EXAMPLE 5

Try It! Model With Sum and Difference Formulas

5. The sound wave for a musical note of A is modeled by $y = \sin(880\pi x)$. The sound wave for a different A note is modeled by $y = \sin\left[880\pi\left(x + \frac{1}{440}\right)\right]$. What is the simplified form of an equation that models the sound wave if the two notes are played at the same time?

HABITS OF MIND

Construct Arguments How do you prove the sum formula for $\tan(\alpha + \beta)$?

Do You UNDERSTAND?

1. ESSENTIAL QUESTION How can you verify and apply relationships between trigonometric functions?

2. **Error Analysis** Sarah said that because of the odd-even identities, both the sine and cosine functions are odd functions. Explain and correct Sarah's error.

3. **Vocabulary** Explain what it means to say that $\cos(-x) = \cos x$ is a trigonometric identity.

4. **Reason** Why do the cofunction identities apply to an angle θ of any size?

5. **Make Sense and Persevere** How can the quotient identity help you to identify angles for which the tangent is undefined?

Do You KNOW HOW?

Verify each identity.

6. $\sin\theta \sec\theta \cot\theta = 1$

7. $\sec\theta \cot\theta = \csc\theta$

Find a simplified form of each expression.

8. $\dfrac{\tan\theta}{\sin\theta}$

9. $\dfrac{\sec\theta}{\sin\theta}(1 - \cos^2\theta)$

Use a sum or difference formula to find the exact value of each of the following.

10. $\sin 15°$

11. $\cos 105°$

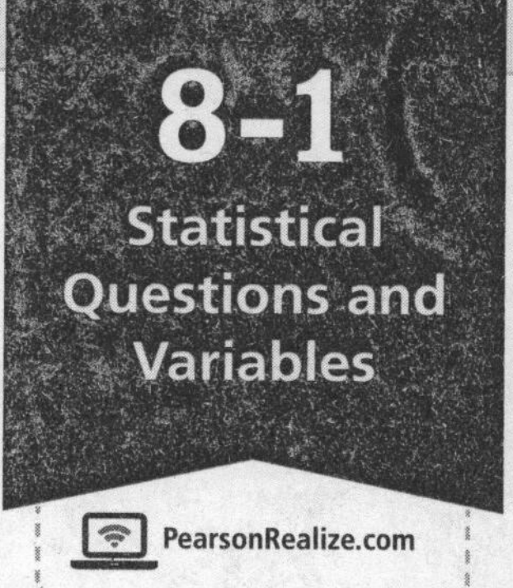

EXPLORE & REASON

A state questioned some of its high schools about the price they were charging for prom tickets. The results are summarized in the histogram.

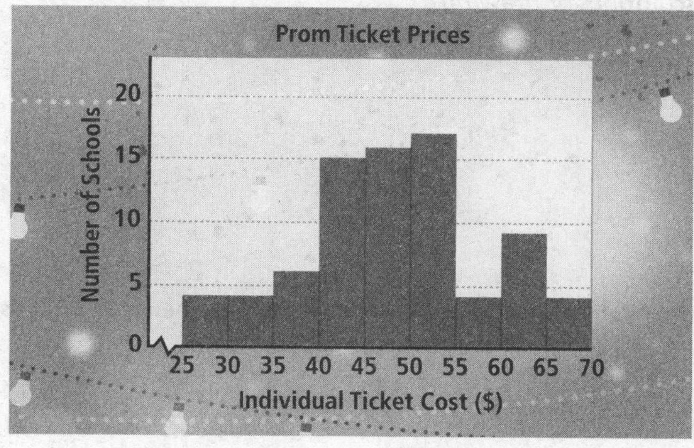

A. What questions can be answered using the data in this histogram?

B. Who might be interested in the answers to these questions? Explain.

C. Construct Arguments Anastasia is surprised that the median cost of a prom ticket is not higher, given that her school is charging $60 per ticket. What are some possible reasons for the data not conforming to her expectations?

HABITS OF MIND

Make Sense and Persevere How many high schools were surveyed? How many charged between $40 and $44 for a ticket to prom?

Notes

EXAMPLE 1 **Try It! Understand Statistical Questions**

1. Is the given question a statistical question?

   a. *"Which is the most popular visual art form: photography, painting, sculpting, or drawing?"*

   b. *"How many lithographs were created by the artist M.C. Escher?"*

EXAMPLE 2 **Try It! Understand Statistical Variables**

2. What is the statistical variable represented by each of the following questions, and is it categorical or quantitative?

   a. *"What breed of dog is most likely to be adopted from an animal shelter?"*

   b. *"What is the average number of students per activity participating in after-school activities at Jefferson High School?"*

HABITS OF MIND

Look for Relationships Consider the sentence, "There are 3 birthdays in our class in the 3rd month." What are the differences in how the 3 is used?

Notes

EXAMPLE 3 **Try It!** **Distinguish Between Populations and Samples**

3. A city worker collects five vials of water from each of ten randomly selected locations all over the city to test the levels of bacteria in the city water supply.
   a. What is the sample in this experiment?
   b. What is the population?

HABITS OF MIND

Construct Arguments Can a sample be the same as the population? Explain.

EXAMPLE 4 **Try It!** **Distinguish Between Parameters and Statistics**

4. Is the given data summary a parameter or statistic?
   a. 53.2% of a district's eligible voters voted for the sitting U.S. House Representative.
   b. The median age of a car in 20 randomly selected spaces in the school parking lot is 7 years.

HABITS OF MIND

Communicate Precisely Describe the difference between a parameter and a statistic.

Do You UNDERSTAND?

1. ESSENTIAL QUESTION What kinds of questions about quantities and relationships among quantities can be answered with statistics?

2. **Error Analysis** Dyani says she identified a quantitative variable and conducted a survey when she asked her fellow classmates in her homeroom about their favorite style of sweatshirt from the categories: hoodie, pullover, or zip-up. Explain her error.

3. **Vocabulary** Explain the difference between a categorical variable and a quantitative variable.

4. **Communicate Precisely** Suppose Hana wants to find out the most commonly driven type of vehicle among the students at her high school. Since 1,560 students attend her high school, she asks every tenth student who enters the building one morning what kind of vehicle he or she drives. What is the population in this scenario?

Do You KNOW HOW?

5. Is the following question a statistical question?

   "During which month did your family take a vacation?"

6. What is the statistical variable represented by the following question, and is it categorical or quantitative?

   "How many TV sets are owned by families?"

7. Forty randomly-selected members of a high school music program were asked to report the number of hours they spend practicing each week. If you were to compute the mean number of hours, would your answer be a parameter or a statistic? Explain.

8-2
Statistical Studies and Sampling Methods

PearsonRealize.com

CRITIQUE & EXPLAIN

Jacinta and Felix were each asked to design a study to answer the question: "What proportion of students at this school listen to music while studying?"

Jacinta

Friends in Gym Class	yes	no
Cameron	X	
Dana	X	
Emma		X
Henry		X
Jung	X	
Keisha		X
Marisol		X

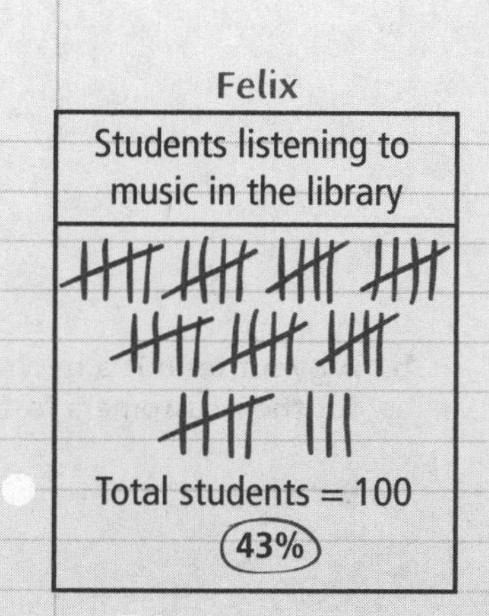

A. What group did Jacinta select from to conduct her study? What group did Felix select from?

B. How did Jacinta choose which members of her group to question? How did Felix choose which members from his group to observe?

C. Look for Relationships Who designed a better study, Jacinta or Felix? Explain.

HABITS OF MIND

Communicate Precisely Did either Jacinta or Felix use randomness? Explain.

 Notes

 Assess

EXAMPLE 1

Try It! Choose a Type of Study

1. What type of study is described?

   a. A gym asks its customers if they would prefer the gym to open earlier in the morning.

   b. A gym tries out a new weightlifting method to see if it will build muscle for their customers faster than their current method.

   c. A gym counts the customers who come before 8 A.M.

HABITS OF MIND

Model With Mathematics The gym wants to know whether or not they should buy more elliptical machines. What kind of statistical study could they use to answer their question? Describe the study you propose.

EXAMPLE 2 

Try It! Determine Sources of Bias

2. A soft drink company calls 500 people at random and asks, "Is our product or our rival's product the best soft drink on the market?" Why is this question a potential source of bias?

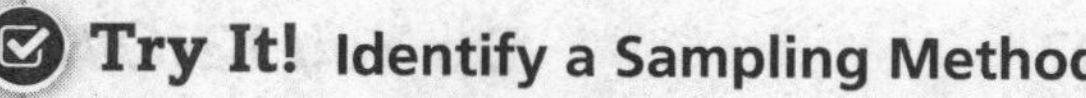

EXAMPLE 3 **Try It! Identify a Sampling Method**

3. What sampling method is used in the following examples? Is the method likely to be biased or not?

   a. The population is grouped according to age, and a random sample is chosen from each group.

   b. A number of hospitals around the country were randomly chosen. Within each hospital, all of the nurses were chosen.

HABITS OF MIND

Make Sense and Persevere Of the five sampling methods, which two are most likely to introduce bias? Explain.

EXAMPLE 4 **Try It! Randomize Experiments**

4. Design an experiment to test whether drinking coffee improves memory. How will you choose the experimental and control groups?

HABITS OF MIND

Construct Arguments Why is it important to have the memory test administered by someone who was not aware of which subjects were in the experimental group?

Assess

Do You UNDERSTAND?

1. ESSENTIAL QUESTION How can you choose the best type of study to answer a given statistical question and choose a reasonable sample?

2. **Vocabulary** A city is weighing whether to increase fares for public transit, or to provide more funding to public transit through the city's general fund, which is primarily funded by local property taxes. A survey of public transit riders was conducted to determine popular opinion. What is this sampling method an example of?

3. **Error Analysis** When Lila conducted an experiment on citywide pond water, all of her samples came from the pond in her uncle's backyard. Explain her error.

Do You KNOW HOW?

4. An ice cream shop asks its customers if they would like the shop to offer containers of ice cream to take home. What type of study does this describe?

5. A television news program asks its viewers to call in to give their opinions on an upcoming ballot question. What type of sampling method does this represent?

6. A doctor assigns people to treatment groups based on data from their medical records. Is this method of selecting treatment groups biased or unbiased? Explain.

8-3 Data Distributions

PearsonRealize.com

CRITIQUE & EXPLAIN

Chen and Dakota were asked to estimate the mean and median of the following data set.

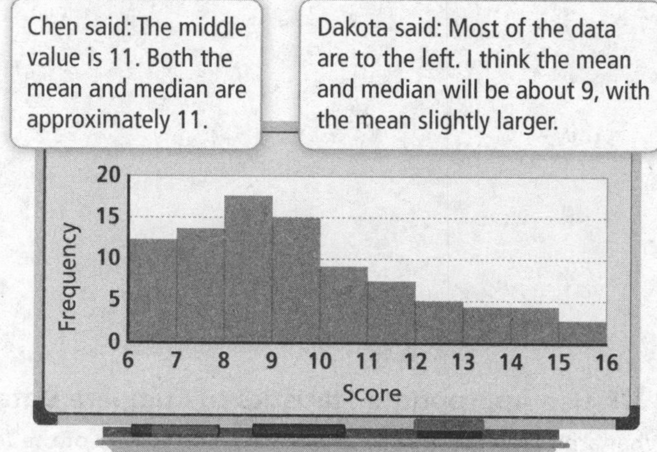

A. Is either Chen or Dakota correct? Explain.

B. What strategies could you use to approximate the exact mean and median?

C. Reason Which measure of center is more representative in this case, the mean or the median? Explain.

HABITS OF MIND

Construct Arguments Kyle thinks that the mode is the most representative measure of center for this set of data. Do you agree? Explain.

EXAMPLE 1

Try It! Find Measures of Center and Spread

1. List the mean, standard deviation, and five-number summary of the following data set.

3 4 9 12 12 14 15 19 25 30 32 33 34 34 35

EXAMPLE 2

Try It! Use Appropriate Statistics to Compare Data Sets

2. What are the better measures of center and spread of the following data sets?

   a. 55 55 57 57 57 58 58 59 59 59 61 61

   b. 110 110 110 120 120 130 140 150 160 170 180 190

HABITS OF MIND

Use Structure How can you determine whether or not a data set is skewed by examining the five-number summary?

Notes

EXAMPLE 3

Try It! Recognize a Normal Distribution

3. Is each situation likely to be normally distributed? Explain.

   a. weight of individuals in a population

   b. the scores on a difficult test

EXAMPLE 4

Try It! Classify a Data Distribution

4. What is the type of distribution and the center and spread of the data?
   20 17 17 12 18 21 19 18 13 14 17 23 25

HABITS OF MIND

Look for Relationships How are the mean and median of a normally distributed data set related?

Do You UNDERSTAND?

1. **ESSENTIAL QUESTION** How can you interpret the distribution of data in a data set?

2. **Vocabulary** Write a definition for *normally distributed* and *normal curve* in your own words.

3. **Error Analysis** A data set has a mean that is approximately equal to the median. Ralph says the median should be used to describe the measure of center, and the quartiles should be used to describe the measure of spread. Explain his error.

4. **Communicate Precisely** Explain how to determine if the data distribution shown is skewed left, right, or is symmetric.

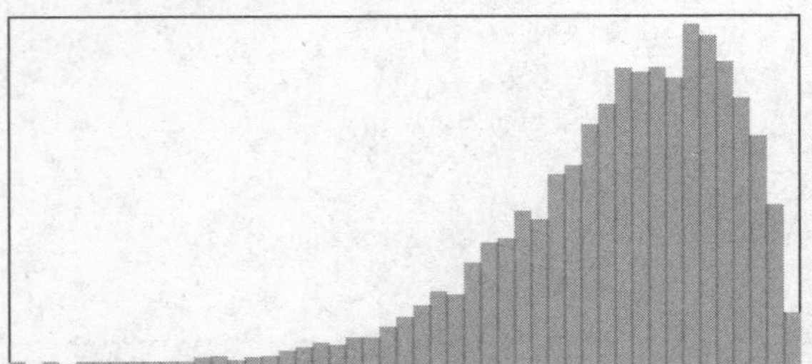

Do You KNOW HOW?

Determine the mean, standard deviation, and five-number summary of each data set. Round to the nearest hundredth, if necessary.

5. 5, 8, 5, 9, 6, 14, 9, 3, 8, 7, 10, 12

6. 10.5, 2.25, 7.75, 8.8, 3.4, 9.2, 6.5, 4.3, 3.9, 6.4

Describe the shape of the data summarized in the histograms.

7.

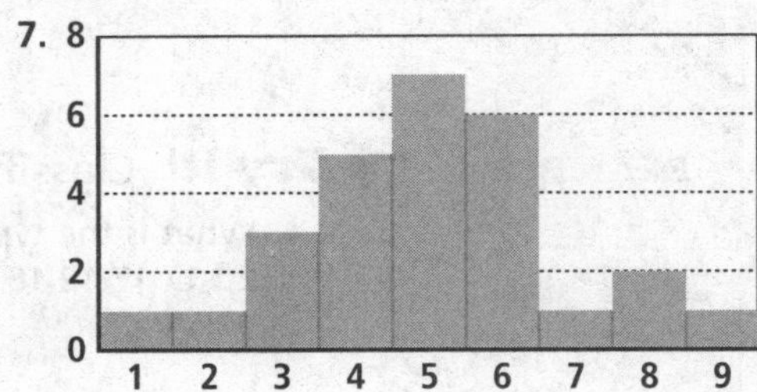

8.

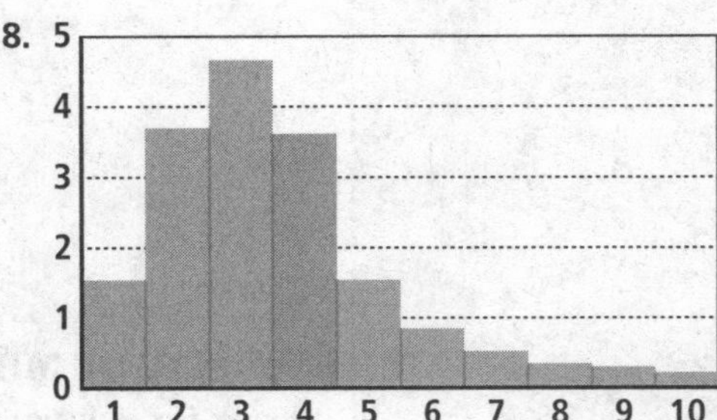

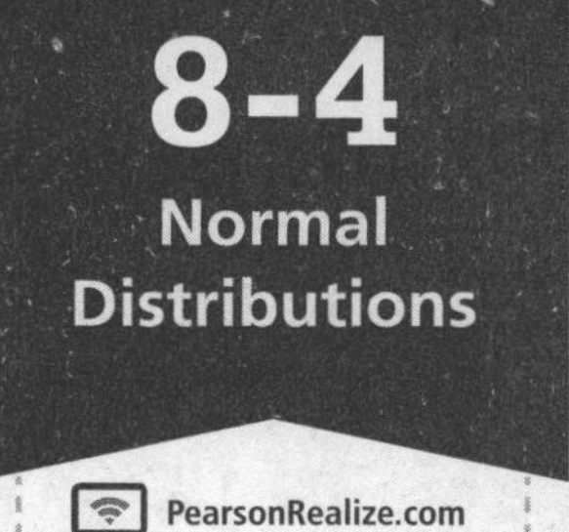

EXPLORE & REASON

The owner of an apple orchard and the owner of an orange grove create histograms to display fruit production data.

mean = 1,750
standard deviation = 296

mean = 210
standard deviation = 47

A. Describe the shape of each distribution. Discuss how the distributions are alike and how they are different.

B. Use Structure Explain how you could estimate the mean from the graphs. The standard deviation measures spread from the mean. Which data values are within a standard deviation of the mean on each graph?

HABITS OF MIND

Reason Could you calculate an exact value for the mean and standard deviation for either of the distributions? Explain.

Notes

EXAMPLE 1

Try It! Find Population Intervals

1. a. What would you expect to be the smallest and largest chest measurements of the "middle" 95% of the men?

   b. What would you expect to be the measurements of the 16% of the men with the largest chests in the population?

EXAMPLE 2

Try It! Use The Empirical Rule

2. Find the proportion of students who earned SAT Math scores in the following ranges.

   a. between 266 and 750

   b. between 266 and 629

HABITS OF MIND

Use Structure A set of data is normally distributed with a mean of 80 and a standard deviation of 10. How do you use the symmetry of the distribution to find the percentage of the values that lie between 80 and 90? Explain.

Notes

EXAMPLE 3

Try It! Compare Values Using *z*-Scores

3. How does an SAT score of 1120 compare to an ACT score of 23?

EXAMPLE 4

Try It! Use a *z*-Score to Compute Percentage

4. Find the percentage of all values in a normal distribution with $z \leq 1.85$.

HABITS OF MIND

Communicate Precisely Why is the *z*-score a good measure to use to compare data values from two different normally distributed data sets?

 Assess

Do You UNDERSTAND?

1. ESSENTIAL QUESTION How can you use the normal distribution to explain where data values fall within a population?

2. **Vocabulary** Write a definition for *z-score* using your own words.

3. **Look for Relationships** Why is it useful to compare a normal distribution to the standard normal distribution?

Do You KNOW HOW?

A data set with a mean of 75 and a standard deviation of 3.8 is normally distributed.

4. What value is three standard deviations above the mean?

5. What percent of the data is from 67.4 to 82.6?

6. What is the z-score for a data value of 69.3?

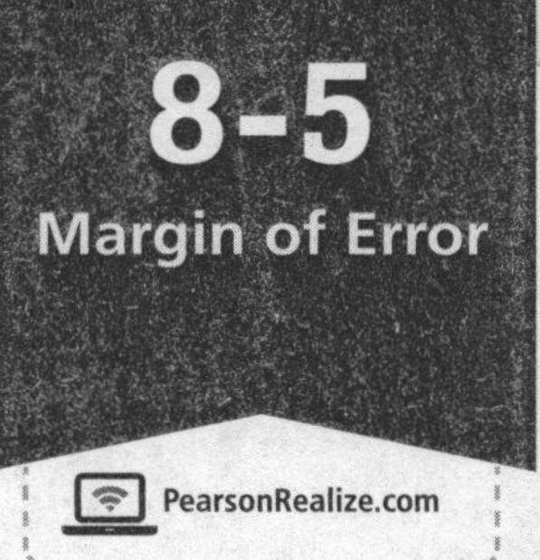

MODEL & DISCUSS

With a partner or a group, toss a number cube 30 times and record the number showing on each toss.

A. Compute the means of the numbers in the first five tosses, the first ten tosses, and all thirty tosses.

B. Use Appropriate Tools Compile the results for your entire class in three sets of data: the means of the first five tosses, the means of the first ten tosses, and the means of all thirty tosses. Create a histogram for each data set.

C. Compare the histograms. Describe how the distribution of the mean changes as the number of tosses increases.

HABITS OF MIND

Generalize One group, on the first set of ten trials, got the same number five times. What does their distribution look like? How do you think their results will affect the overall distribution of the class' results?

✎ Notes

EXAMPLE 1

Try It! Estimate a Population Parameter

1. Use the sample data to estimate the mean distance from home. Estimate the proportion of seniors to the total population at the college.

EXAMPLE 2

Try It! Make an Inference Using Multiple Samples

2. Each classmate calculates the mean distance from home in miles reported by participants. Seth and Tia create this histogram to investigate the sample statistics. How many samples reported an average distance from home between 101 and 125 mi? Use the histogram to suggest a reasonable interval to estimate the population parameter.

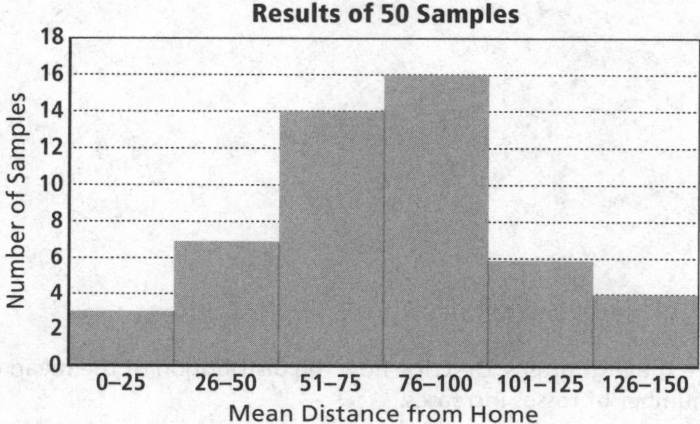

HABITS OF MIND

Look for Relationships As the number of samples increases, what is the relationship between the statistic you calculate and the population parameter?

Notes

EXAMPLE 3

Try It! Use a Simulation to Evaluate a Claim

3. How would your conclusion in Example 3 differ if you did 100 simulations of 10 shots each? How would it differ if you did 100 simulations of 1,000 shots each?

EXAMPLE 4

Try It! Use a Margin of Error for a Mean

4. A random sample of 100 Washington High seniors reveals that 40% plan to take the SAT this year. Use the margin of error to predict the actual proportion of seniors planning to take the exam.

HABITS OF MIND

Reason As the number of samples increases, what happens to the margin of error? Explain.

Assess

Do You UNDERSTAND?

1. ESSENTIAL QUESTION How can you determine how far a statistic is likely to be from a parameter?

2. **Error Analysis** In a sample of 16 students from a teacher's physical education classes, students attempted to do as many sit-ups as possible in one minute. The mean was 10 with a standard deviation of 2. The teacher said that the margin of error was $\frac{1}{4}$. What is the teacher's error?

3. **Vocabulary** Explain what a sampling distribution is in your own words.

4. **Communicate Precisely** Suppose you want to find the margin of error for a certain sample. Explain when to use the formula Margin of Error $\frac{2\sigma}{\sqrt{n}}$ and when to use the formula Margin of Error $= \frac{1}{\sqrt{n}}$.

Do You KNOW HOW?

Suppose an event occurs *x* times in a sample size of *n*. Find the sample proportion and the margin of error to the nearest percent.

5. $x = 80$ and $n = 700$

6. $x = 45$ and $n = 1{,}200$

Suppose a sample has a standard deviation of σ and a sample size of *n*. Find the margin of error to the nearest tenth.

7. $\sigma = 21.26$ and $n = 500$

8. $\sigma = 122.18$ and $n = 850$

9. **Model with Mathematics** In a sample of 400 adults, 348 have never been to Australia. Find the sample proportion for those who have never been to Australia. Write the answer as a percent.

8-6 Introduction to Hypothesis Testing

PearsonRealize.com

EXPLORE & REASON

The tables below each show the results of flipping a coin 30 times.

Coin 1					
H	H	H	H	H	T
H	T	T	H	H	T
T	T	H	H	T	H
H	H	T	T	T	H
H	T	T	H	T	H

Coin 2					
T	T	H	T	H	H
H	T	T	T	H	T
T	T	H	T	T	T
H	T	T	T	T	T
T	T	T	H	T	T

A. How many heads and how many tails resulted from flipping each coin 30 times?

B. How many heads and how many tails would you expect from flipping a fair coin 30 times? Are either of these coins close to what you would expect?

C. Construct Arguments Can you conclude with certainty that either of the coins is fair? Can you conclude that either of the coins is unfair?

HABITS OF MIND

Reason If you got exactly 15 heads and 15 tails, could you say for certain that the coin was fair? Explain.

Notes

EXAMPLE 1

Try It! Write Hypotheses

1. A soccer goalie saved 46.4% of her opponents' tiebreaker attempts. After her coach adjusted her position in the goal, she saved 47.3% of the attempts. Write the null hypothesis and alternative hypothesis for a statistical study to evaluate the population parameter *P*, the proportion of tiebreaker goals she saves after working with her coach.

HABITS OF MIND

Make Sense and Persevere In the Try It! problem, what are the quantities of interest? How do you know?

EXAMPLE 2

Try It! Examine Data from an Experiment

2. In one particular randomization one group has these data values:

   34.1, 36.7, 35.1, 36.1, 36.8

   a. Identify the data values for the other group.

   b. Calculate the difference of the means for the two groups.

HABITS OF MIND

Look for Relationships If you perform a random resampling of the data and get a greater difference between the two new sample means, what conjecture could you make?

Notes

EXAMPLE 3 Try It! Use Simulation Results to Test Hypotheses

3. The fuel additive was tested again, resulting in the data displayed below. Use a simulation to randomly assign the data into two new groups. Find the difference of the means of the original sample and the new groups you just created. How do they differ? Explain what additional information you need to be able to test the hypotheses from Example 2.

Without Additive	34.1	32.8	33.8	30.9	36.7
	33.4	35.1	32.1	30.4	33.1
With Additive	34.8	35.1	32.9	35.3	36.1
	36.9	36.0	37.2	36.3	36.8

EXAMPLE 4 Try It! Evaluate a Report Based on Data

4. Best Bet revises their claim and now reports an average retail price of \$1.60. A second marketing study sampled 300 prices for Best Bet Mac & Cheese finding a mean price of \$1.64.

   a. What is the margin of error for the new sample?

   b. Is Best Bet's revised claim supported by this new study? Explain why or why not.

HABITS OF MIND

Make Sense and Persevere You want to determine whether the difference between sample means is due to the treatment or to natural variation. How do you do this through resampling? Through margin of error?

Do You UNDERSTAND?

1. ESSENTIAL QUESTION How do you formulate and test a hypothesis using statistics?

2. **Error Analysis** When presented with an experiment about teeth whitening strips claiming to deliver visibly whiter teeth within two weeks, Mercedes said the null hypothesis of the experiment was that the teeth would become significantly whiter after two weeks of using the whitening strips. Explain Mercedes' error.

3. **Vocabulary** Explain the difference between a *null hypothesis* and an *alternative hypothesis*.

4. **Communicate Precisely** If the null hypothesis of an experiment is H_0: $\mu \leq 10.8$, then what is the alternative hypothesis, H_a?

Do You KNOW HOW?

5. A baseball player's career batting average was .278. After working with a new coach, the player batted .315. Write the null hypothesis and alternative hypothesis for a study of the effect of the change.

6. A a lumber company claims that at least 80% of its plywood is made from recycled materials. It tests 25 pieces of the plywood and finds that the mean of the percentage of recycled material in the sample is 78%. The standard deviation of the population is 3%. Give an interval of reasonable values for the percentage of recycled material in the plywood. Is the company's claim likely true?

7. Terrence grows two varieties of tomatoes, TomTom and Hugemato. Hugemato claims to grow 10% heavier tomatoes. Find the difference of the sample means for the samples shown. Resample randomly and find the new difference of sample means. How do they compare?

TomTom	10.1	10.5	9.9	10.4	11.2
Hugemato	13.1	11	12.1	11.4	12.9

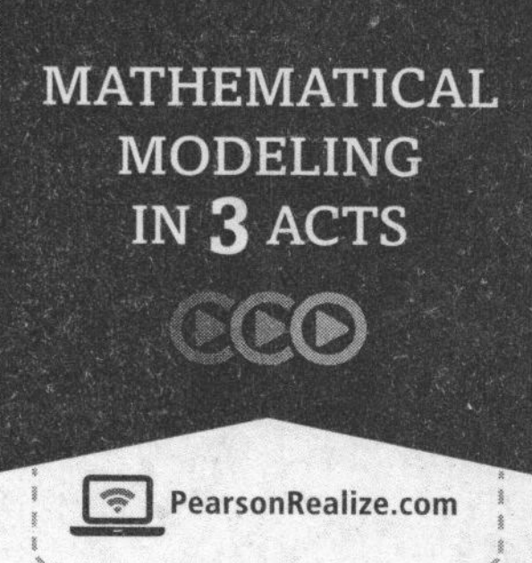

Mark and Recapture

It wouldn't take very long for you to count the number of people who live in your home or the number of socks in your drawer. How about the number of deer in Yellowstone National Park or the number of sharks in the waters around Hawaii?

The mark and recapture method is a popular way researchers can estimate an animal population. You will see an example of this method in the Mathematical Modeling in 3 Acts lesson.

ACT 1 Identify the Problem

1. What is the first question that comes to mind after watching the video?

2. Write down the Main Question you will answer.

3. Make an initial conjecture that answers this Main Question.

4. Explain how you arrived at your conjecture.

5. What information will be useful to know to answer the main question? How can you get it? How will you use that information?

Video

ACT 2 Develop a Model

6. Use the math that you have learned in the topic to refine your conjecture.

ACT 3 Interpret the Results

7. Did your refined conjecture match the actual answer exactly? If not, what might explain the difference?

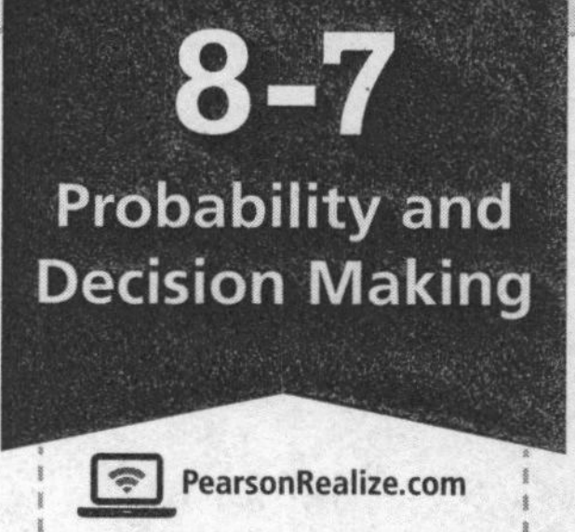

CRITIQUE & EXPLAIN

Your friend offers to play the following game with you. "If the product of the rolls of two number cubes is 10 or less, I win. If not, you win!"

A. If you were to play the game many times, what percent of games would you expect to win?

B. Is the game fair? Should you take the offer? Explain.

C. Make Sense and Persevere Suggest a way to change the game from fair to unfair, or vice versa, while still using the product of the two number cubes. Explain.

HABITS OF MIND

Use Structure Change the game from using products to using a different mathematical number operation. Can you make the game fair? Explain your reasoning.

Notes

EXAMPLE 1

Try It! Use Probability to Make Fair Decisions

1. Your trainer creates training programs for you. How can you use index cards to randomly choose the following: Strength training 1 day per week; Cardio training 2 days per week, with no consecutive days; Swimming 1 day per week.

EXAMPLE 2

Try It! Determine Whether a Decision Is Fair or Unfair

2. Justice and Tamika use the same 3 cards, but change the game. In each round, a player draws a card and replaces it, and then the other player draws. The differences between the two cards are used to score each round. Order matters, so the difference can be negative. Is each game fair? Explain.

   a. If the difference between the first and second cards is 2, Justice gets a point. Otherwise Tamika gets a point.

   b. They take turns drawing first. Each round, the first player to draw subtracts the second player's number from her own and the result is added to her total score.

EXAMPLE 3 **Try It!** **Make a Decision Based on Expected Value**

3. Additional data is collected for the TAB5000 and TAB5001. The manufacturing cost and the replacement cost for the TAB5001 remain unchanged.

   a. The production and replacement costs for the TAB5000 increased by \$10. What would the expected profit be for the TAB5000?

   b. The failure rate for the TAB5001 increased by 1%. What would the expected profit be for the TAB5001?

   c. As a consultant for the company, what would you recommend they do to maximize their profit?

HABITS OF MIND

Construct Arguments When do you need to compute and compare expected values instead of just comparing probabilities? Explain.

EXAMPLE 4 **Try It!** **Use a Binomial Distribution to Make Decisions**

4. A play calls for a crowd of 12 extras with non-speaking parts. Because 10% of the extras have not shown up in the past, the director selects 15 students as extras. Find the probabilities that 12 extras show up to the performance, 15 extras show up to the performance, and more than 12 extras show up to the performance.

HABITS OF MIND

Use Structure What three expressions are multiplied together in the binomial probability formula and what do they represent?

Assess

Do You UNDERSTAND?

1. ESSENTIAL QUESTION How can you use probability to make decisions?

2. **Reason** How can you use random numbers to simulate rolling a standard number cube?

3. **Error Analysis** Explain the error in Diego's reasoning.

4. **Use Structure** Describe what conditions are needed for a fair game.

5. **Use Appropriate Tools** Explain how you can visualize probability distributions to help you make decisions.

6. **Reason** Why must the expected value of a fair game of chance equal zero?

Do You KNOW HOW?

7. A teacher assigns each of 30 students a unique number from 1 to 30. The teacher uses the random numbers shown to select students for presentations. Which student was selected first? second?

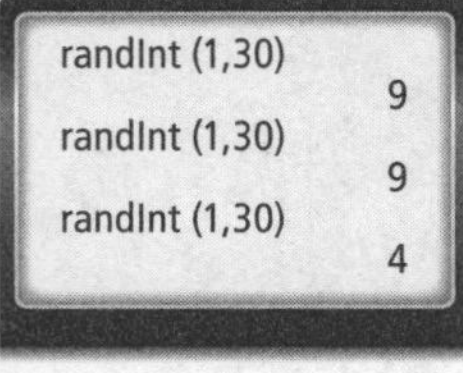

8. Three friends are at a restaurant and they all want the last slice of pizza. Identify three methods involving probability that they can use to determine who gets the last slice. Explain mathematically why each method will guarantee a fair decision.

9. Edgar rolls one number cube and Micah rolls two. If Edgar rolls a 6, he wins a prize. If Micah rolls a sum of 7, she gets a prize. Is this game fair? Explain.

10. The 10 parking spaces in the first row of the parking lot are reserved for the 12 members of the Student Council. Usually an average of ten percent of the Student Council does not drive to school dances. What is the probability that more members of the Student Council will drive to a dance than there are reserved parking spaces?

9-1 Basic Constructions

PearsonRealize.com

EXPLORE & REASON

Using a compass, make a design using only circles like the one shown.

A. What instructions can you give to another student so they can make a copy of your design?

B. Make Sense and Persevere Use a ruler to draw straight line segments to connect points where the circles intersect. Are any of the segments that you drew the same length? If so, why do you think they are?

HABITS OF MIND

Communicate Precisely What mathematical terms or concepts can you use to describe your design?

Assess

EXAMPLE 1

Try It! Copy a Segment

1. How can you construct a copy of $\overline{XY}$?

X ——— Y

EXAMPLE 2

Try It! Copy an Angle

2. How can you construct a copy of $\angle B$?

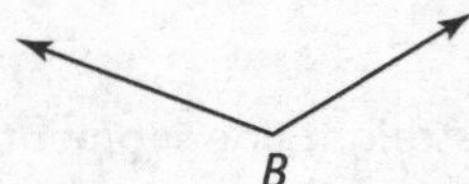

HABITS OF MIND

Construct Arguments Leo says a copy of a segment or angle is always congruent to the original, even if the orientation of the copy is different from the orientation of the original. Construct an argument to support or refute Leo's statement.

Notes

EXAMPLE 3

Try It! Construct a Perpendicular Bisector

3. How can you construct the perpendicular bisector of $\overline{JK}$?

J K

EXAMPLE 4

Try It! Construct an Angle Bisector

4. How can you construct the angle bisector of $\angle G$?

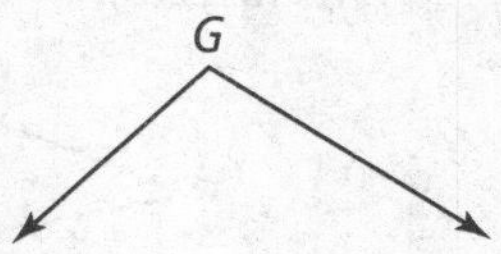

EXAMPLE 5

Try It! Use Constructions

5. Where should the sculpture be placed if it is to be center-aligned with the museum entrance and the center of the ticket sales desk?

HABITS OF MIND

Look for Relationships How is constructing a perpendicular bisector similar to constructing an angle bisector?

Do You UNDERSTAND?

1. ESSENTIAL QUESTION How are a straightedge and compass used to make basic constructions?

2. **Error Analysis** Chris tries to copy $\angle T$ but is unable to make an exact copy. Explain Chris's error.

3. **Vocabulary** What is the difference between a line that is perpendicular to a segment and the perpendicular bisector of a segment?

4. **Look for Relationships** Darren is copying $\triangle ABC$. First, he constructs $\overline{DE}$ as a copy of $\overline{AB}$. Next, he constructs $\angle D$ as a copy of $\angle A$, using $\overline{DE}$ as one of the sides. Explain what he needs to do to complete the copy of the triangle.

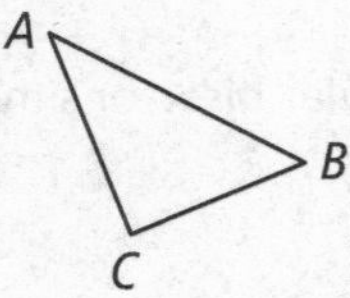

Do You KNOW HOW?

Construct a copy of each segment, and then construct its perpendicular bisector.

5. 6.

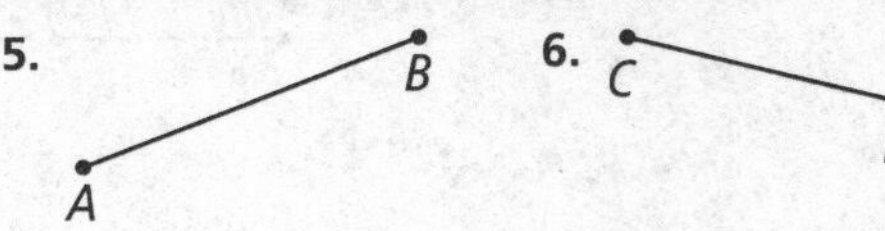

Construct a copy of each angle, and then construct its bisector.

7. 8.

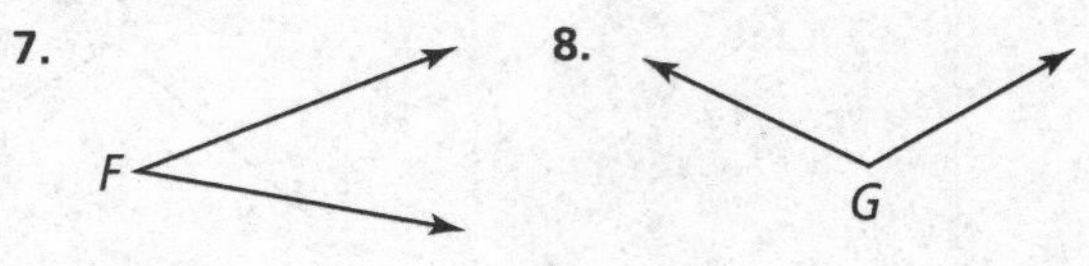

9. A new sidewalk is perpendicular to and bisecting the existing sidewalk. At the point where new sidewalk meets the fence around the farmer's market, a gate is needed. At about what point should the gate be placed?

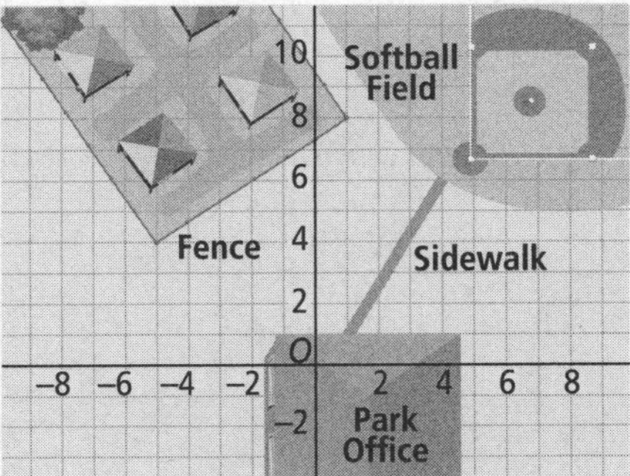

Notes

Assess

EXTENSION 9-1a Constructions in Triangles

PearsonRealize.com

EXAMPLE 1

Try It! Construct the Circumscribed Circle of a Triangle

1. Draw an obtuse triangle. Construct the circumscribed circle of the triangle

EXAMPLE 2

Try It! Construct the Inscribed Circle of a Triangle

2. Draw an obtuse triangle. Construct the inscribed circle of the triangle

HABITS OF MIND

Look for Structure Can the incenter of a triangle ever be located on a side of the triangle?

Do You UNDERSTAND?

1. ESSENTIAL QUESTION How can you construct the circumscribed and inscribed circles of a triangle?

2. **Vocabulary** What parts of the triangle is the *circumcenter* equidistant from? What parts of the circle is the *incenter* equidistant from?

Do You KNOW HOW?

3. Draw an acute triangle and label is $\triangle GHJ$. Construct the circumscribed circle of $\triangle GHJ$.

4. Draw an obtuse triangle and label is $\triangle RST$. Construct the inscribed circle of $\triangle RST$.

9-2 Slopes of Parallel and Perpendicular Lines

PearsonRealize.com

MODEL & DISCUSS

Pilar and Jake begin climbing to the top of a 100-ft monument at the same time along two different sets of steps at the same rate. The tables show their distances above ground level after a number of steps.

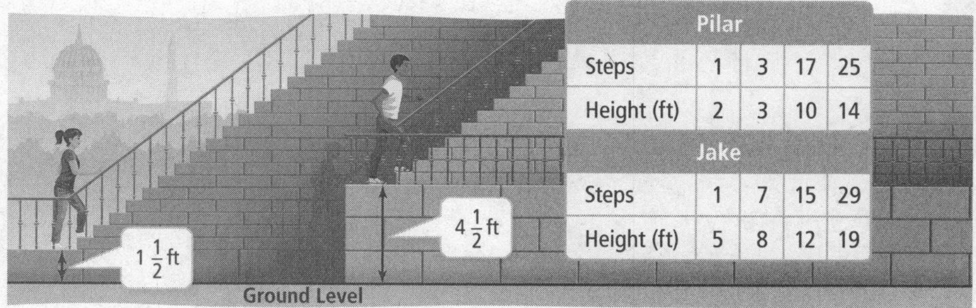

Pilar				
Steps	1	3	17	25
Height (ft)	2	3	10	14

Jake				
Steps	1	7	15	29
Height (ft)	5	8	12	19

A. How many feet does each student climb after 10 steps? Explain.

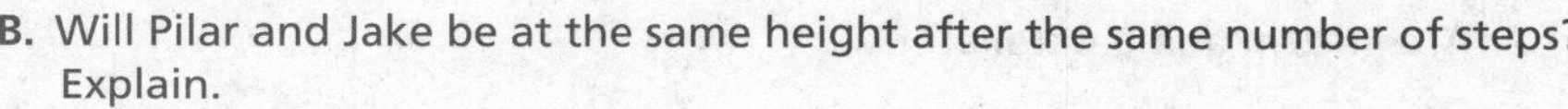

B. Will Pilar and Jake be at the same height after the same number of steps? Explain.

C. Reason What would you expect the graphs of each to look like given your answers to parts A and B? Explain.

HABITS OF MIND

Model With Mathematics What would it mean if the graphs intersected?

Notes

EXAMPLE 1  **Try It! Slopes of Parallel Lines**

1. Suppose another line for a chair lift is placed at a constant distance c below the gondola line. What is an equation of the new line? Is the new line also parallel to the hill? Explain.

EXAMPLE 2  **Try It! Check Parallelism**

2. Are lines m and q parallel?

HABITS OF MIND

Reason Could two lines that are parallel ever pass through the same point?

Notes

EXAMPLE 3 **Try It!** **Check Perpendicularity**

3. a. Are lines h and ℓ perpendicular?

b. Are lines k and m perpendicular?

EXAMPLE 4 **Try It!** **Write Equations of Parallel and Perpendicular Lines**

4. What are equations of lines parallel and perpendicular to the given line k passing through point T?

a. $y = -3x + 2$; $T(3, 1)$

b. $y = \frac{3}{4}x - 5$; $T(12, -2)$

HABITS OF MIND

Generalize How can you use slope to determine if two lines are perpendicular, parallel, or neither perpendicular or parallel?

Do You UNDERSTAND?

1. ESSENTIAL QUESTION How do the slopes of the lines that are parallel to each other compare? How do the slopes of the lines that are perpendicular to each other compare?

2. **Error Analysis** Katrina said that the lines $y = -\frac{2}{3}x + 5$ and $y = -\frac{3}{2}x + 2$ are perpendicular. Explain Katrina's error.

3. **Reason** Give an equation for a line perpendicular to the line $y = 0$. Is there more than one such line? Explain.

4. **Communicate Precisely** What are two different if-then statements implied by Theorem 2-13?

5. **Error Analysis** Devin said that $\overleftrightarrow{AB}$ and $\overleftrightarrow{CD}$ for $A(-2, 0)$, $B(2, 3)$, $C(1, -1)$, and $D(5, -4)$ are parallel. Explain and correct Devin's error.

slope of $\overleftrightarrow{AB}$: $\frac{3-0}{2-(-2)} = \frac{3}{4}$

slope of $\overleftrightarrow{CD}$: $\frac{-1-(-4)}{5-1} = \frac{3}{4}$

slopes are equal, so $\overleftrightarrow{AB} \parallel \overleftrightarrow{CD}$

Do You KNOW HOW?

Use the diagram for Exercises 6–9.

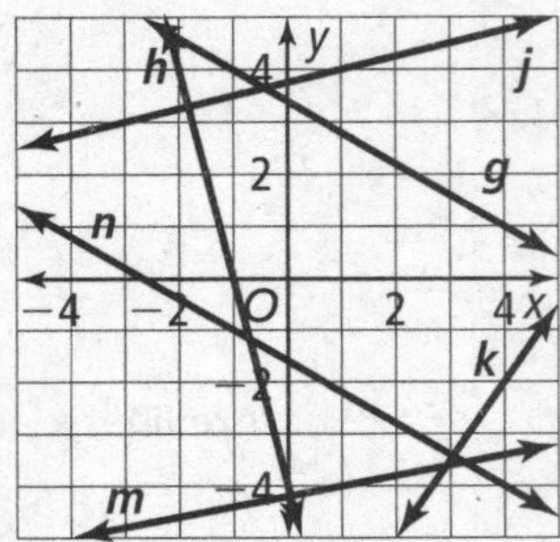

6. Are lines g and n parallel?

7. Are lines j and m parallel?

8. Are lines n and k perpendicular?

9. Are lines h and j perpendicular?

10. What is an equation for the line parallel to $y = -x + 7$ that passes through $(7, -2)$?

11. What is an equation for the line perpendicular to $y = 3x - 1$ that passes through $(-9, -2)$?

12. The graph of a roller coaster track goes in a straight line through coordinates (10, 54) and (42, 48), with coordinates in feet. A support beam runs parallel 12 feet below the track. What equation describes the support beam?

9-3 Polygons in the Coordinate Plane

PearsonRealize.com

EXPLORE & REASON

Players place game pieces on the board shown and earn points from the attributes of the piece placed on the board.

- 1 point for a right angle
- 2 points for a pair of parallel sides
- 3 points for the shortest perimeter

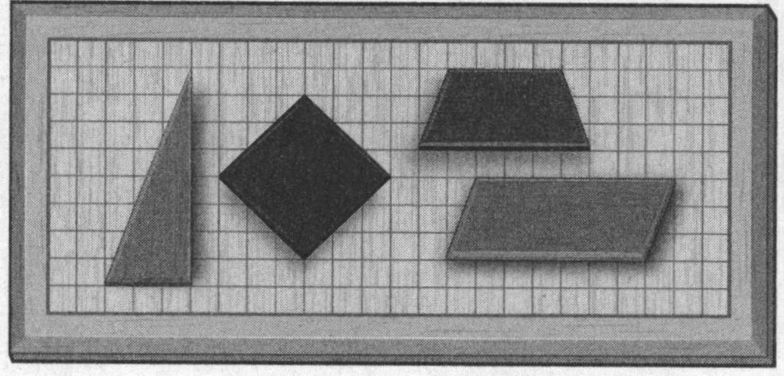

A. Which game piece is worth the greatest total points? Explain.

B. Make Sense and Persevere Describe a way to determine the perimeters that is different from the way you chose. Which method do you consider better? Explain.

HABITS OF MIND

Communicate Precisely How can you compare the lengths of sides of polygons that are placed on grids?

Notes

EXAMPLE 1

Try It! Connect Algebra and Geometry Through Coordinates

1. Given $\triangle ABC$ in Example 1, what is the length of the line segment connecting the midpoints of $\overline{AC}$ and $\overline{BC}$?

EXAMPLE 2

Try It! Classify a Triangle on the Coordinate Plane

2. The vertices of $\triangle PQR$ are $P(4, 1)$, $Q(2, 7)$, and $R(8, 5)$.

a. Is $\triangle PQR$ equilateral, isosceles, or scalene? Explain.

b. Is $\triangle PQR$ a right triangle? Explain.

HABITS OF MIND

Look for Relationships Given the vertices of a triangle on a coordinate plane, what formulas can you use to determine the type of triangle? Explain.

Notes

EXAMPLE 3 **Try It! Classify a Parallelogram on the Coordinate Plane**

3. The vertices of a parallelogram are $A(-2, 2)$, $B(4, 6)$, $C(6, 3)$, and $D(0, -1)$.

   a. Is *ABCD* a rhombus? Explain.

   b. Is *ABCD* a rectangle? Explain.

EXAMPLE 4 **Try It! Classify Quadrilaterals as Trapezoids and Kites on a Coordinate Plane**

4. Is each quadrilateral a kite, trapezoid, or neither?

   a.

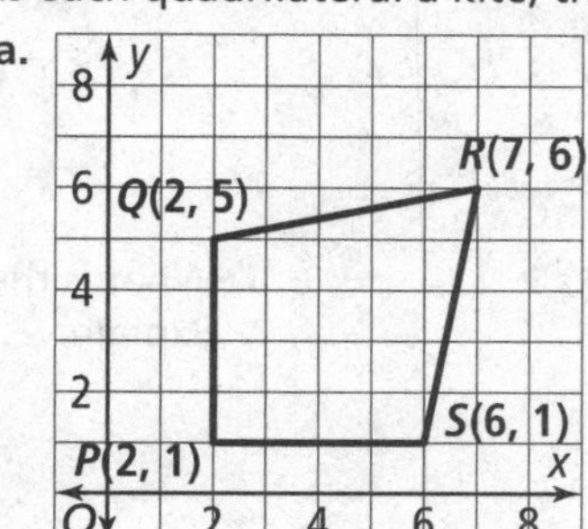

   b.

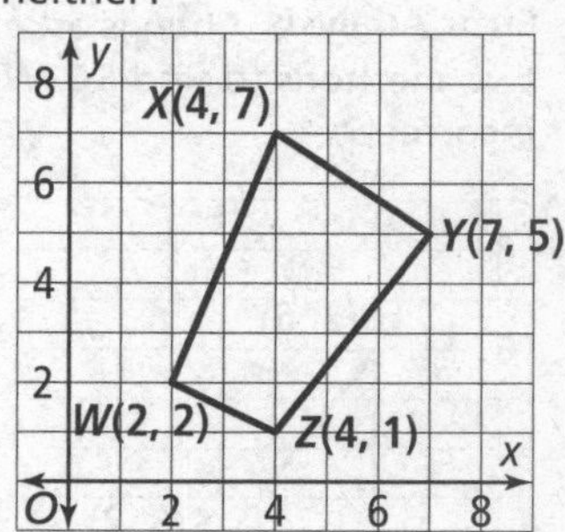

EXAMPLE 5 **Try It! Find Perimeter and Area**

5. The vertices of *WXYZ* are $W(5, 4)$, $X(2, 9)$, $Y(9, 9)$, and $Z(8, 4)$.

   a. What is the perimeter of *WXYZ*?

   b. What is the area of *WXYZ*?

HABITS OF MIND

Use Structure Can the slopes of three of the four sides of a quadrilateral be equal? Explain.

Do You UNDERSTAND?

1. **ESSENTIAL QUESTION** How are properties of geometric figures represented in the coordinate plane?

2. **Error Analysis** Chen is asked to describe two methods to find *BC*. Why is Chen incorrect?

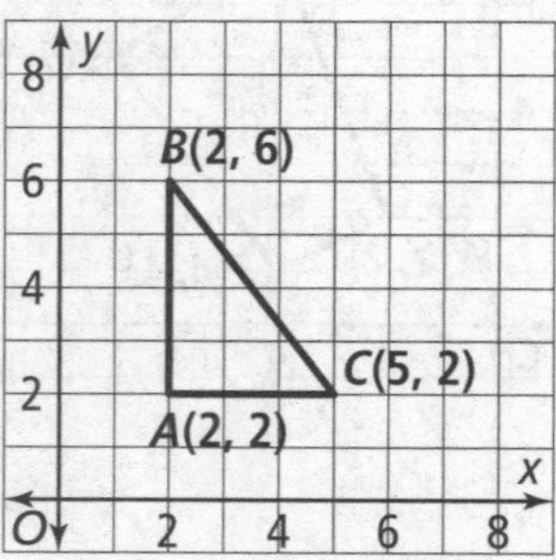

The only possible method is to use the Distance Formula because you only know the endpoints of $\overline{BC}$.

3. **Communicate Precisely** Describe three ways you can determine whether a quadrilateral is a parallelogram given the coordinates of the vertices.

Do You KNOW HOW?

Use *JKLM* for Exercises 4–6.

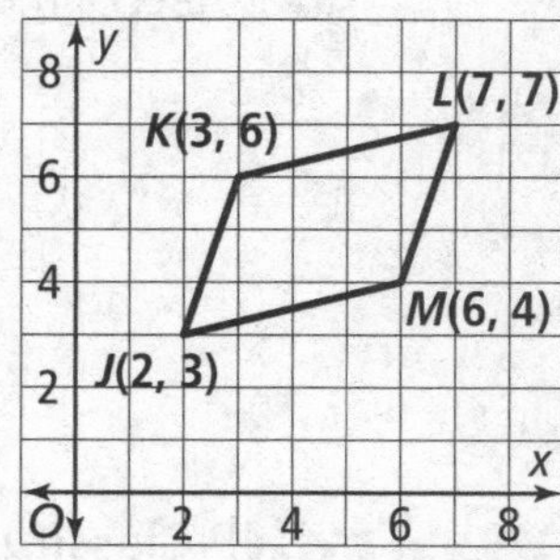

4. What is the perimeter of *JKLM*?

5. What is the relationship between $\overline{JL}$ and $\overline{KM}$? Explain.

6. What type of quadrilateral is *JKLM*? Explain.

Use △*PQR* for Exercises 7 and 8.

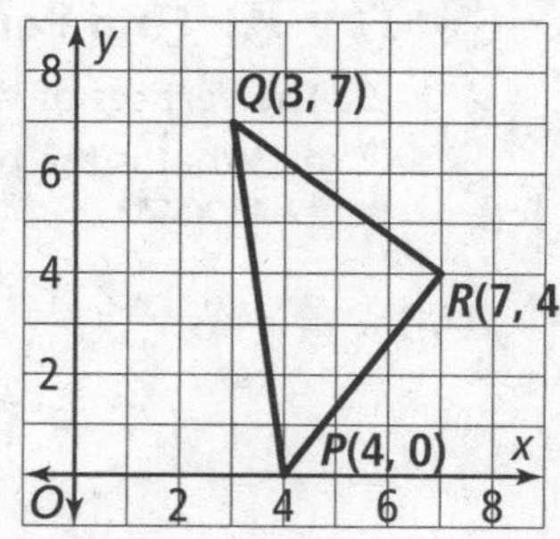

7. What kind of triangle is *PQR*? Explain.

8. What is the area of *PQR*?

You Be the Judge

Have you ever been a judge in a contest or competition? What criteria did you use to decide the winner? If you were one of many judges, did you all agree on who should win?

Often there is a set of criteria that judges use to help them score the performances of the contestants. Having criteria helps all of the judges be consistent regardless of the person they are rating. Think of this during the Mathematical Modeling in 3 Acts lesson.

ACT 1 Identify the Problem

1. What is the first question that comes to mind after watching the video?

2. Write down the main question you will answer.

3. Make an initial conjecture that answers this main question.

4. Explain how you arrived at your conjecture.

5. What information will be useful to know to answer the main question? How can you get it? How will you use that information?

Video

ACT 2 Develop a Model

6. Use the math that you have learned in the Topic to refine your conjecture.

ACT 3 Interpret the Results

7. Did your refined conjecture match the actual answer exactly? If not, what might explain the difference?

9-4

Proofs Using Coordinate Geometry

CRITIQUE & EXPLAIN

Dakota and Jung are trying to show that $\triangle ABC$ is a right triangle. Each student uses a different method.

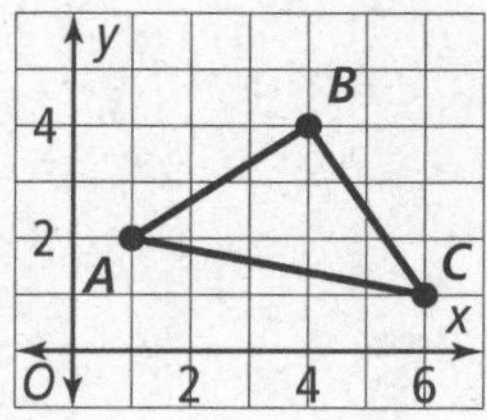

Dakota

slope of $\overline{AB} = \frac{2}{3}$, slope of $\overline{BC} = -\frac{3}{2}$

slope of $\overline{AB}$ • slope of $\overline{BC} = -1$

Triangle *ABC* is a right triangle.

Jung

$AB = BC = \sqrt{13}$, $AC = \sqrt{26}$

$(\sqrt{13})^2 + (\sqrt{13})^2 = (\sqrt{26})^2$

Triangle *ABC* is a right triangle.

A. Did Dakota and Jung both show $\triangle ABC$ is a right triangle? Explain.

B. Reason If the coordinates of $\triangle ABC$ were changed to (2, 3), (5, 5), and (7, 2), how would each student's method change? Explain.

HABITS OF MIND

Make Sense and Persevere What information about angles or sides might you use to show that a triangle is not a right triangle? Explain.

EXAMPLE 1

Try It! Plan a Coordinate Proof

1. Plan a proof to show that the diagonals of a square are congruent and perpendicular.

EXAMPLE 2

Try It! Write a Coordinate Proof

2. Use coordinate geometry to prove that the diagonals of a rectangle are congruent.

HABITS OF MIND

Use Structure If a figure has a pair of parallel sides, how could that help you in determining coordinates to use for your figure?

Notes

EXAMPLE 3

Try It! Plan and Write a Coordinate Proof

3. To complete the proof in Example 3, use the coordinates to show that $AP = \frac{2}{3}AD$, $BP = \frac{2}{3}BE$, and $CP = \frac{2}{3}CF$.

EXAMPLE 4

Try It! Use Coordinate Proofs to Solve Problems

4. A table has a top that is a right triangle and a single support leg. Where should the center of the leg be placed so it corresponds with the center of gravity of the table top? Plan a coordinate geometry proof to find its location.

HABITS OF MIND

Construct Arguments Why might you decide to have one vertex of a figure at the origin? Why might you decide not to?

Assess

Do You UNDERSTAND?

1. ESSENTIAL QUESTION How can geometric relationships be proven algebraically in the coordinate plane?

2. **Error Analysis** Venetta tried to find the slope of $\overline{AB}$. What is her error?

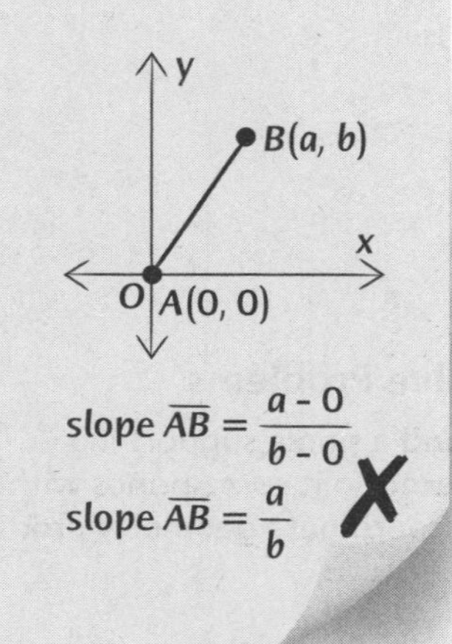

$\text{slope } \overline{AB} = \frac{a - 0}{b - 0}$

$\text{slope } \overline{AB} = \frac{a}{b}$ ✗

3. **Communicate Precisely** What is a coordinate geometry proof?

4. **Reason** Describe why it is important to plan a coordinate proof.

5. **Use Structure** What coordinates would you use to describe an isosceles triangle on a coordinate plane? Explain.

Do You KNOW HOW?

For Exercises 6–8, write a plan for a coordinate proof.

6. The diagonals of a rhombus are perpendicular.

7. The area of a triangle with vertices $A(0, 0)$, $B(0, a)$ and $C(b, c)$ is $\frac{ab}{2}$.

8. The lines that contain the altitudes of a triangle are concurrent.

For Exercises 9–12, plan and write a coordinate proof.

9. A point on the perpendicular bisector of a segment is equidistant from the endpoints.

10. The diagonals of a kite are perpendicular.

11. All squares are similar.

12. The area of a rhombus is half the product of the lengths of its diagonals.

Notes

 Assess

EXTENSION 9-4a
Partitioning a Line Segment

PearsonRealize.com

EXAMPLE 1 **Try It! Partition a Segment**

1. Find the coordinates of each point described.

   a. Point Q partitions $\overline{AB}$ into a ratio of 7 : 3.

   b. Point R partitions $\overline{AB}$ into a ratio of 4 : 1.

   c. Point T partitions $\overline{BA}$ into a ratio of 4 : 1.

HABITS OF MIND

Solve a Simpler Problem How does using a simpler ratio help you solve the problem?

EXAMPLE 2 **Try It! Use Similar Triangles**

2. Use similar triangles to find the coordinates of P that partition the line segment between $A(-5, 6)$ and $B(5, -18)$ into a ratio of 2 : 3.

 Assess

Do You UNDERSTAND?

1. ESSENTIAL QUESTION How can you find a point on a directed line segment between two given points that partitions the segment in a given ratio?

2. **Vocabulary** Compare and contrast directed line segment $\overline{AB}$ with directed line segment $\overline{BA}$.

3. **Error Analysis** Corey found the coordinates of *P* that divides the line segment between (1, 1) and (7, 13) into a ratio of 1 : 2. What Is Corey's error?

Horizontal: $\frac{1}{2}(7 - 1) = 3$

Vertical: $\frac{1}{2}(13 - 1) = 6$

$P = (1 + 3, 1 + 6) = (4, 7)$

Do You KNOW HOW?

***PQ* has endpoints *P*(–5, 4) and *Q*(7 –5).**

4. What are the coordinates of the point that partitions $\overline{PQ}$ in a ratio of 2 : 1?

5. What are the coordinates of the point that partitions $\overline{PQ}$ in a ratio of 2 : 1?

6. A chair lift at a ski resort travels along the cable shown.

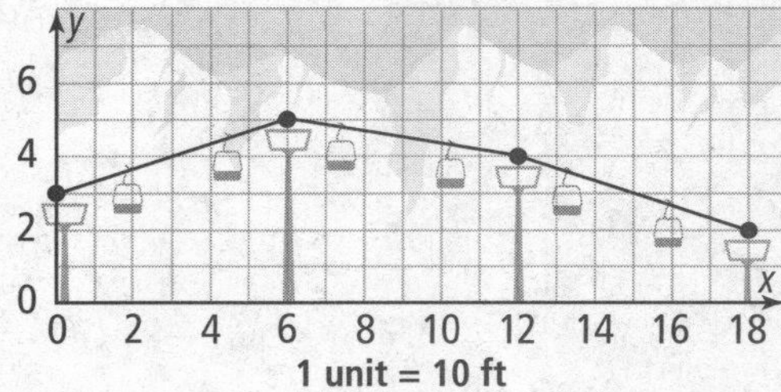

Additional supports will be added along each section of cable so that the ratio of the lower length of cable to the higher length of cable is 3 : 2.

a. Where will each support be placed?

b. How tall will each support need to be?

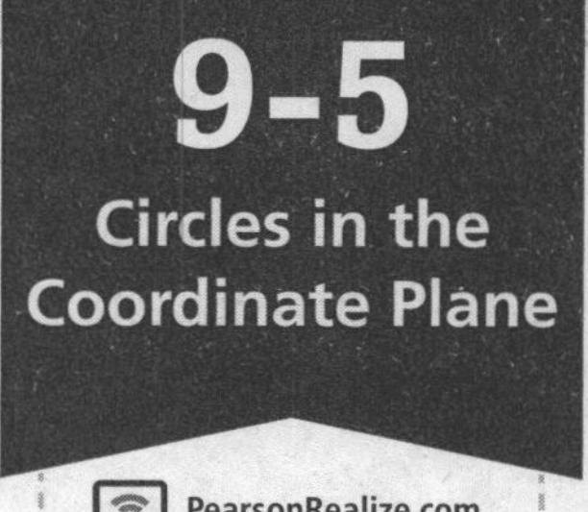

MODEL & DISCUSS

Damian uses an app to find all pizza restaurants within a certain distance of his current location.

A. What is the shape of the region that the app uses to search for pizza restaurants? Explain how you know.

B. What information do you think the app needs to determine the area to search?

C. **Construct Arguments** If Damian's friend is using the same app from a different location, could the app find the same pizza restaurant for both boys? Explain.

HABITS OF MIND

Use Appropriate Tools What geometric figure could you use with a paper map to locate points within a given distance from a given location? What tool would you use?

EXAMPLE 1 

Try It! Derive the Equation of a Circle

1. What are the radius and center of the circle with the equation $(x - 2)^2 + (y - 3)^2 = 25$?

EXAMPLE 2

Try It! Write the Equation of a Circle

2. What is the equation for each circle?

a. 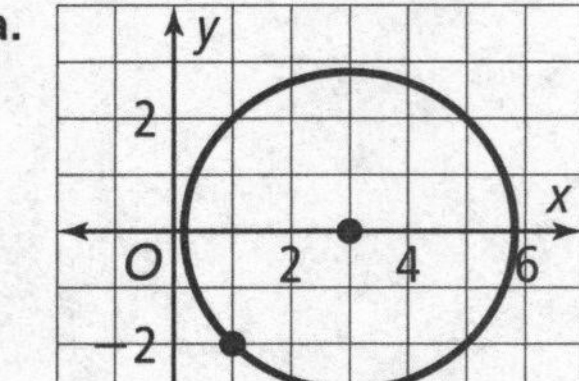

b. 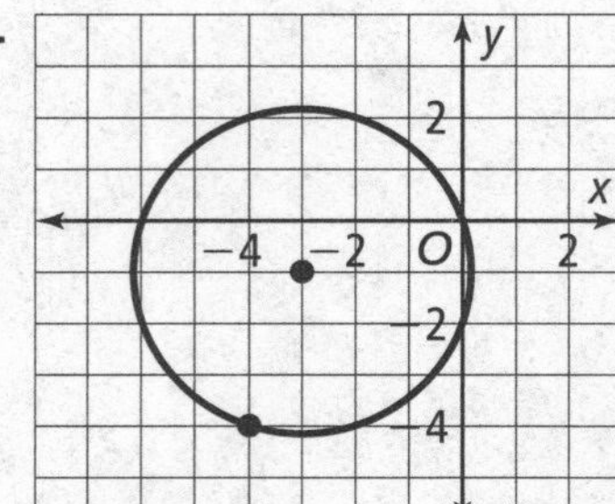

HABITS OF MIND

Use Structure Given the endpoints of the diameter of a circle, how would you find the equation of the circle?

EXAMPLE 3 **Try It! Determine Whether a Point Lies on a Circle**

3. Determine whether each point lies on the given circle.

a. $(-3, \sqrt{11})$; circle with center at the origin and radius $2\sqrt{5}$

b. (6, 3); circle with center at (2, 4) and radius $3\sqrt{3}$

EXAMPLE 4 **Try It! Complete the Square to Find the Center and Radius of a Circle**

4. What is the graph of each circle?

a. $x^2 + 4x + y^2 = 21$

a. $x^2 + 2x + y^2 - 4x = -4$

EXAMPLE 5 **Try It! Use the Graph and Equation of a Circle to Solve Problems**

5. If one or both of the existing radar stations could be moved, would three radar stations be sufficient to cover all the towns? Explain.

HABITS OF MIND

Use Structure How can you verify that an equation of a circle agrees with the graph of the circle?

Do You UNDERSTAND?

1. ESSENTIAL QUESTION How is the equation of a circle determined in the coordinate plane?

2. **Error Analysis** Leo says that the equation for the circle is $(x-1)^2 + (y-2)^2 = 3$. What is his error?

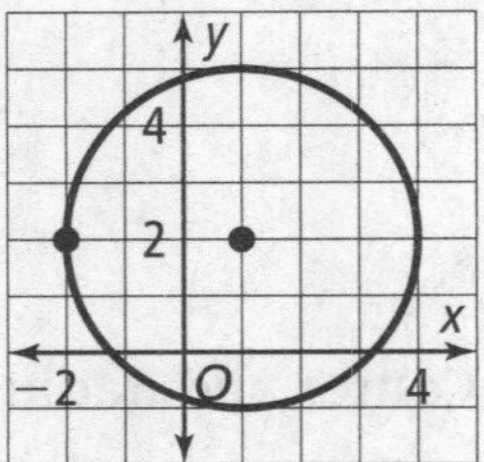

3. **Construct Arguments** If you are given the coordinates of the center and one point on a circle, can you determine the equation of the circle? Explain.

4. **Make Sense and Persevere** How could you write the equation of a circle given only the coordinates of the endpoints of its diameter?

Do You KNOW HOW?

5. What are the center and radius of the circle with equation $(x-4)^2 + (y-9)^2 = 1$?

6. What is the equation for the circle with center (6, 2) and radius 8?

7. What are the center and radius of the circle with equation $(x+7)^2 + (y-1)^2 = 9$?

8. What is the equation for the circle with center (−9, 5) and radius 4?

For Exercises 9 and 10, write an equation for each circle shown.

9.

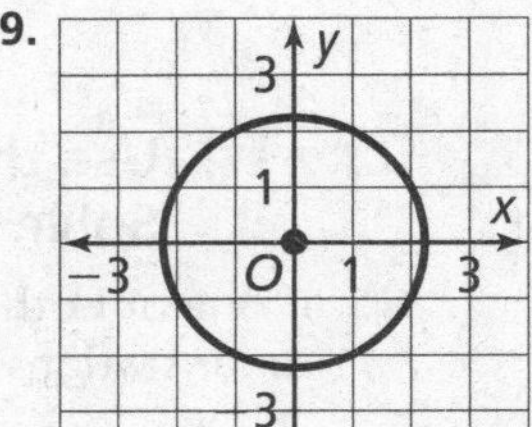

10.

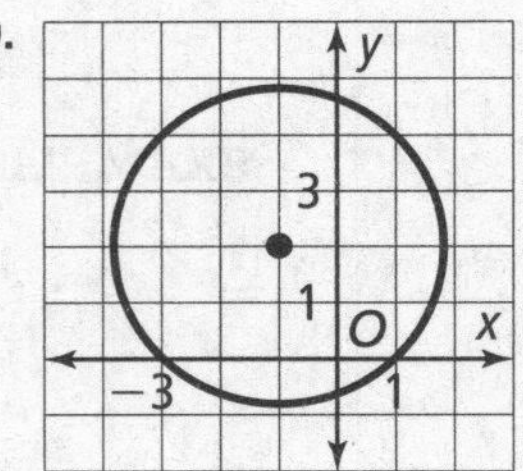

11. Is point (5, −2) on the circle with radius 5 and center (8, 2)?

12. What is the equation for the circle with center (5, 11) that passes through (9, −2)?

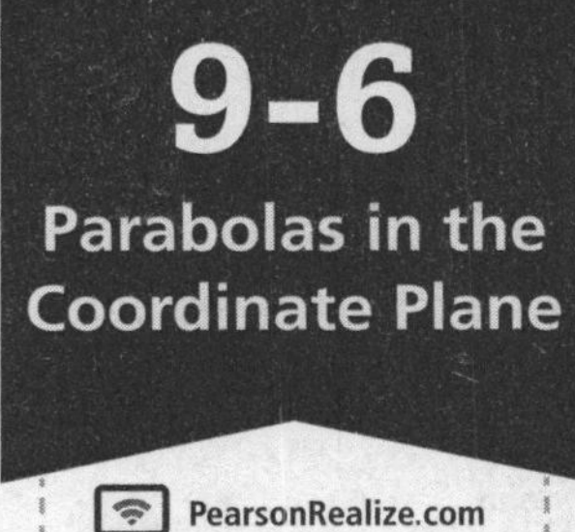

Activity

EXPLORE & REASON

Consider two points and two intersecting lines.

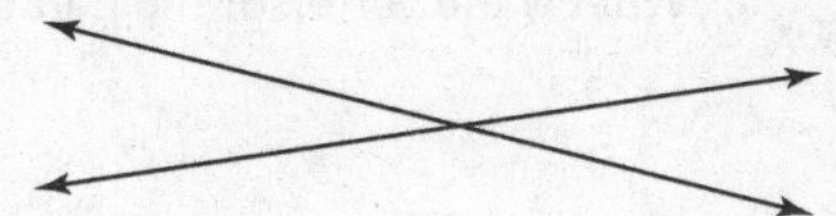

A. Describe the set of points that is equidistant from two points. Draw a diagram to support your answer.

B. Describe the set of points that is equidistant from two intersecting lines. Draw a diagram to support your answer.

C. **Look for Relationships** What do you think a set of points that is equidistant from a line and a point would look like? Draw a diagram to support your answer.

HABITS OF MIND

Make Sense and Persevere What is the point or set of points in a plane equidistant from two parallel lines? Explain how you know.

Notes

Assess

EXAMPLE 1 **Try It!** **Explore the Graph of a Parabola**

1. The set of points equidistant from (3, 5) and the line $y = 9$ is also a parabola.

   a. What is the vertex of the parabola?

   b. Describe the graph of the parabola.

EXAMPLE 2 **Try It!** **Derive the Equation of a Parabola**

2. What expression represents the distance between the focus and the directrix?

HABITS OF MIND

Use Structure How would the parabola be different if the directrix is above the focus on the coordinate plane?

Notes

EXAMPLE 3

Try It! Write the Equation of a Parabola

3. a. What equation represents the parabola with focus $(-1, 4)$ and directrix $y = -2$?

b. What equation represents the parabola with focus $(3, 5)$ and vertex $(3, -1)$?

EXAMPLE 4

Try It! Apply the Equation of a Parabola

4. On a different satellite dish, the feed horn is 38 inches above the vertex. If the height of the dish is 22 inches, what is its width?

HABITS OF MIND

Communicate Precisely How can you find the focus of parabola given the vertex and the directrix?

Do You UNDERSTAND?

1. ESSENTIAL QUESTION How does the geometric description of a parabola relate to its equation?

2. **Error Analysis** Arthur says that an equation of the parabola with directrix $y = 0$ and focus $= (0, 6)$ is $y - 3 = \frac{1}{24}x^2$. What is his error?

3. **Vocabulary** How could the word *direction* help you remember that the directrix is a line?

4. **Reason** What are the coordinates of point *P*? Show your work.

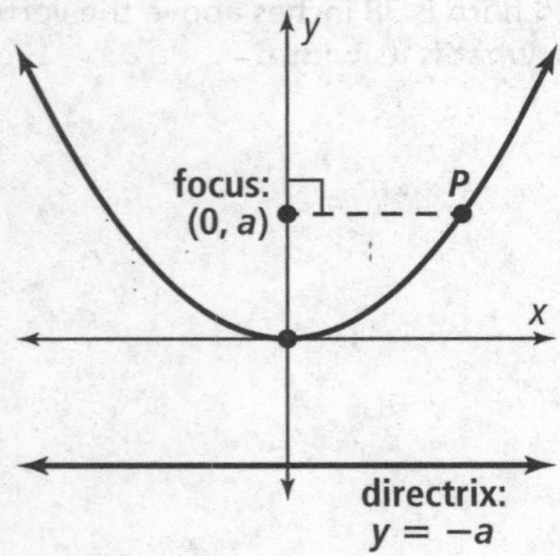

5. **Communicate Precisely** Given vertex (a, b) and focus (a, c), describe how you would write an equation for the parabola.

Do You KNOW HOW?

For Exercises 6–9, write an equation of each parabola with the given focus and directrix.

6. focus: (0, 4); directrix: $y = -4$

7. focus: (5, 1); directrix: $y = -5$

8. focus: (4, 0); directrix: $y = -4$

9. focus: (2, −1); directrix: $y = -4$

For Exercises 10–13, give the vertex, focus, and directrix of each parabola.

10. $y = \frac{1}{8}x^2$

11. $y - 2 = \frac{1}{6}x^2$

12. $y - 6 = \frac{1}{4}(x - 1)^2$

13. $y + 3 = \frac{1}{20}(x - 9)^2$

For Exercises 14–17, write an equation of each parabola with the given focus and vertex.

14. focus: (6, 2); vertex: (6, −4)

15. focus: (−1, 8); vertex: (−1, 7)

16. focus: (4, 0); vertex: (4, −2)

17. focus: (−3, −1); vertex: (−3, −4)

18. Consider the parabola $y = \frac{1}{36}x^2$.
    a. What are the focus and directrix?
    b. The parabola passes through (12, 4). Show that this point is equidistant from the focus and the directrix.

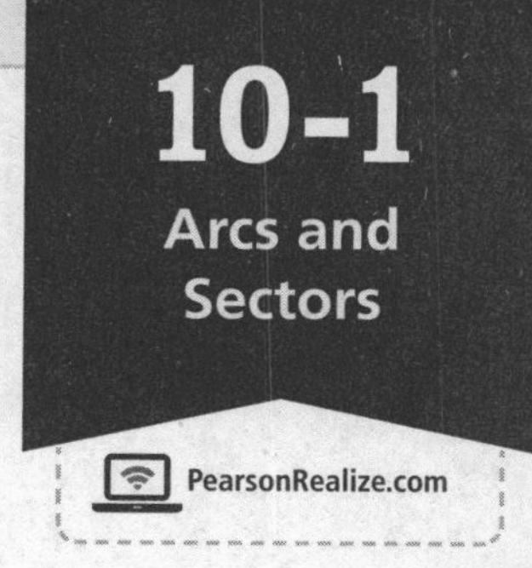

EXPLORE & REASON

Darren bends a piece of wire using a circular disc to make the shape as shown.

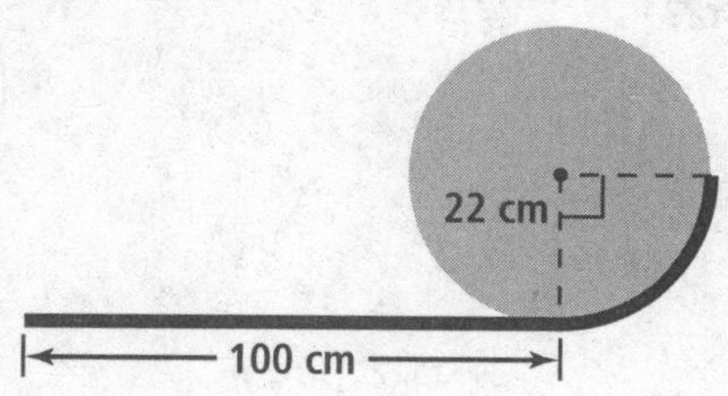

A. How long does the piece of wire need to be to make the shape? Explain.

B. Construct Arguments What information do you think is needed to find part of the circumference of a circle? Justify your answer.

HABITS OF MIND

Model With Mathematics Write an expression that represents the curved part of the wire. Explain what each part of your expression represents.

EXAMPLE 1 **Try It!** **Relate Central Angles and Arc Measures**

1. Use $\odot W$.

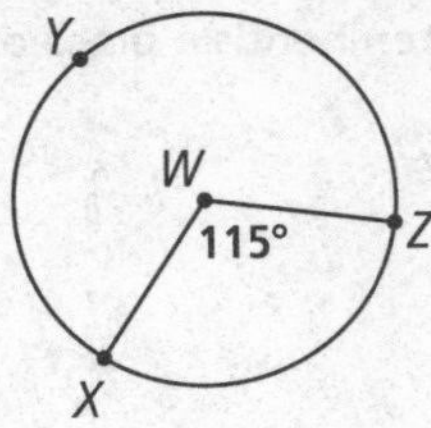

a. What is $m\widehat{XZ}$?

b. What is $m\widehat{XYZ}$?

EXAMPLE 2 **Try It!** **Relate Arc Length to Circumference**

2. a. In a circle with radius 4, what is the length of an arc that has a measure of 80? Round to the nearest tenth.

b. In a circle with radius 6, what is the length of an arc that has a measure of π radians? Round to the nearest tenth.

Notes

EXAMPLE 3

Try It! Apply Arc Length

3. Use ⊙Q. Express answers in terms of π.

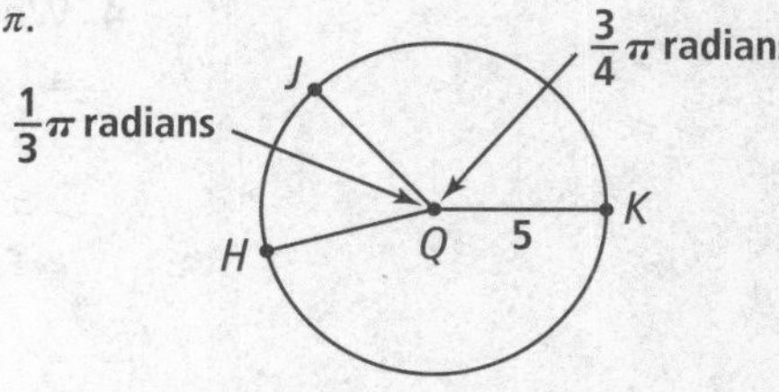

a. What is the length of $\widehat{JK}$?

b. What is the length of $\widehat{HK}$?

HABITS OF MIND

Reason How would you describe the relationships between arc length, arc measure, and circumference?

EXAMPLE 4 **Try It!** **Relate the Area of a Circle to the Area of a Sector**

4. What is the area of each sector?

a.

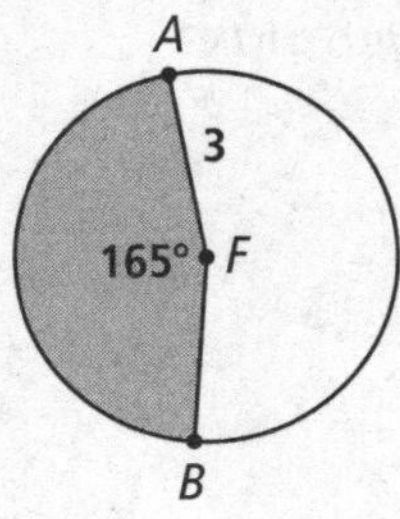

b.

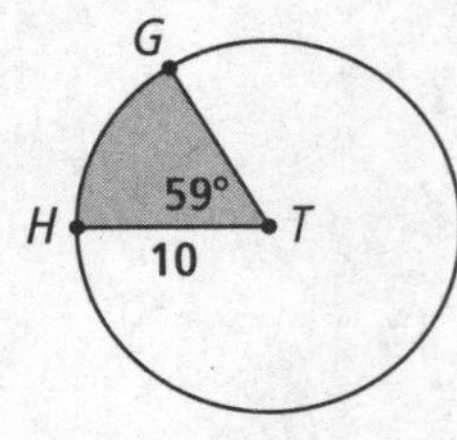

EXAMPLE 5 **Try It!** **Find the Area of a Segment of a Circle**

5. What is the area of each segment?

a.

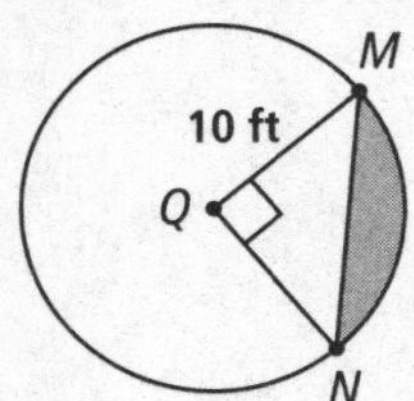

b.

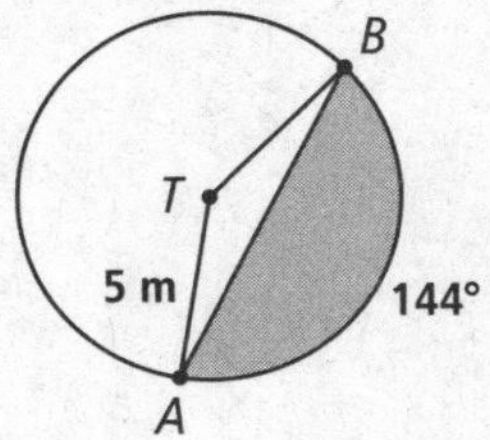

Notes

EXAMPLE 6

Try It! Solve Problems Involving Circles

6. What is the area and perimeter of sector QNR? Round to the nearest tenth.

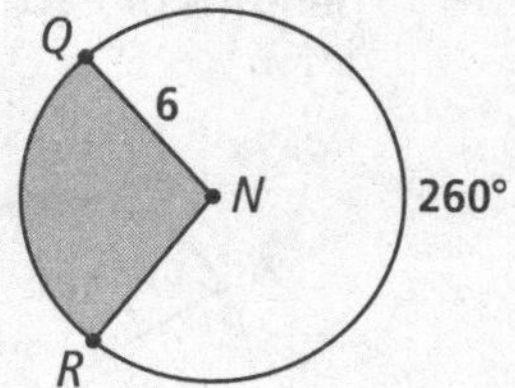

HABITS OF MIND

Generalize Is it always true that the area of a segment is less than the area of the corresponding sector? Explain.

Do You UNDERSTAND?

1. ESSENTIAL QUESTION How are arc length and sector area related to circumference and area of a circle?

2. **Error Analysis** Luke was asked to compute the length of $\overset{\frown}{AB}$. What is Luke's error?

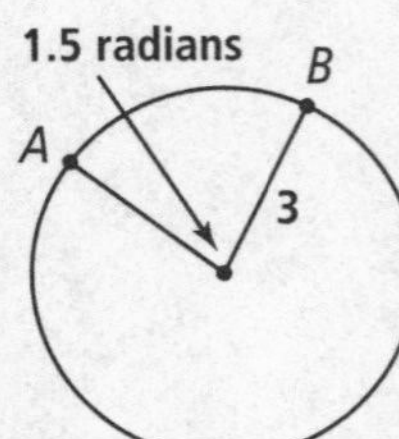

$$S = \frac{n}{360} \cdot 2\pi r$$
$$= \frac{1.5}{360} \cdot 2\pi(3)$$
$$= 0.0785$$

✗

3. **Vocabulary** How can the word *segment* help you remember what a *segment of a circle* is?

4. **Reason** Mercedes says that she can find the area of a quarter of a circle using the formula $A = \frac{1}{4}\pi r^2$. Using the formula for the area of a sector, explain why Mercedes is correct.

Do You KNOW HOW?

For Exercises 5 and 6, find the measures and lengths of each arc. Express the answers in terms of π.

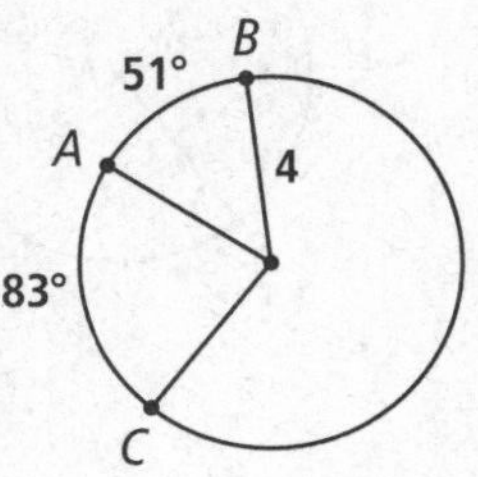

5. $\overset{\frown}{BC}$

6. $\overset{\frown}{ABC}$

7. Circle *P* has radius 8. Points *Q* and *R* lie on circle *P*, and the length of $\overset{\frown}{QR}$ is 4π. What is $m\angle QPR$ in radians?

8. What is the area of sector *EFG*? Express the answer in terms of π.

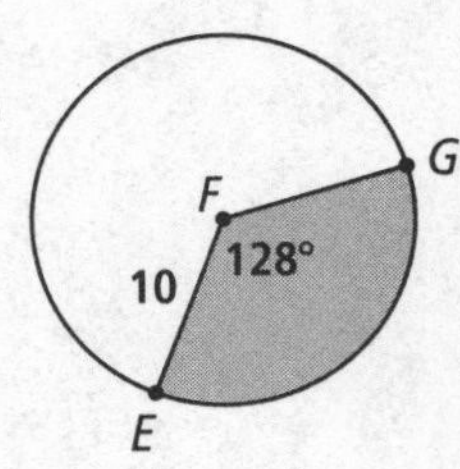

9. What is the area of the segment? Express the answer in terms of π.

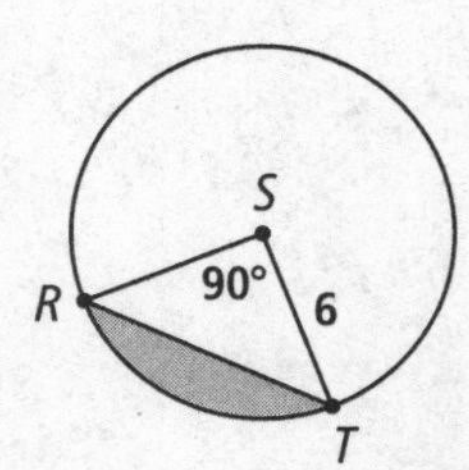

10-2 Lines Tangent to a Circle

CRITIQUE & EXPLAIN

Alicia and Renaldo made conjectures about the lines that intersect a circle only once.

Alicia

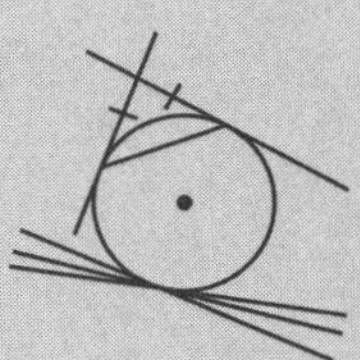

- Many lines intersect the circle once at the same point.
- Two lines that intersect the circle once and the segment connecting the points form an isosceles triangle.

Renaldo

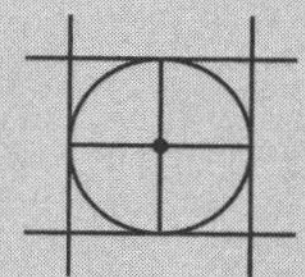

- Parallel lines intersect the circle at opposite ends of the same diameter.
- The lines intersecting the circle at one point are perpendicular to a diameter of the circle.

A. Use Appropriate Tools Which of the four conjectures do you agree with? Which do you disagree with? Draw sketches to support your answers.

B. What other conjectures can you make about lines that intersect a circle at one point?

HABITS OF MIND

Communicate Precisely What mathematical terms apply in this situation?

Notes

EXAMPLE 1

Try It! Understand Tangents to a Circle

1. Does Example 1 support Renaldo's conjecture that parallel lines intersect the circle at opposite ends of the same diameter? Explain.

EXAMPLE 2

Try It! Use Tangents to Solve Problems

2. Use ⊙N.

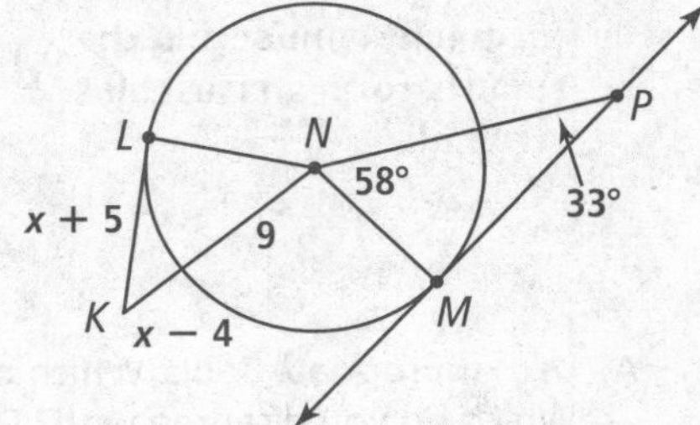

a. Is $\overleftrightarrow{MP}$ tangent to ⊙N? Explain.

b. If $\overline{LK}$ is tangent to ⊙N at L, what is KN?

HABITS OF MIND

Construct Arguments What are some ways that you can determine whether a line is tangent to a circle?

Notes

EXAMPLE 3 **Try It!** **Find Lengths of Segments Tangent to a Circle**

3. If $TX = 12$ and $TZ = 20$, what are XZ and YZ?

EXAMPLE 4 **Try It!** **Find Measures Involving Tangent Lines**

4. What is the perimeter of *ABCD*?

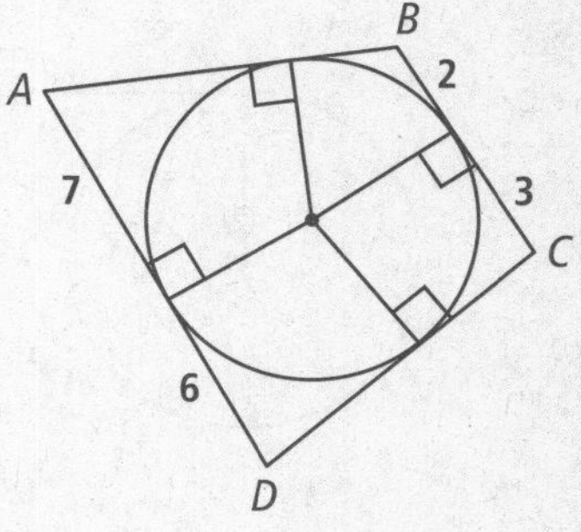

EXAMPLE 5 **Try It!** **Construct Tangent Lines**

5. Prove that $\overline{TC}$ is tangent to $\odot P$.

Given: Concentric circles with center *P*, points *A* and *C* on the smaller circle, points *T* and *B* on the larger circle, $\overline{AB} \perp \overline{PT}$

Prove: $\overline{TC}$ is tangent to $\odot P$ at *C*.

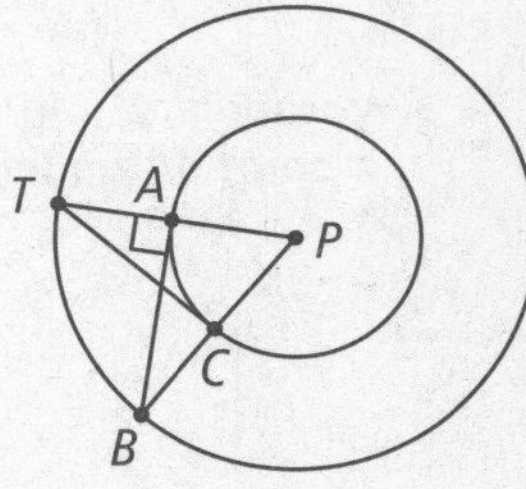

HABITS OF MIND

Generalize Is it always true that there are exactly two tangent lines from a point on the exterior of a circle to the circle? Explain.

Do You UNDERSTAND?

1. **ESSENTIAL QUESTION** How is a tangent line related to the radius of a circle at the point of tangency?

2. **Error Analysis** Kona looked at the figure shown and said that $\overline{AB}$ is tangent to ⊙G at A because it intersects ⊙G only at A. What was Kona's error?

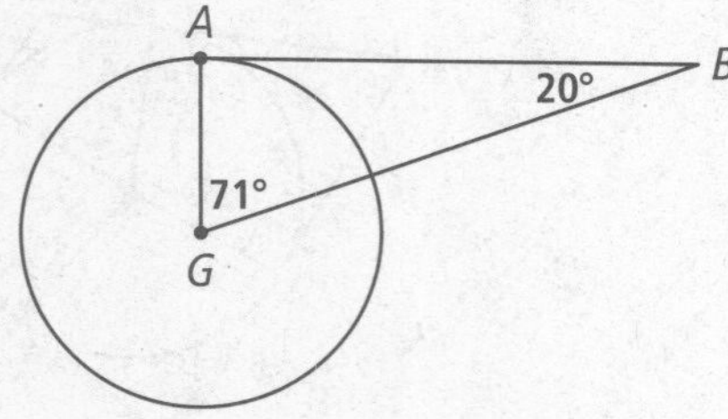

3. **Vocabulary** Can any point on a circle be a *point of tangency*? Explain.

4. **Reason** Lines m and n are tangent to circles A and B. What are the relationships between ∠PAS, ∠PQS, ∠RQS, and ∠RBS? Explain.

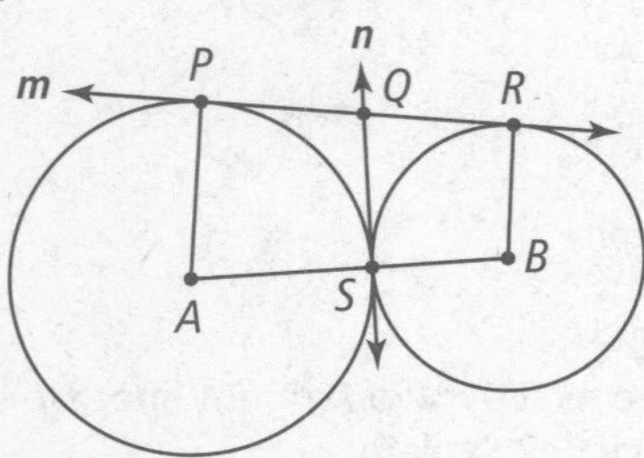

Do You KNOW HOW?

Tell whether each line or segment is a tangent to ⊙B.

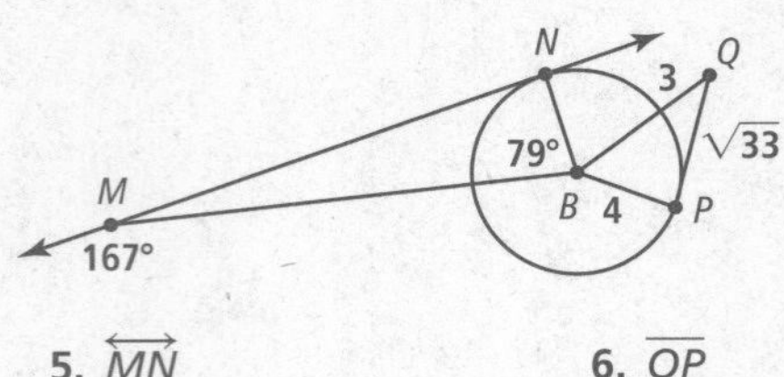

5. $\overleftrightarrow{MN}$

6. $\overline{QP}$

Segment AC is tangent to ⊙D at B. Find each value.

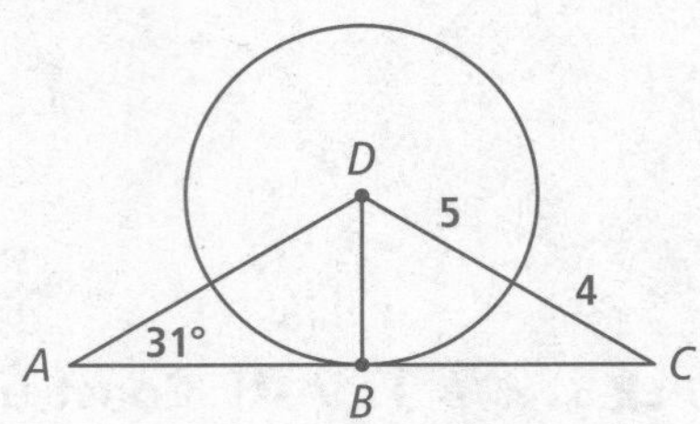

7. $m\angle ADB$

8. BC

Segment FG is tangent to ⊙K at F and $\overline{HG}$ is tangent to ⊙K at H. Find each value.

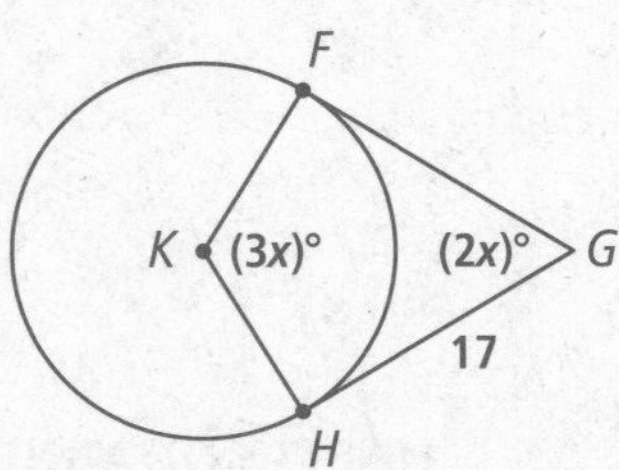

9. FG

10. $m\angle FGH$

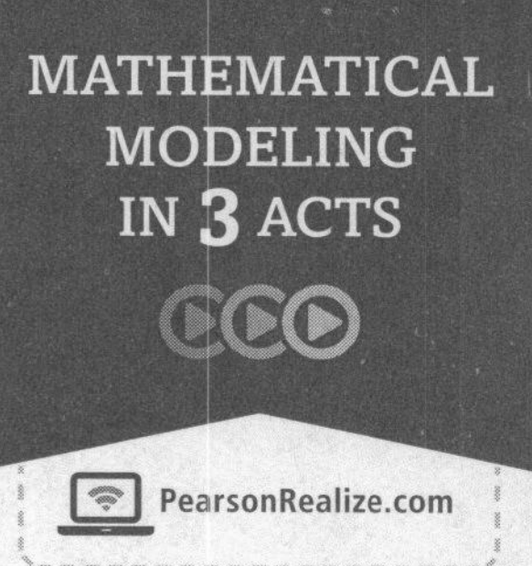

Earth Watch

Scientists estimate that there are currently about 3,000 operational man-made satellites orbiting Earth. These satellites serve different purposes, from communication to navigation and global positioning. Some are weather satellites that collect environmental information.

The International Space Station is the largest man-made satellite that orbits Earth. It serves as a space environment research facility, and it also offers amazing views of Earth. Think about this during the Mathematical Modeling in 3 Acts lesson.

ACT 1 Identify the Problem

1. What is the first question that comes to mind after watching the video?

2. Write down the main question you will answer about what you saw in the video.

3. Make an initial conjecture that answers this main question.

4. Explain how you arrived at your conjecture.

5. What information will be useful to know to answer the main question? How can you get it? How will you use that information?

Video

ACT 2 Develop a Model

6. Use the math that you have learned in the Topic to refine your conjecture.

ACT 3 Interpret the Results

7. Did your refined conjecture match the actual answer exactly? If not, what might explain the difference?

10-3
Chords

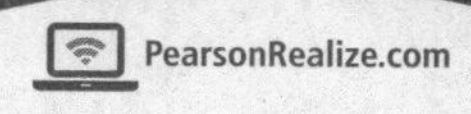

EXPLORE & REASON

Use the diagram to answer the questions.

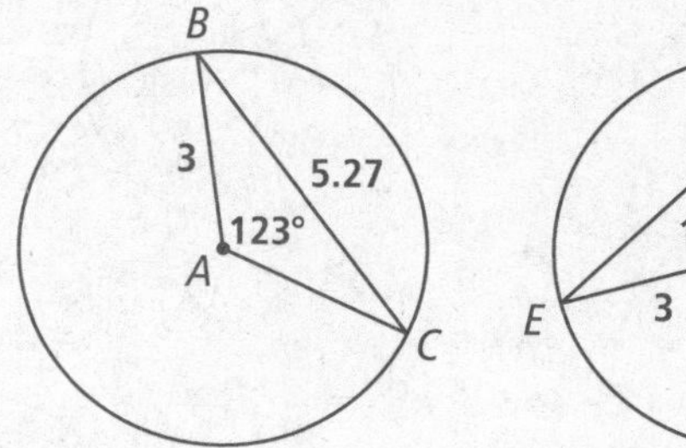

A. What figures in the diagram are congruent? Explain.

B. Look for Relationships How can you find *EF*?

HABITS OF MIND

Use Structure What is true of the radii of both circles? Explain.

EXAMPLE 1

Try It! Relate Central Angles and Chords

1. Why is $\angle BAC \cong \angle DAE$?

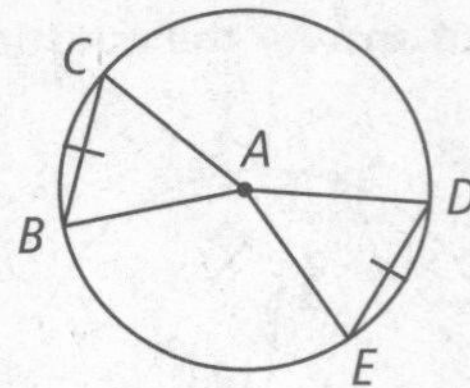

EXAMPLE 2

Try It! Relate Arcs and Chords

2. Write a flow proof of the Converse of Theorem 10-4.

EXAMPLE 3

Try It! Relate Chords Equidistant from the Center

3. Write a flow proof of the Converse of Theorem 10-5.

HABITS OF MIND

Generalize In the same circle or in congruent circles, what is true about congruent chords?

Notes

EXAMPLE 4

Try It! Construct a Regular Hexagon Inscribed in a Circle

4. Construct an equilateral triangle inscribed in a circle.

EXAMPLE 5

Try It! Solve Problems Involving Chords of Circles

5. Fresh cut flowers need to be in at least 4 inches of water. A spherical vase is filled until the surface of the water is a circle 5 inches in diameter. Is the water deep enough for the flowers? Explain.

HABITS OF MIND

Reason What is the first thing to look for when solving problems involving chords and diameters?

Do You UNDERSTAND?

1. ESSENTIAL QUESTION How are chords related to their central angles and intercepted arcs?

2. **Error Analysis** Sasha writes a proof to show that two chords are congruent. What is her error?

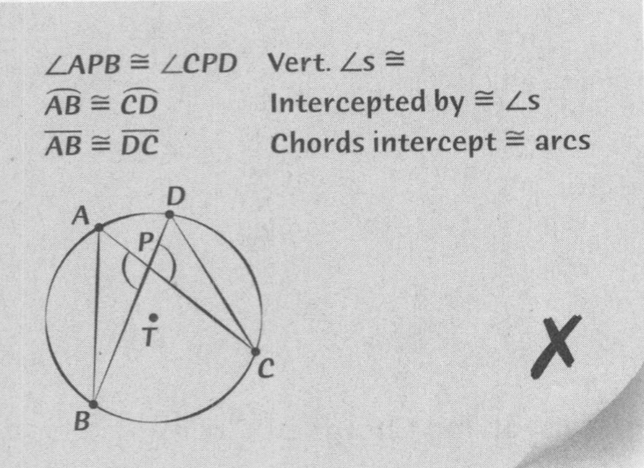

3. **Vocabulary** Explain why all diameters of circles are also chords of the circles.

4. **Reason** Given $\overline{RS} \cong \overline{UT}$, how can find UT?

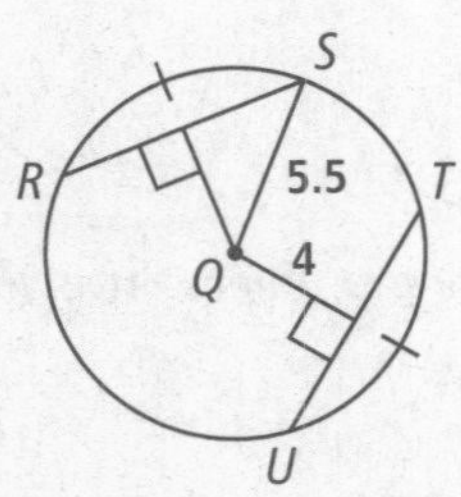

Do You KNOW HOW?

For Exercises 5–10, in ⊙P, $m\widehat{AB} = 43°$, and $AC = DF$. Find each measure.

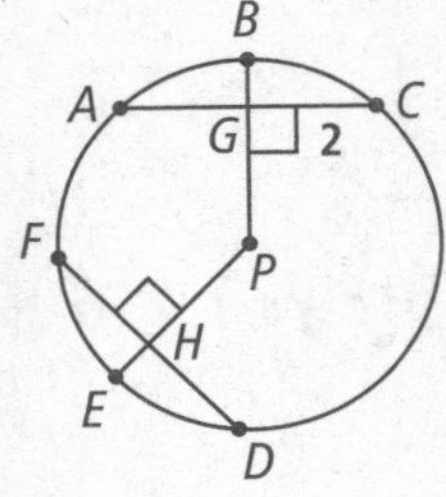

5. DF

6. $m\widehat{AC}$

7. FH

8. $m\widehat{DE}$

9. AC

10. $m\widehat{DF}$

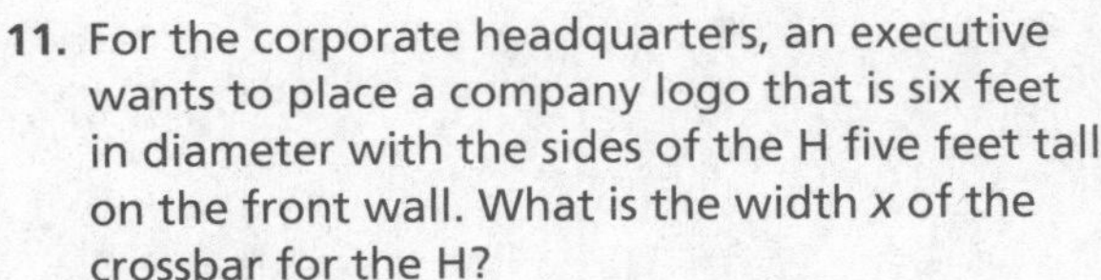

11. For the corporate headquarters, an executive wants to place a company logo that is six feet in diameter with the sides of the H five feet tall on the front wall. What is the width x of the crossbar for the H?

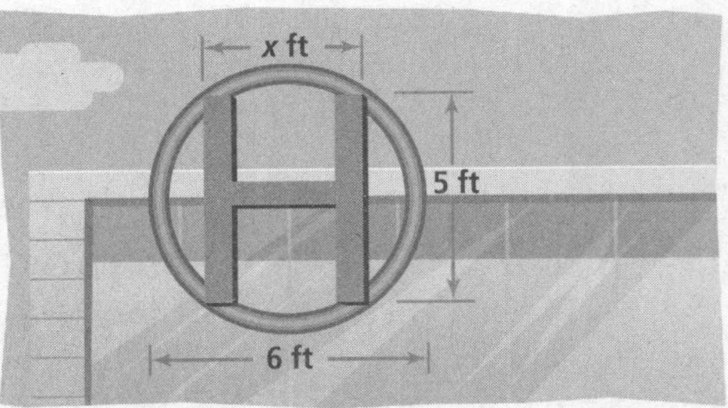

10-4 Inscribed Angles

PearsonRealize.com

EXPLORE & REASON

Consider ⊙*T*.

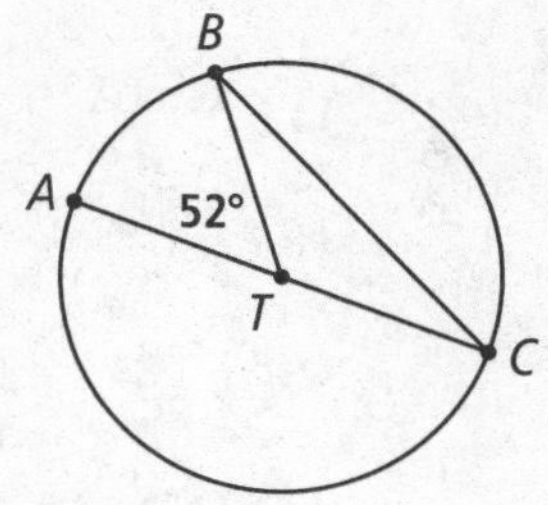

A. Make Sense and Persevere List at least seven things you can conclude about the figure.

B. How is ∠*ACB* related to ∠*ATB*? Explain.

HABITS OF MIND

Use Structure What is the relationship between a central angle and its intercepted arc?

Notes

EXAMPLE 1

Try It! Relate Inscribed Angles to Intercepted Arcs

1. Given $\odot P$ with inscribed angle $\angle S$, if $m\widehat{RT} = 47$, what is $m\angle S$?

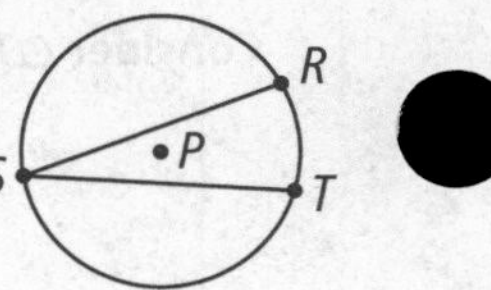

EXAMPLE 2

Try It! Use the Inscribed Angles Theorem

2. a. If $m\widehat{RST} = 164$, what is $m\angle RVT$?

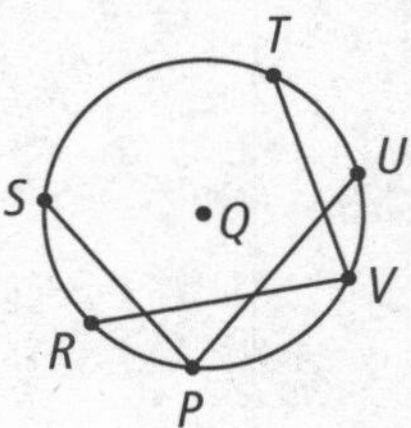

b. If $m\angle SPU = 79$, what is $m\widehat{STU}$?

HABITS OF MIND

Communicate Precisely If the center of a circle is in the exterior of an inscribed angle, can the inscribed angle be a right angle? Explain.

Notes

Assess

EXAMPLE 3 Try It! Explore Angles Formed by a Tangent and a Chord

3. a. Given $\overleftrightarrow{BD}$ tangent to ⊙P at point C, if $m\widehat{AC} = 88$, what is $m\angle ACB$?

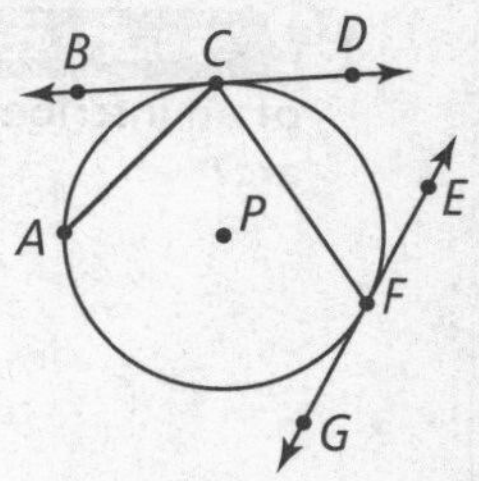

b. Given $\overleftrightarrow{EG}$ tangent to ⊙P at point F, if $m\angle GFC = 115$, what is $m\widehat{FAC}$?

EXAMPLE 4 Try It! Use Arc Measure to Solve a Problem

4. a. Given $\overleftrightarrow{WY}$ tangent to ⊙C at point X, what is $m\widehat{XZ}$?

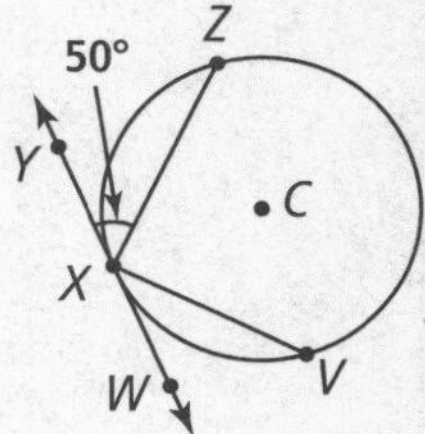

b. What is $m\angle VXW$?

HABITS OF MIND

Reason What can you conclude about the intercepted arc when a tangent and a diameter form an angle? Explain.

Do You UNDERSTAND?

1. ESSENTIAL QUESTION How is the measure of an inscribed angle related to its intercepted arc?

2. **Error Analysis** Darren is asked to find $m\widehat{XZ}$. What is his error?

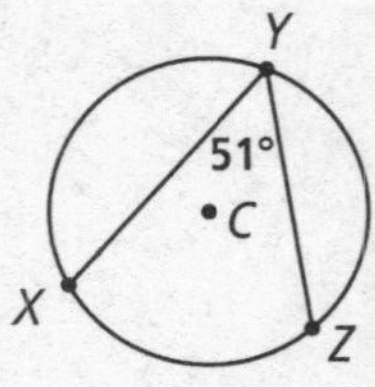

$$m\widehat{XZ} = \frac{1}{2}\, m\angle XYZ$$
$$= \frac{1}{2}(51)$$
$$= 25.5$$

✗

3. **Reason** Can the measure of an inscribed angle be greater than the measure of the intercepted arc? Explain.

4. **Make Sense and Persevere** Is there enough information in the diagram to find $m\widehat{RST}$? Explain.

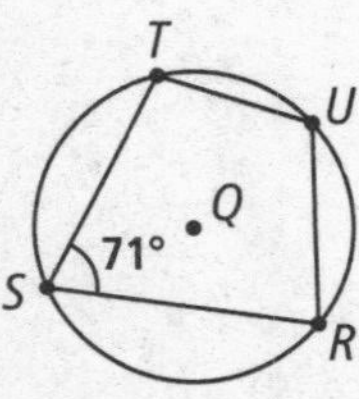

Do You KNOW HOW?

For Exercises 5–8, find each measure in ⊙*Q*.

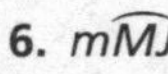

5. $m\widehat{JL}$

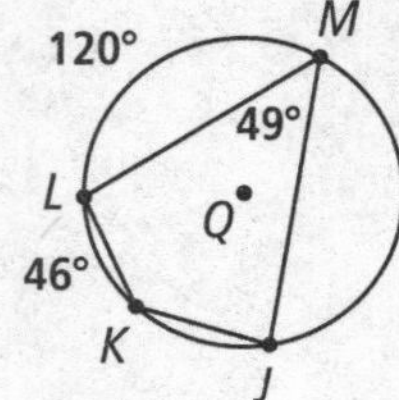

6. $m\widehat{MJ}$

7. $m\angle KJM$

8. $m\angle KLM$

For Exercises 9–12, $\overleftrightarrow{DF}$ is tangent to ⊙*O* at point *E*. Find each measure.

9. $m\widehat{EH}$

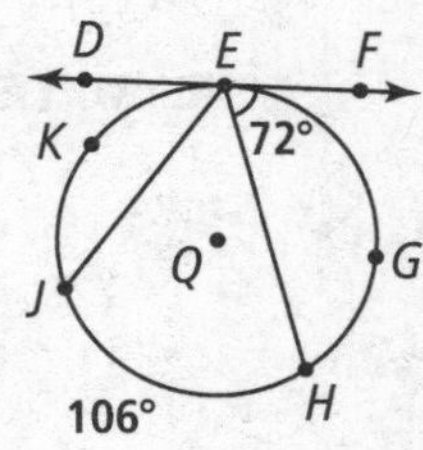

10. $m\widehat{EJ}$

11. $m\angle HEJ$

12. $m\angle DEJ$

For Exercises 13–16, find each measure in ⊙*M*.

13. $m\angle PRQ$

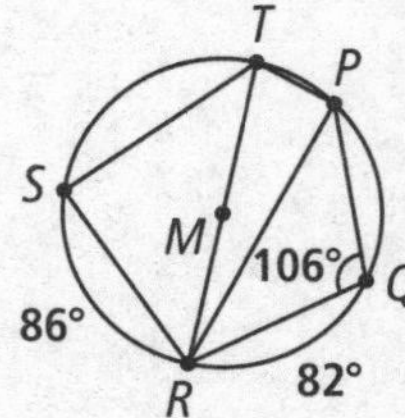

14. $m\angle PTR$

15. $m\angle RST$

16. $m\angle SRT$

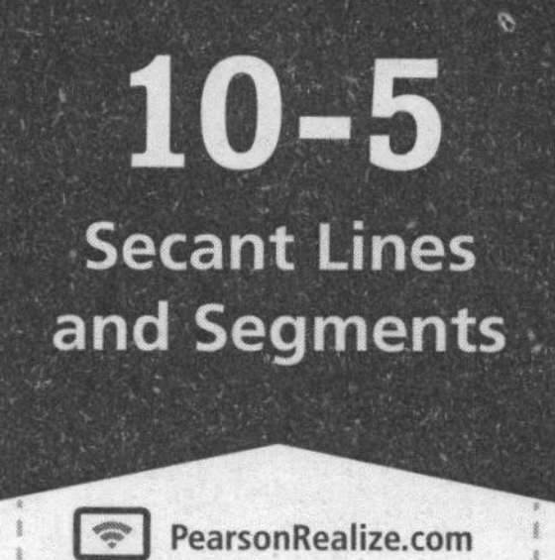

EXPLORE & REASON

Skyler made the design shown. Points *A*, *B*, *C*, and *D* are spaced evenly around the circle.

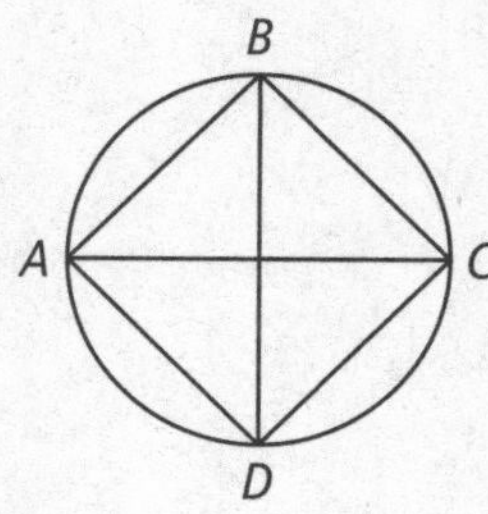

A. Using points *A*, *B*, *C*, and *D* as vertices, what congruent angles can you find? How can you justify that they are congruent?

B. Make Sense and Persevere What strategy did you use to make sure you found all congruent angles?

HABITS OF MIND

Generalize How does the fact that the points are evenly spaced affect your answers?

EXAMPLE 1

Try It! Relate Secants and Angle Measures

1. If $m\widehat{AD} = 155$ and $m\widehat{BC} = 61$, what is $m\angle 1$?

EXAMPLE 2

Try It! Prove Theorem 10-11, Case 1

2. Prove Theorem 10-11, Case 2.

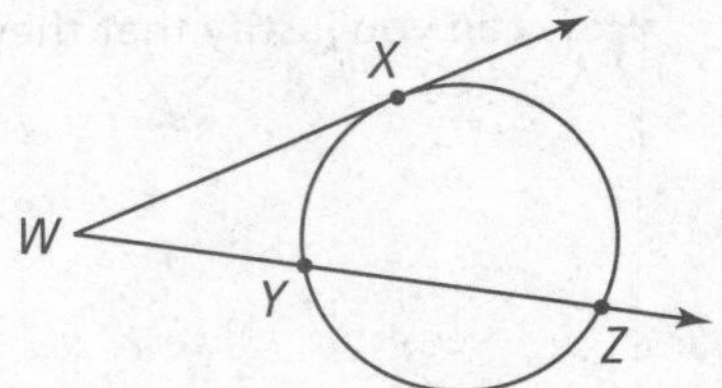

EXAMPLE 3

Try It! Use Secants and Tangents to Solve Problems

3. a. What is $m\widehat{WX}$?

b. What is $m\angle PSQ$?

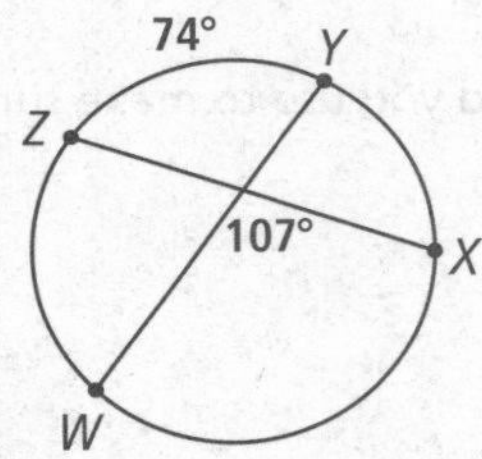

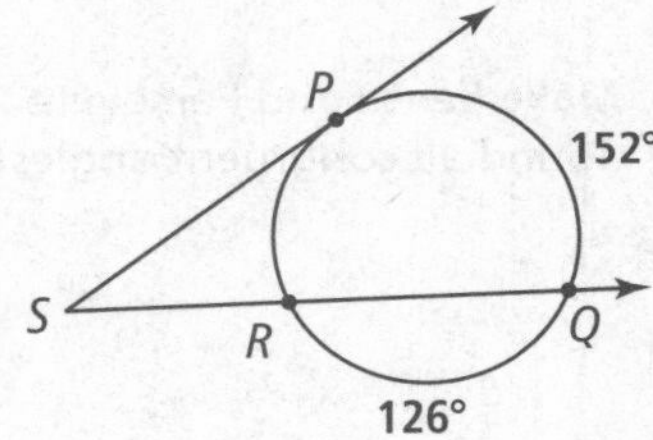

HABITS OF MIND

Look for Relationships What are the same and what are different about angles formed by intersecting chords, intersecting secants, intersecting tangents, and intersecting secant and tangent?

Notes

EXAMPLE 4 **Try It!** **Develop Chord Length Relationships**

4. What is the value of *y*?

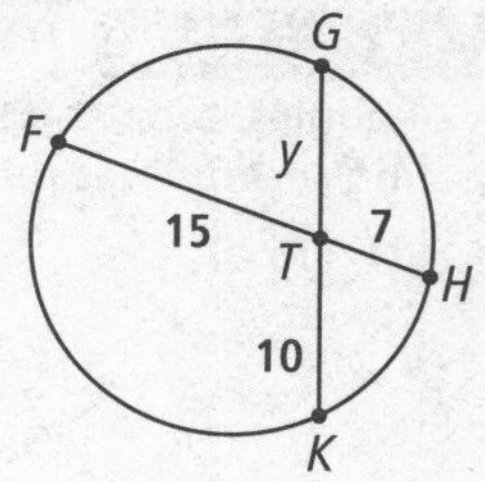

EXAMPLE 5 **Try It!** **Use Segment Relationships to Find Lengths**

5. a. What is the value of *a*?

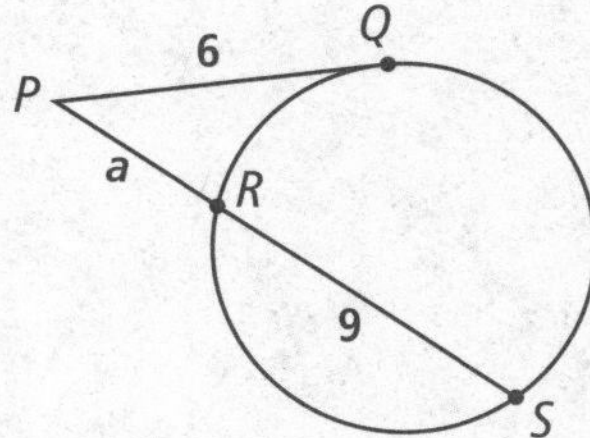

b. What is *EC*?

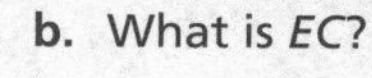

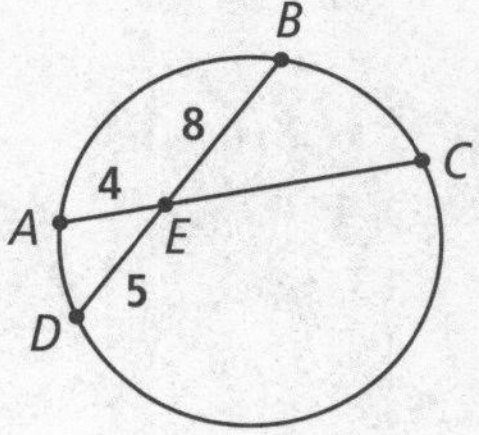

HABITS OF MIND

Generalize What mathematical consistencies do you notice between the three cases of Theorem 10-12?

Do You UNDERSTAND?

1. ESSENTIAL QUESTION How are the measures of angles, arcs, and segments formed by intersecting secant lines related?

2. **Error Analysis** Derek is asked to find the value of x. What is his error?

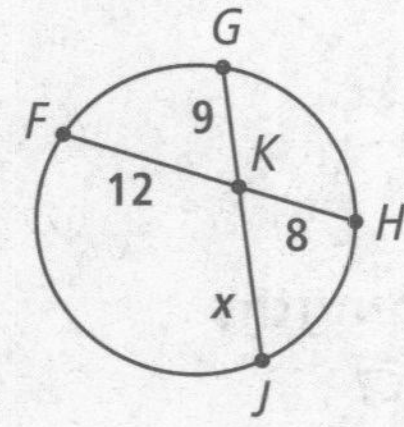

$GK \cdot FK = HK \cdot JK$
$12 \cdot 9 = 8 \cdot x$
$x = 13\frac{1}{2}$

X

3. **Vocabulary** How are *secants* and *tangents* to a circle alike and different?

4. **Construct Arguments** The rays shown are tangent to the circle. Show that $m\angle 1 = (x - 180)$.

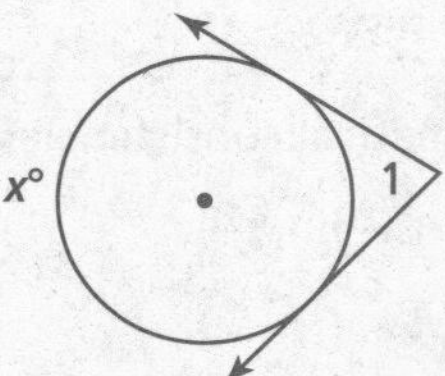

Do You KNOW HOW?

For Exercises 5 and 6, find each angle measure. Rays *QP* and *QR* are tangent to the circle in Exercise 6.

5. $m\angle BEC$

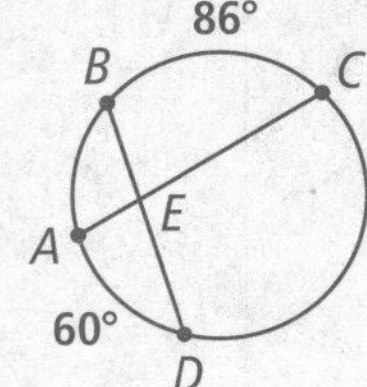

6. $m\angle PQR$

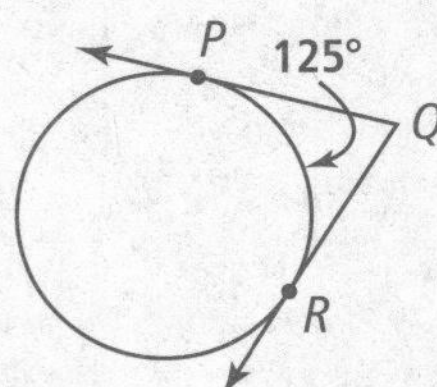

For Exercises 7 and 8, find each length. Ray *HJ* is tangent to the circle in Exercise 7.

7. *GF*

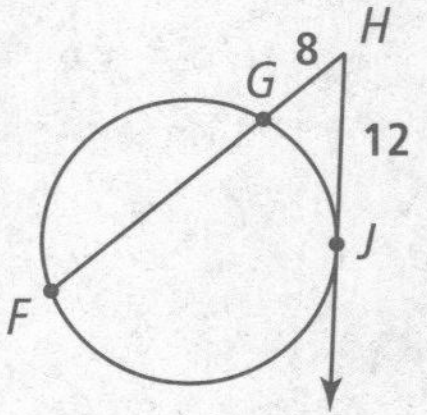

8. *LM*

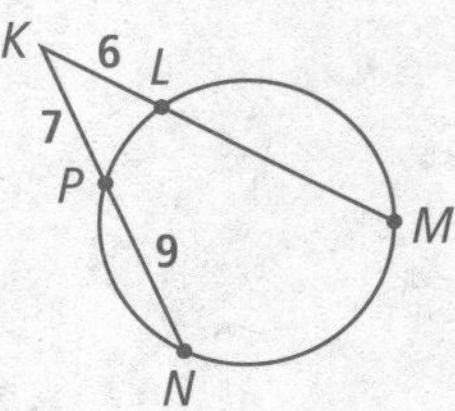

For Exercises 9 and 10, $\overline{AE}$ is tangent to ⊙*P*. Find each length.

9. *BC*

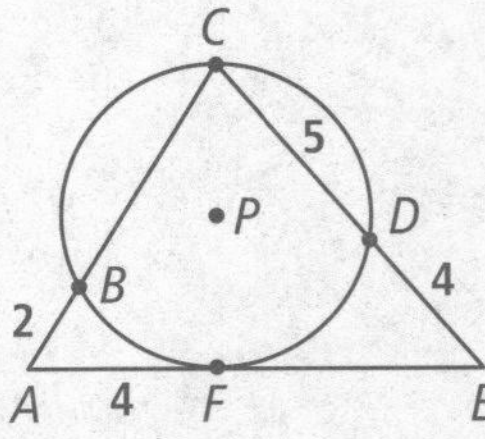

10. *EF*

11-1 Three-Dimensional Figures and Cross Sections

PearsonRealize.com

EXPLORE & REASON

Consider a cube of cheese. If you slice straight down through the midpoints of four parallel edges of the cube, the outline of the newly exposed surface is a square.

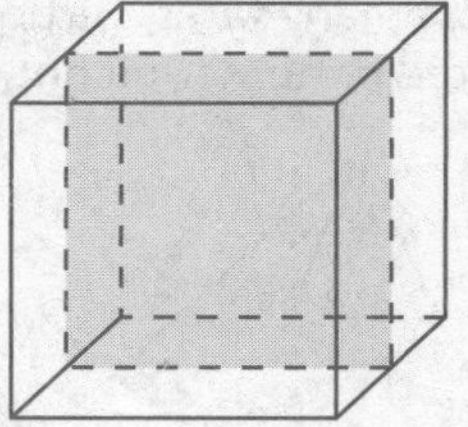

A. How would you slice the cube to expose a triangular surface?

B. Communicate Precisely How would you slice the cube to expose a triangular surface with the greatest possible area?

HABITS OF MIND

Use Structure How could you slice a cube to expose a rectangle that is not a square?

Notes

EXAMPLE 1  **Try It!** **Develop Euler's Formula**

1. How many faces, vertices, and edges do the pyramids have? Name at least three patterns you notice.

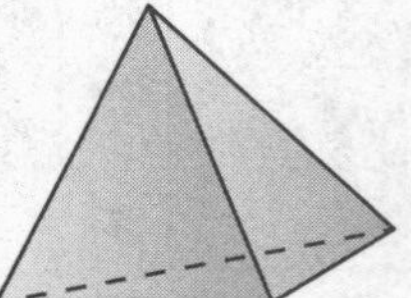 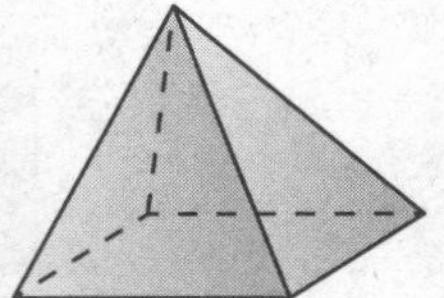 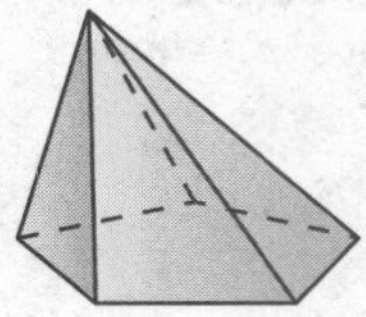 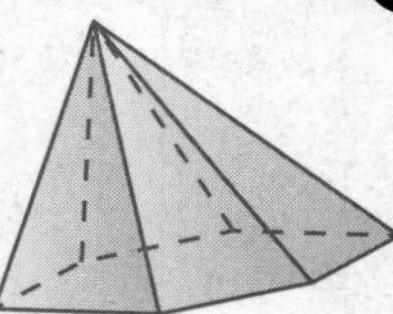

EXAMPLE 2  **Try It!** **Apply Euler's Formula**

2. a. A polyhedron has 12 faces and 30 edges. How many vertices does it have?

b. Can a polyhedron have 4 faces, 5 vertices, and 8 edges? Explain.

HABITS OF MIND

Reason Could a polyhedron ever have the same number of vertices and edges? Explain.

EXAMPLE 3 **Try It! Describe a Cross Section**

3.

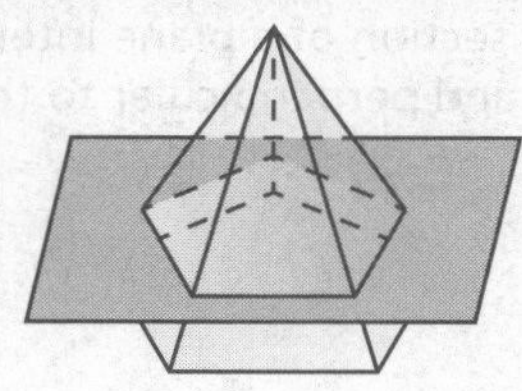

a. What shape is the cross section shown?

b. What shape is the cross section if the plane is perpendicular to the base and passes through the vertex of the pyramid?

Notes

Assess

EXAMPLE 4 **Try It! Draw a Cross Section**

4. a. Draw the cross section of a plane intersecting the tetrahedron through the top vertex and perpendicular to the base.

b. Draw the cross section of a plane intersecting a hexagonal prism perpendicular to the base.

HABITS OF MIND

Generalize Is it always true, sometimes true, or never true that a right prism and a plane can intersect to form a rectangular cross section? Explain.

Notes

Assess

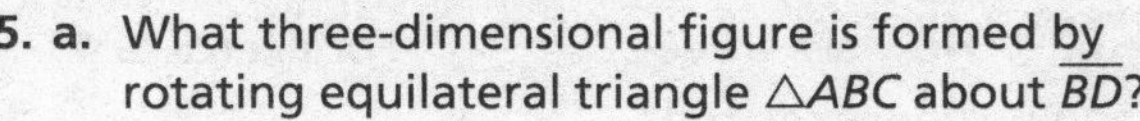

EXAMPLE 5 **Try It!** **Rotate a Polygon to Form a Three-Dimensional Figure**

5. a. What three-dimensional figure is formed by rotating equilateral triangle $\triangle ABC$ about $\overline{BD}$?

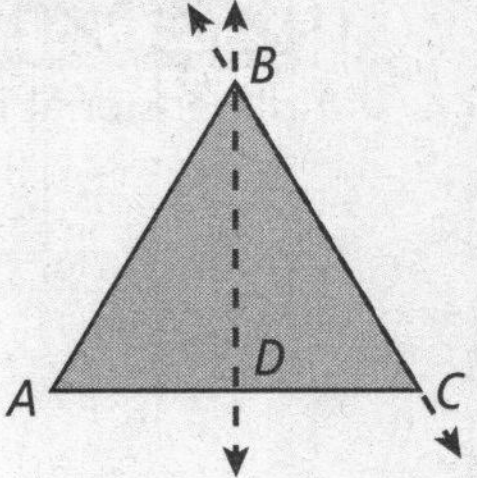

b. What three-dimensional figure is formed by rotating $\triangle ABC$ about $\overline{BC}$?

HABITS OF MIND

Communicate Precisely Can a polyhedron be formed by rotating a polygon about its side? Explain.

Do You UNDERSTAND?

1. ESSENTIAL QUESTION How are three-dimensional figures and polygons related?

2. **Error Analysis** Nicholas drew a figure to find a cross section of an icosahedron, a polyhedron with 20 faces. What is Nicholas's error?

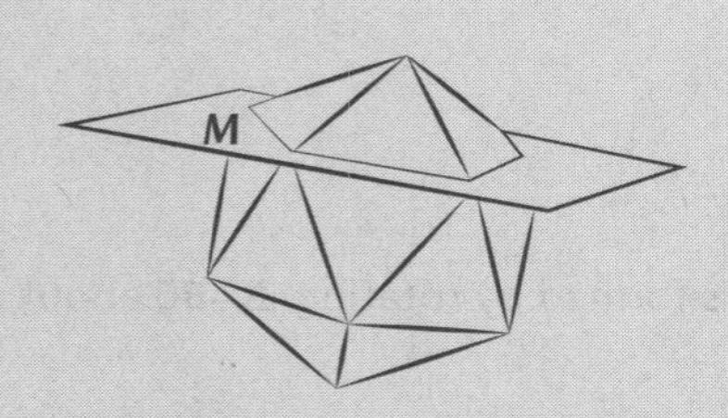

Because the plane that intersects the icosahedron is a rectangle, the cross section is a rectangle. ✗

3. **Reason** Can a polyhedron have 3 faces, 4 vertices, and 5 edges? Explain.

Do You KNOW HOW?

For Exercises 4–7, complete the table.

	Faces	Vertices	Edges
4.	5	6	
5.	8		18
6.		12	44
7.	22	44	

8. What polygon is formed by the intersection of plane *N* and the octagonal prism shown?

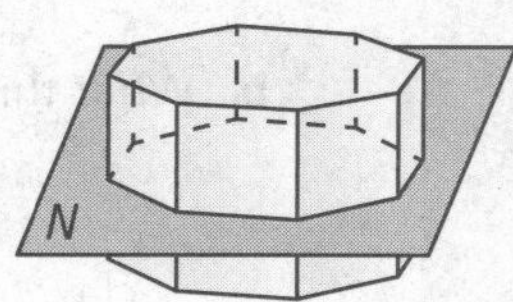

9. Describe the three-dimensional figure that is formed from rotating the isosceles right triangle about the hypotenuse.

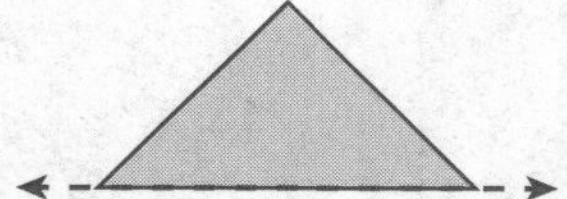

11-2
Volumes of Prisms and Cylinders

PearsonRealize.com

MODEL & DISCUSS

The Environmental Club has a piece of wire mesh that they want to form into an open-bottom and open-top compost bin.

A. Using one side as the height, describe how you can form a compost bin in the shape of a rectangular prism using all of the mesh with no overlap.

B. Construct Arguments Which height would result in the largest volume? Explain.

C. Suppose you formed a cylinder using the same height as a rectangular prism. How would the volumes compare?

HABITS OF MIND

Reason How are the dimensions of the wire mesh related to the dimensions of the compost bin?

EXAMPLE 1  **Try It! Develop Cavalieri's Principle**

1. Do you think that right and oblique cylinders that have the same height and cross-sectional area also have equal volume? Explain.

EXAMPLE 2 **Try It! Find the Volumes of Prisms and Cylinders**

2. a. How would the volume of the storage shed change if the length of the triangular base is reduced by half?

   b. How would the volume of the canisters change if the diameter is doubled?

HABITS OF MIND

Construct Arguments What is the same and what is different about finding area and finding volume?

EXAMPLE 3  **Try It! Apply the Volumes of Prisms to Solve Problems**

3. Kathryn is using cans of juice to fill a cylindrical pitcher that is 11 in. tall and has a radius of 4 in. Each can of juice is 6 in. tall with a radius of 2 in. How many cans of juice will Kathryn need?

Notes

EXAMPLE 4  **Try It!** **Apply the Volumes of Cylinders to Solve Problems**

4. Benito is considering the aquarium shown. What is the maximum number of neon tetras that this aquarium can hold?

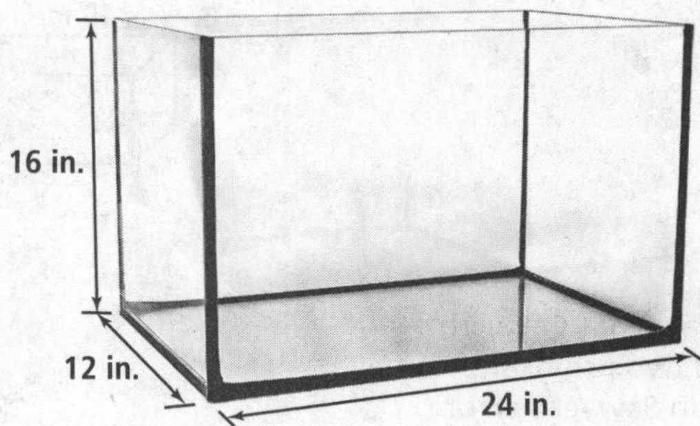

HABITS OF MIND

Communicate Precisely How can you confirm that your answers to Examples 3 and 4 are reasonable?

EXAMPLE 5  **Try It!** **Determine Whether Volume or Surface Area Best Describes Size**

5. Describe a situation when surface area might be a better measure of size than volume.

HABITS OF MIND

Model With Mathematics What do you know in Example 5 that is not stated in the problem?

Do You UNDERSTAND?

1. **ESSENTIAL QUESTION** How does the volume of a prism or cylinder relate to a cross section parallel to its base?

2. **Error Analysis** Sawyer says that Cavalieri's Principle proves that the two prisms shown have the same volume. Explain Sawyer's error.

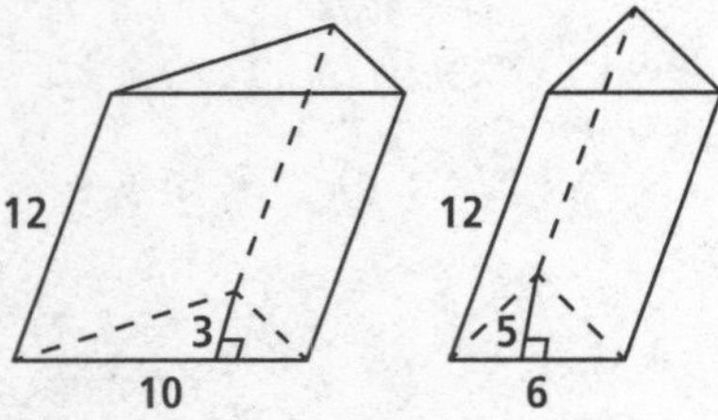

3. **Vocabulary** How are an oblique prism and an oblique cylinder alike and different?

4. **Reason** The circumference of the base of a cylinder is x, and the height of the cylinder is x. What expression gives the volume of the cylinder?

5. **Construct Arguments** Denzel kicks a large dent into a trash can and says that the volume does not change because of Cavalieri's Principle. Do you agree with Denzel? Explain.

Do You KNOW HOW?

For Exercises 6–11, find the volume of each figure. Round to the nearest tenth.

6. 7.

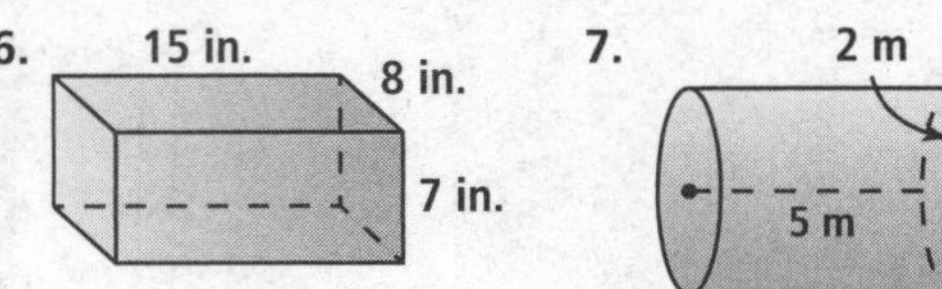

8. 9.

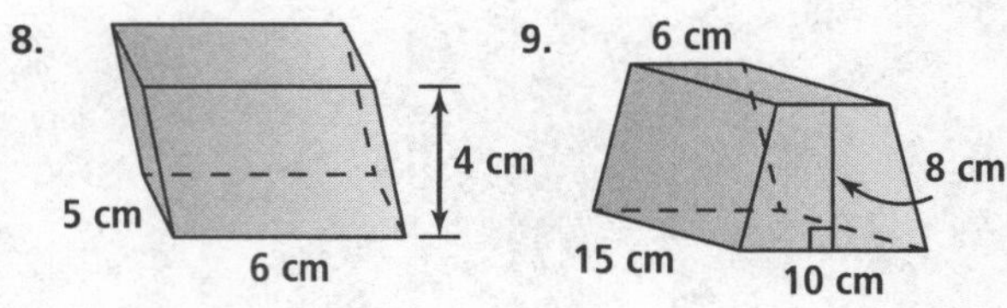

10. 11.

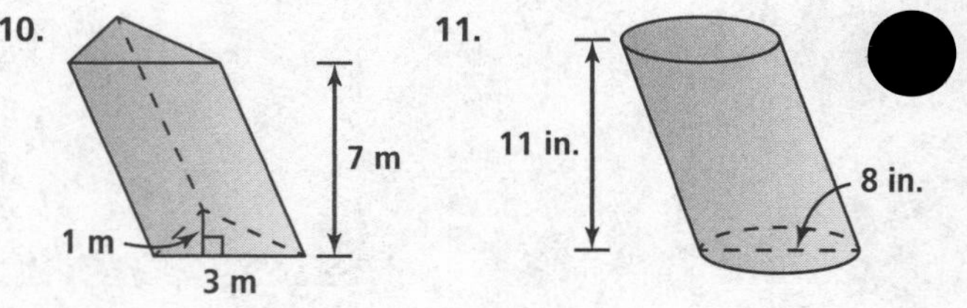

12. Which figures have the same volume? Explain.

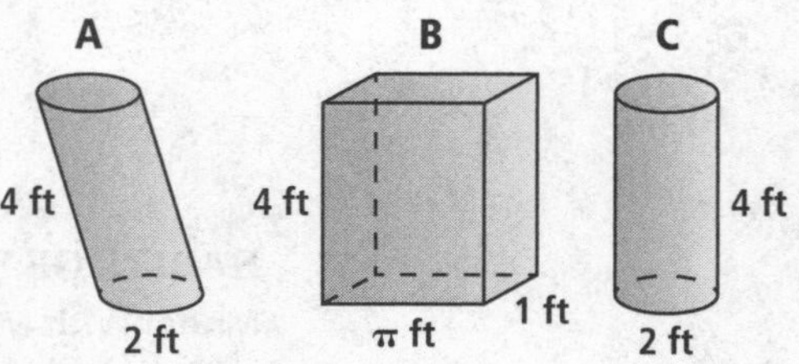

Video

MATHEMATICAL MODELING IN 3 ACTS

PearsonRealize.com

Box 'Em Up

With so many people and businesses shopping online, retailers, and especially e-retailers, ship more and more packages every day. Some of the products people order have unusual sizes and shapes and need custom packaging. Imagine how you might package a surfboard, or a snow blower, or even live crawfish to ship to someone's house!

Think about this during the Mathematical Modeling in 3 Acts lesson.

ACT 1 Identify the Problem

1. What is the first question that comes to mind after watching the video?

2. Write down the main question you will answer about what you saw in the video.

3. Make an initial conjecture that answers this main question.

4. Explain how you arrived at your conjecture.

5. What information will be useful to know to answer the main question? How can you get it? How will you use that information?

Video

ACT 2 Develop a Model

6. Use the math that you have learned in this Topic to refine your conjecture.

ACT 3 Interpret the Results

7. Did your refined conjecture match the actual answer exactly? If not, what might explain the difference?

Activity

11-3 Pyramids and Cones

PearsonRealize.com

EXPLORE & REASON

Consider the cube and pyramid.

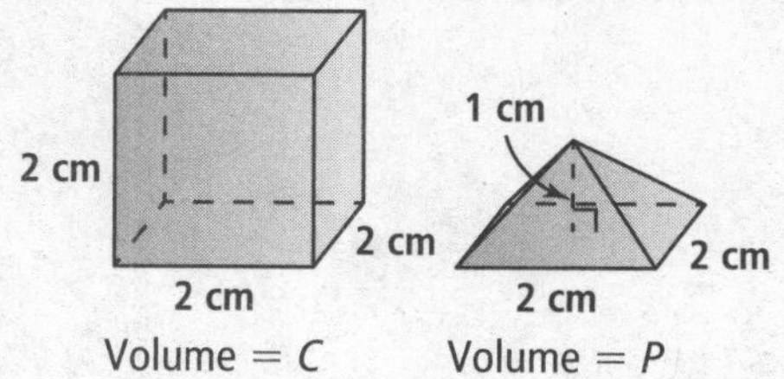

A. How many pyramids could you fit inside the cube? Explain.

B. Write an equation that shows the relationship between C and P.

C. Look for Relationships Make a conjecture about the volume of any pyramid. Explain your reasoning.

HABITS OF MIND

Use Structure Does the same pattern you found in Part A apply to other types of prisms and pyramids? Do you think the mathematical rule you found in Part B applies to all pyramids and prisms with the same size base?

Notes

EXAMPLE 1  **Try It!** **Apply Cavalieri's Principle to Pyramids and Cones**

1. Is it possible to use only Cavalieri's Principle to show that a cone and a cylinder have equal volume? Explain.

EXAMPLE 2  **Try It!** **Find the Volumes of Pyramids and Cones**

2. a. What is the volume of a cone with base diameter 14 and height 16?

   b. What is the volume of a pyramid with base area 10 and height 7?

HABITS OF MIND

Use Appropriate Tools What mathematical tools are helpful when solving problems about cones and pyramids?

 Notes

EXAMPLE 3

Try It! Apply the Volumes of Pyramids to Solve Problems

3. A rectangular pyramid has a base that is three times as long as it is wide. The volume of the pyramid is 75 ft^3 and the height is 3 ft. What is the perimeter of the base?

EXAMPLE 4

Try It! Apply the Volumes of Cones to Solve Problems

4. A cone has a volume of 144π and a height of 12.
   a. What is the radius of the base?

   b. If the radius of the cone is tripled, what is the new volume? What is the relationship between the volumes of the two cones?

EXAMPLE 5

Try It! Measure a Composite Figure

5. A cone-shaped hole is drilled in a prism. The height of the triangular base is 12 cm. What is the volume of the remaining figure? Round to the nearest tenth.

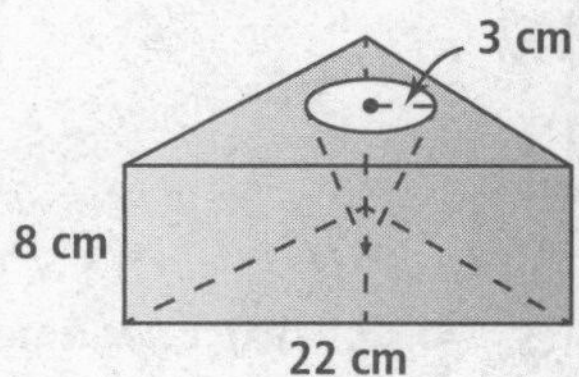

HABITS OF MIND

Communicate Precisely How do you know that your solutions are reasonable?

Do You UNDERSTAND?

1. ESSENTIAL QUESTION How are the formulas for volume of a pyramid and volume of a cone alike?

2. **Error Analysis** Zhang is finding the height of a square pyramid with a base side length of 9 and a volume of 162. What is his error?

$V = Bh$

$162 = 9^2(h)$

$h = 2$

✗

3. **Reason** A cone and cylinder have the same radius and volume. If the height of the cone is h, what is the height of the cylinder?

4. **Construct Arguments** Do you have enough information to compute the volume of the cone? Explain.

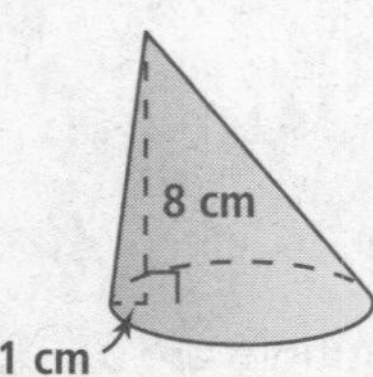

Do You KNOW HOW?

For Exercises 5–10, find the volume of each figure. Round to the nearest tenth. Assume that all angles in each polygonal base are congruent.

5.

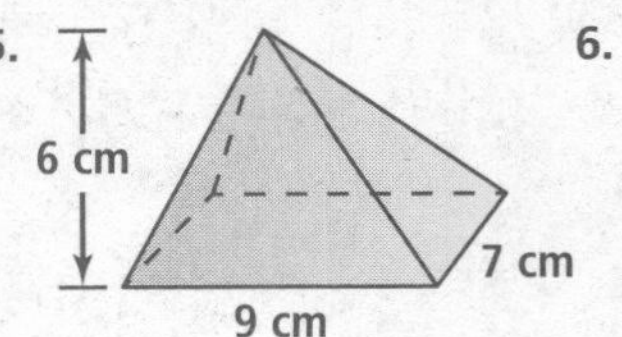

6.

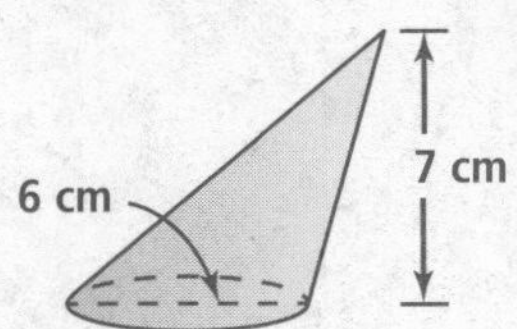

7. 8 in. 3 in.

8.

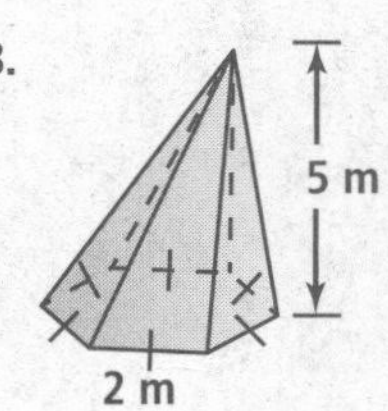

9. 24 ft 11 ft 18 ft 12 ft

10.

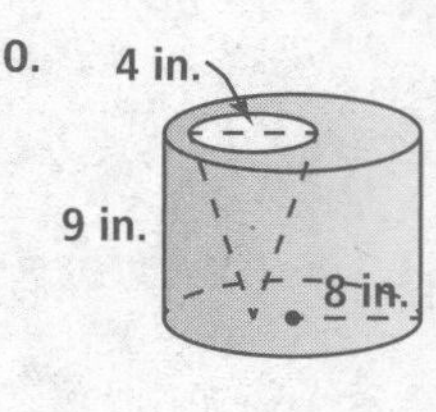

11. A solid metal square pyramid with a base side length of 6 in. and height of 9 in. is melted down and recast as a square pyramid with a height of 4 in. What is the base side length of the new pyramid?

CRITIQUE & EXPLAIN

Ricardo estimates the volume of a sphere with radius 2 by placing the sphere inside a cylinder and placing two cones inside the sphere. He says that the volume of the sphere is less than 16π and greater than $\frac{16}{3}\pi$.

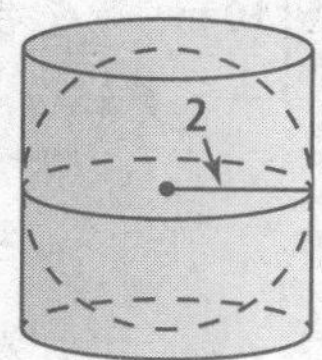

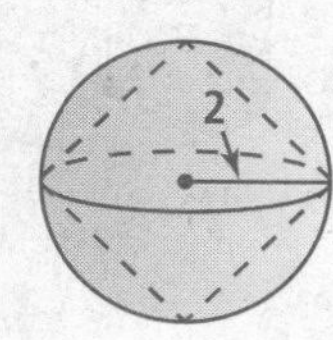

11-4
Spheres

A. Do you agree with Ricardo? Explain.

B. Reason How might you estimate the volume of the sphere?

HABITS OF MIND

Make Sense and Persevere What other figures could you contain within a sphere?

EXAMPLE 1  **Try It!** **Explore the Volume of a Sphere**

1. Find the volumes of the three solids. What do you notice?

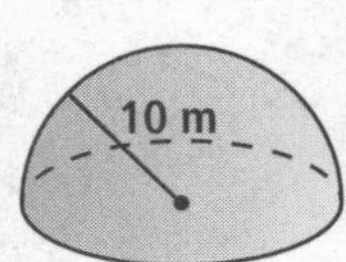

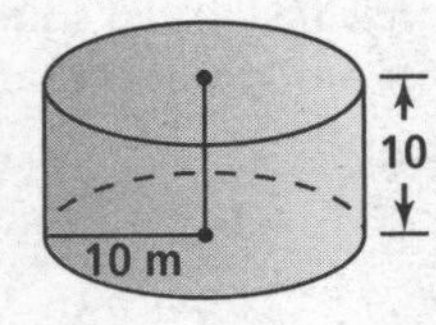

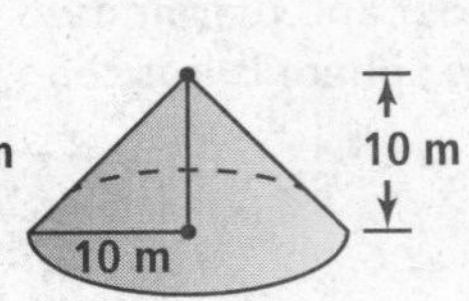

EXAMPLE 2 **Try It!** **Use the Volumes of Spheres to Solve Problems**

2. What is the largest volume a sphere can have if it is covered by 6 m^2 of fabric?

HABITS OF MIND

Use Structure Do cross sections parallel to the base of a half sphere, cylinder, or cone ever have zero area? Explain.

Notes

EXAMPLE 3 **Try It! Find the Volumes of Hemispheres**

3. a. What is the volume of a hemisphere with radius 3 ft?

b. What is the volume of a hemisphere with diameter 13 cm?

EXAMPLE 4 **Try It! Find the Volumes of Composite Figures**

4. What is the volume of the space between the sphere and the cylinder?

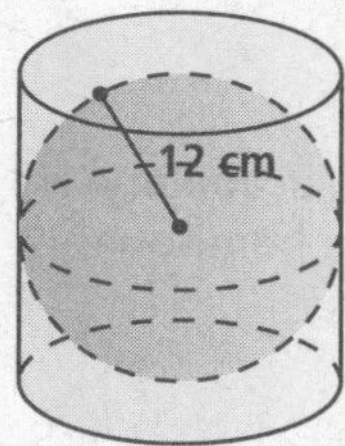

HABITS OF MIND

Make Sense and Persevere How do you know if a plane divides a sphere into equal volumes? Explain.

Do You UNDERSTAND?

1. ESSENTIAL QUESTION How does the volume of a sphere relate to the volumes of other solids?

2. **Error Analysis** Reagan is finding the volume of the sphere. What is her error?

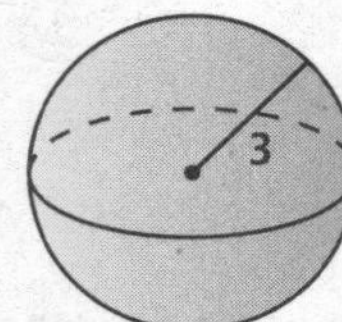

$$\text{S.A.} = \frac{4}{3}\pi r^3$$

$$\text{S.A.} = \frac{4}{3} \cdot \pi \cdot 3^3$$

$$\text{S.A.} \approx 113.1 \text{ square units}$$

3. **Vocabulary** How does a great circle define a hemisphere?

4. **Reason** The radius of a sphere, the base radius of a cylinder, and the base radius of a cone are *r*. What is the height of the cylinder if the volume of the cylinder is equal to the volume of the sphere? What is the height of the cone if the volume of the cone is equal to the volume of the sphere?

Do You KNOW HOW?

For Exercises 5 and 6, find the surface area of each solid.

5.

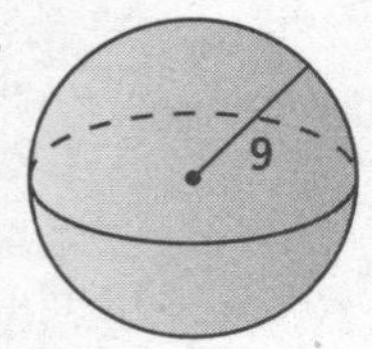

6.

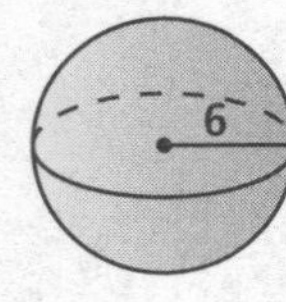

For Exercises 7 and 8, find the volume of each solid.

7.

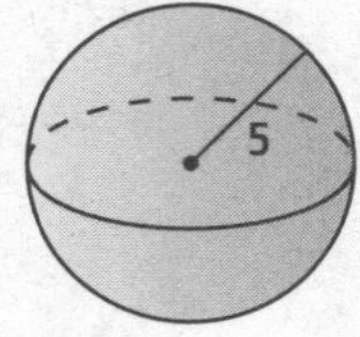

8.

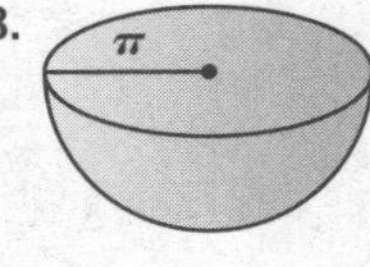

9. Find the volume of the largest sphere that can fit entirely in the rectangular prism.

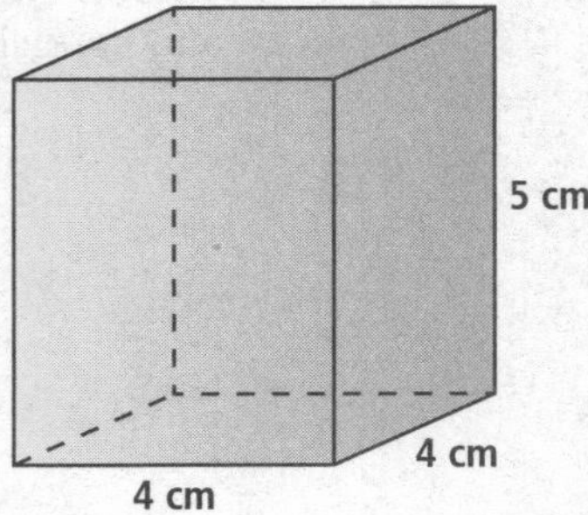

10. Find the volume and surface area of a sphere with radius 1.